D1017499

THE

WEST

LOST LEGENDS
& TREASURES

BRAD WILLIAMS &
CHORAL PEPPER

PROMONTORY
PRESS

Published By
Promontory Press
A Division of BBS Publishing Corporation
252 W. 38th Street
New York, NY 10018

Promontory Press is a registered trademark of
BBS Publishing Corporation.

Published by arrangement with Henry Holt and Company, Inc.

Library of Congress Catalog Card Number: 2008923911

ISBN 10: 0-88394-102-3
ISBN 13: 978-0-88394-102-7

Printed in the United States of America.

To Isabel

LOST LEGENDS
OF THE WEST

CONTENTS

Sixteen pages of black and white photographs follow page 114.

PREFACE

Located some one hundred and twenty miles west of San Diego, California, is a small island nation that does not exist, a country that the United States Government would dearly like to see become lost. It has been given three names, Albonia, Aqualandia, and Taluga, and none of them appear on any map. Although its three potential rulers are squabbling among themselves, they agree that this new nation will be independent, that all of its permanent residents will be employed by the government, and that it will not be a democratic society.

The site of this country, that is not, is the Cortes Bank, a shallow reef about 12 miles wide and 35 miles long which presently is between 14 and 30 feet below the surface of the sea. The news of this emerging nation first came to public attention when motion-picture actor Joe Kirkwood, Jr., and two associates bought an old concrete-hulled freighter named *Jalisco*, announced that they were going to sink it on the reef, and that the wreck would be the cornerstone of a new land known as Albonia. The announcement was greeted with the skepticism accorded many Hollywood press releases, until Kirkwood entered a low bid with the city of Los Angeles to haul away its trash for $1.25 a ton. He told reporters that Albonia would rise on six thousand tons of solid trash a day from Los Angeles. About the same time, a Coast

Guard patrol plane noticed the *Jalisco* anchored off the southwest corner of the reef.

The military took a dim view of the new nation so close to the borders of the United States and, although Albonia was some thirty miles farther from California than Cuba is from Florida, the military were successful in obtaining an injunction from the federal courts which prohibited Kirkwood from scuttling the *Jalisco*. The City of San Diego suddenly became fearful that the nation of Albonia quite possibly could break up in a heavy storm and that the city would become inundated by Los Angeles trash.

A few hours after the injunction was granted, a large swell rolled in from the Pacific, effortlessly scuttled the *Jalisco* on the spot and so, according to Kirkwood, established the cornerstone for this new nation.

It was at this point that the conflict between Albonia and the United States reached the attention of a Seattle attorney named Jack England. He promptly announced that he had claimed the reef as early as 1959, that his backers were prepared to build a new nation on the site and upon a much more solid foundation than Los Angeles rubbish. The name of the new nation was Taluga, not Albonia. He exhibited documents and artists' conceptions of the new nation with its three cities, Aurora, Bonaventura, and Tirana, and detailed plans as to how the reef would be encircled by huge granite boulders such as those used on the ten-mile levee surrounding Los Angeles Harbor. The interior then would be filled by dredging and more boulders brought out from California. Then would come the hotels, the airport, and possibly a few gambling casinos to attract the nomadic, playful American tourist.

"Kirkwood and England are both out of line," then announced Mike Austin of Los Angeles. "I claimed this nation many years ago and named it Aqualandia." He, too, produced documents and the great seal of the nation of Aqualandia which proclaimed him as regent.

The United States then began seriously to concern itself with the nation that was yet to be. United States attorney Edwin Miller of the Federal Department of Justice called a press conference in San Diego. There will be no foreign country emerging this close to the United States, he announced. Although the Cortes Bank is more than one hundred miles offshore, he said, it is located on the United States continental shelf and under the 1899 Rivers and Harbors Act, it is under United States control. "All navigable waters surrounding the United States and extending as far as the continental shelf are under our government's control," he told the Associated Press. "It is unlawful to build any construction without permission of the Army."

"The Army?"

"Yes. This is under control of the Army Corps of Engineers and the Department of the Interior," Miller replied.

This should have ended the story, but, unhappily, someone in the American Tuna Fleet Association read Miller's remarks. The Association is very sensitive to any claims of jurisdiction outside the three-mile limit of any nation. Tuna clippers more than one hundred and fifty miles at sea have been impounded by Ecuador and Peru. To have a United States attorney even hint that this country would recognize any jurisdictional claim beyond three miles was equivalent to treason. Telegrams of protest were dispatched to the President and the Congress.

Someone turned to Army Brigadier General John Dillard for comment. "We ought to blow it up," he replied. "Blow it up and the whole issue will become lost."

It was not necessary to blow up the Cortes Bank. There were no more diplomatic exchanges between the heads of government of Albonia, Aqualandia, or Taluga. In the late spring of 1969, someone telephoned Marvin Gray, a talk-show commentator in Los Angeles, and asked him if he ever had heard of the legend of the lost continent of Taluga which sank off the coast of

California about a thousand years ago. Gray replied that so far as he was concerned, even the legend had become lost.

Most legends have their roots in fact, although few are so far apart as the lost continent of Taluga and an idea from a Seattle attorney. Most legends of the West evolve around something lost, ranging from mines to heads. Some of the most intriguing of these have been chosen as the theme for this book. The writers have purposely avoided the lost-mine syndrome, where derelict prospectors expire in the arms of a friendly family physician only seconds before the location of a fabulously rich gold mine can be divulged.

Such stories are not so much legend as adult fairy tales. Instead, the writers have taken legends which are known to have been based on fact and, in many instances, they have substantiated them by comparatively recent developments.

The adamant young lady who called Marvin Gray was convinced that there was a lost nation of Taluga. When the conversation was over, she was still convinced that there had been a lost nation of Taluga and that Marvin Gray was not very bright.

Legends start from fact. They are kept alive through faith.

The writers particularly wish to thank the following for the help they have given in preparing this book: The Hon. John McManus, Fred A. Carleson, John J. (Cactus Jack) Jeffrey, Dana Burden, Dora Heap, Arda Haenszel, Betty Lou Waters, Don Turner, Mick Jirack, Midge Walker, Larry Meyer, Chuck Hillinger, Jack Pepper, and Bill Knyvett.

Los Angeles, California
June 1969

Brad Williams
Choral Pepper

A FEW LOST BONES

Which my name is Bowers, and
my crust was busted
Falling down a shaft in Calavaras
County
But I'd take it kindly if you'd
send the pieces
Home to old Missouri!

—"To the Pliocene Skull,"
Bret Harte

The West certainly is the newest part of the United States, but it is equally certain that it is the oldest part of the continent. Man was living in southern California for many thousands of years before there even was a Plymouth Rock.

Probably the best authority on California's anthropological popularity is Dr. Louis S. B. Leakey, the prominent British anthropologist and archaeologist, "who has come up with evidence that man was living around what is now the Mojave Desert at least 40,000 years ago, and possibly as long as 100,000 years before this section of the United States was besieged by smog. Dr. Leakey based his assumptions upon a find in the Calico Mountains

1

where 170 man-made implements were found by an archaeological team headed by Dr. Ruth D. Simpson of San Bernardino.

Finds of early human habitation are being made with remarkable regularity throughout the West, and it appears almost axiomatic that when someone digs up an ancient skull, someone other than the original owner is due for a headache.

In the Calico Mountain discovery, the headache came first to Glen S. Gunn, a prospector who held several mining claims in the area, including one that stretched across the archaeologists' trenches. At about the same time the ancient tools were discovered, Gunn discovered that the area contained valuable mineral deposits. To Gunn, the minerals were worth a lot more than a stone tool abandoned by some squatter 100,000 years ago. He promptly served an eviction notice upon the archaeologists. They took the matter up with the Bureau of Land Management, who referred it to the United States Department of the Interior. With all this pressure, Gunn stayed his eviction notice and although the issue has been solved temporarily, there is still a touch of migraine on both sides of the trenches, when either party thinks of the unreasonableness of the other.

Recently a 13,000-year-old skull was dug up near the confluence of the Snake and Palouse rivers in southeastern Washington by Professor Ronald Fryxell. The area in which this skull was found soon will be flooded by back-up waters from the new Lower Monumental Dam, a fact which causes some concern to archaeologists who would like more time for exploration than is in the present timetable. Human bones, found along with this skull, indicated that this 13,000-year-old man had provided a meal for some other 13,000-year-old neighbors. At last reports, this skull was in the possession of Senator Warren Magnuson of Washington.

About thirty-five years ago, another skull was found on what is now the outskirts of Laguna Beach, California. The skull

2

was found by Howard Wilson, who was digging in the area for arrowheads and came across it about five feet below the surface of the ground. Wilson kept his find in a shoebox for a couple of years before he reported it to the Southwest Museum in Los Angeles. Here the skull was named the Laguna Man and was described as prehistoric.

Two years later, the Laguna Man was taken to the Museum of Natural History in Santa Barbara, where an opinion was rendered that it probably belonged to a member of the "Oak Grove people" who preceded the modern California Indian. Its age was estimated at about 9,000 years. A short time later an anthropologist at the University of Southern California decided that it was once part of the skeleton of a California Indian of comparatively recent origin. The skull was returned to Wilson, who put it back in his shoebox, where it remained until 1953. In that year, he lent it to a friend who took it to experts in London, Paris, Madrid, Rome, and Brussels. The opinions of these experts were not announced publicly, but eight years elapsed before the skull of Laguna Man was returned to its shoebox in Laguna Beach.

In 1967, the discovery of the Laguna Man came to the attention of the ubiquitous Dr. Leakey. He went to Laguna, studied it, then took it to the University of California at Los Angeles. Officials at UCLA became excited and sent it on to the Smithsonian Institution in Washington where Carbon-14 tests revealed that the skull of the Laguna Man was approximately 17,000 years old. The skull of the Laguna Man started back to the shoebox, via the anthropological department at UCLA where, this time, it came to the attention of Dr. Ranier Berger. Dr. Berger made still another significant discovery. The skull of the Laguna Man was no man at all. It was the skull of a woman.

No bones have caused such furor as that raised across the nation in 1866, however, when a miner by the name of Mattison, from Angels Camp, California, found a skull almost 130 feet underground in a shaft of his mine in Calavaras County. The discovery shook the foundations of Genesis. What intrigued Mr. Mattison was why some Indian would dig a grave that deep in the ground when anything over six feet would suffice. He knew the skull belonged to a very old Indian because it was fossilized and encrusted with the same kind of gravel distinctive to the earth in which he had come across it. He took it into one of the bars in Angels Camp on his next visit to town. Here he eventually ran across a doctor who told Mattison that if it was an Indian, it was a deformed one. The doctor pointed out the heavy brow ridges which extended entirely across the eyes and nose, and he pointed out several other differences in the cranium between this and other Indian skulls of a more contemporary period which were dug up occasionally around the mining camp.

The unknown doctor prevailed upon Mattison to report the find to Mr. J. D. Whitney, who, at the time, was the geologist for the State of California. Although Whitney knew nothing about skulls, he was an excellent geologist and when he was shown the gravel-encrusted skull, he checked it with the gravel in its burial place and found the two to match. The skull had been found under four strata of lava and three strata of gold-bearing gravels and thus, Whitney reported, it probably had been buried near the end of the Pliocene Era, or roughly a million years earlier.

If the announcement had been restricted to the area around Angels Camp, everyone probably would have laughed and the skull probably would have wound up as back-bar furniture in some tavern. Whitney announced the discovery, however, in San Francisco, thus incurring the immediate enmity of most of the nation's clergy who knew that Adam was the first man that ever was invented and he wasn't anywhere near a million years old.

Whitney discovered that he had some other enemies also.

4

Some months earlier, because of his testimony, some local San Francisco financiers had become considerably embarrassed when caught selling stock in mining properties which were worthless and had been forced to refund investors large sums of money. This group immediately sided with the clergy, accusing Whitney of heresy and questioning Whitney's mental health, as well as his qualifications as a geologist. One of these confidence men called in the press and announced that the skull really was the property of an Angels Camp dentist and had been planted in the mine as a practical joke on Mattison. He even displayed a headless skeleton, which he said had been in the fictional Dr. Kelley's office.

Anthropologists joined in the attack upon Whitney because, if the skull was a million years old, it destroyed every theory on record about the age of man on earth. Whitney apparently had a remarkable disposition. He kept the skull and whenever he was questioned about it, he would reply that the skull had been discovered *in situ* (that it had not been planted where it was found), and that the area in which it had been found dated back to the end of the Pliocene Era. He did not get upset even over such vitriolic attacks as one from a high-spirited evangelist who claimed that God had told him that Whitney was in reality Satan and that there was no such thing as the Pliocene Era.

The charges were raised constantly for almost fifteen years, until finally Whitney, with Mattison's permission, sent the notorious skull to the Peabody Museum of Archaeology and Ethnology in Cambridge, Massachusetts.

In 1903, Professor John C. Merriam of the Museum solved the controversy with diplomatic finesse. In a paper read before the Anthropological Association, Merriam said, "Taken as a whole, the problem seemed to present as remarkable a case of absolutely contradictory evidence as ever has appeared in science or law. After so long a lapse of years, it will probably never be possible to trace out the history of the Calavaras Skull with certainty." He added that Whitney was right in stating that the skull came from a very ancient cave deposit, "but how ancient is still a matter to be determined."

The skull is still in the Peabody Museum at Harvard. Its age will never be known. "From the condition of its finding it will never be possible to get any kind of a date for it," W. W. Howells, Professor of Anthropology at Harvard, recently told the writers.

In Angels Camp, they have a different memory of the skull. "Isn't anything to it," one old-timer said recently. "Now, if I remember correctly, someone took the skull from a dentist's office and planted it in a mineshaft as a joke. The dentist just got so mad about it, he just up and left town."

Bret Harte apparently was not convinced as to its authenticity either. Its discovery prompted his writing an ode "To the Pliocene Skull."

There is still another skull that figures prominently in the lore of the West, but unlike the Calavaras skull, this one has yet to be found.

PANCHO VILLA'S LOST HEAD

Fly, fly, little dove
Perch among the castor beans
And tell to all the gringos
That Pancho Villa's dead.
—Mexican Mariachi Song

Early in the morning of July 20, 1923, Francisco "Pancho" Villa was assassinated in the small city of Parral, Mexico, a few miles south of Chihuahua. Two and one half years later, his grave at Parral was broken open and Villa's head was severed from his body. There have been many theories advanced as to the reason for this. The most popular in Mexico is that the United States wanted proof that Villa was really dead and offered a $50,000 reward to the first person who could deliver Villa's head in El Paso. Most scholars scoff at this solution to the riddle, yet recently there died in New Mexico an old man who may have found the answer to this mystery. It is not far removed from the

7

popular thought in Mexico. The key to the posthumous decapitation is the notorious raid by Villa on the sleepy New Mexican
town of Columbus in the early morning hours of March 9, 1916.

In 1915, President Woodrow Wilson recognized
Venustiano Carranza as the head of government for Mexico, a
diplomatic gesture which upset several of the revolutionary contenders for the oft-changing presidency. Of all the applicants,
Villa was the most vehement in expressing his disapproval. The
first positive indication of his anger came on January 10, 1916,
when a section of his army, commanded by Rafael Castro and
Pablo Lopez, ambushed a train near Santa Isabel in Chihuahua.
On the train was a large party of North American mining engineers and miners. All had been assured of safe passage by a recently installed Carrancista governor in Chihuahua who needed
the mining experts to help reopen a long-closed mine.

Villa stopped the train, robbed all of the passengers, then
shot and killed sixteen of the North American mining experts to
demonstrate that Carranza was not in a position to guarantee safe
passage to anyone in northern Mexico.

The second demonstration of his rage came two months
later when a horde of Villistas swept across the border and attacked Columbus, thus assuring the loss of Pancho's head a little
less than a decade later. Villa quite probably was motivated by
reasons other than revenge for his assault on Columbus. The
Thirteenth Cavalry Encampment was stationed here and they
were well supplied with arms, ammunition, and other vital military equipment which Villa needed desperately. Villa also had
some unfinished business with one of his major suppliers, Sam
Ravel, who operated a general store in the town. When President
Wilson recognized the Carranza government, the United States
embargoed all arms shipments to Villa. Ravel had been one of
Villa's principal suppliers and had accepted payment for another
shipment immediately prior to the embargo. Having already pur-

chased the arms he could not deliver, Ravel thought it poor business to refund the money to Villa until he had found another customer.

At the time of the raid, the warden of the New Mexico State Penitentiary was a young man named John B. McManus. A native of Ireland, McManus had lived in Wisconsin briefly, then headed for the West, where he got a job as a telegrapher for the railroad in Columbus. In 1912, shortly after New Mexico was admitted to the Union, McManus was appointed warden by Governor W. C. McDonald, whom he had met when McDonald was in Columbus.

McManus had a great fondness for Mexico, particularly the wide desert country in the northern part of that nation. He spoke a "bastard Spanish, enough to get by on." Early in March of 1916, he had gone to visit friends in El Paso, Texas. In spite of warnings that Villa was on a rampage, he crossed the border into Juarez, where he bought a horse. He then started out on a cross-country trip just below the border, planning to re-enter the United States near Columbus, where he would stay with friends a few days before returning to Santa Fe.

On the morning of the raid, McManus was sleeping on the desert a few miles south of Columbus. He was awakened abruptly by the thrust of a rifle muzzle in his belly and was surrounded by what appeared to be an army. As he struggled out of his blanket, he heard one of the Mexicans order that he be shot. Another instantly countermanded the order, warning that the shot might be heard by someone else ahead of them who would alert the town.

There was a brief discussion. "Who would be sleeping on the desert?"

"Here is one," a bandit said. "If there is one, there may be some others."

The argument seemed reasonable. McManus was led to

his horse, lifted onto its back, and then his feet were tied together by a rope passing beneath the animal's belly. His saddle, his blankets, and other gear disappeared somewhere amid the mass of silent men. A bandanna was placed in his mouth as a gag and a line was attached to the horse's bridle, with the other end fastened to the saddle of one of the bandits.

The thought that remained with McManus for the rest of his life was a wonder as to how so many men could move so silently and so swiftly. Not a man uttered a word. Even the horses seemed to be trained to be quiet, as the bandit army moved across the desert toward Columbus. When they arrived at the small town, three of the bandits went ahead. A moment later, by the light of the moon, McManus saw one of them climb a pole and cut the telegraph wires. The falling of the wires was a signal, for suddenly the bandits swooped down upon the town and its adjacent military encampment, screaming and shouting and shooting their rifles.

McManus' horse was cut loose from the other, but it raced along with the bandits into the center of the town.

For more than two hours, McManus watched the looting of stores and of the military base from his uncomfortable bare-backed-perch on the high-withered horse. The animal, untethered and not in the least disconcerted by the gunfire, ambled around the town, pausing occasionally to nibble a tuft of grass.

Villa himself did not accompany his horde on the raid, but everyone in Columbus thought he did because of the raiders' constant cries of "Viva Villa, Viva Mexico!" Soon they were answered by cries in Spanish of, "One thousand dollars for Villa's head!"

Sam Ravel's store was first to be looted and put to the torch, then went the others, but there was no organized resistance, except mistakenly when one gang of bandits raced around the corner of a building and was cut down by gunfire from another gang. Through it all, McManus and the horse wandered about unscathed. Bodies were lying everywhere on the streets and the screams of the dying mingled eerily with the cries of the bandits still praising their leader. McManus was convinced that his luck could not last.

The raid ended with the arrival of the false dawn. As the bandits began their retreat, one galloped up to McManus and raised his rifle. Then he paused and stared at McManus with an expressionless face. Suddenly he laughed and placed the rifle back into a saddle holster. He next quickly picked up the line to the bridle and, with McManus still tied to the animal, galloped after his companions with the horse in tow. The ride was incredibly painful. McManus' feet were tied under the animal's belly, but his hands had been left free so he was able to hold his balance on the horse's back by wrapping his arms around its neck.

About two hours later, when well inside of Mexico, the bandits paused. The man who had been towing McManus and the horse dismounted and walked a short distance ahead to confer with some men who apparently also held positions of rank in the Villa forces. By now, McManus was in such pain that he was in a semiconscious condition. Only vaguely was he aware of being the subject of conversation among the bandit leaders. Occasionally they stared at him and gesticulated. Finally, all but one shrugged and turned away.

The exception walked back toward him. It was the same man who had hesitated before taking him captive in Columbus. The bandit untied the ropes that bound McManus' feet under the horse and then, as McManus started to fall, the bandit helped him to the ground. McManus could not stand upright. The circulation in his legs had been cut off too long. When he sank to the sand, expecting to be executed, the bandit laughed. Slowly, he began to massage McManus' legs.

"I do you a favor," he said presently, in Spanish. "You understand?"

McManus nodded.

11

"Then someday maybe you will do me a favor?"

Again McManus nodded. He wanted to be a hero but he was too frightened.

The bandit laughed again, rose, and led the horse over to some others that had been captured from the United States Cavalry Encampment. Presently he returned, carrying a United States Army canteen full of water and a piece of dried beef. These he gave to McManus. Ten minutes later, the Villa horde was gone. An hour later, McManus was able to move and start his painful journey back to Columbus. Afterward, he could never understand how he was able to make his way on foot back to the border, but shortly before dark he was intercepted by a military patrol on the North American side and was given a horse. He rode "sidesaddle" the rest of the way into Columbus. The first night he spent in military custody. Interrogators found it difficult to believe his story, but eventually they released him.

The raid had been a costly one for Villa. Approximately five hundred men had crossed the border and of these, exactly one hundred had been killed in Columbus. The raiders, however, had taken back with them more than one hundred of the cavalry's horses and most of its arsenal, including machine guns and rifles. Eighteen Americans had been killed, eight wounded, and virtually everyone in the town had been robbed of money and any possessions of value to the raiders. Sam Ravel lost his shipment of arms which had been destined for the Villa forces.

There were many repercussions from the raid. The United States, over the objections of the Carranza government it so recently had recognized, sent in troops on a punitive expedition commanded by General John Pershing. The expedition never could find Villa nor any of his men, but three months after the raid, Pershing found himself fighting Carranza forces who objected to the invasion. In June there was a battle near Carrizal, in which General Felix U. Gomez, along with eighty-four men, was killed. Eight United States soldiers also lost their lives in this engagement.

Peace talks were scheduled and held in New London, Connecticut, and Atlantic City, New Jersey, but they amounted to nothing. Pershing continued his futile search for Villa in Chihuahua, while at the same time, Villa issued manifestos accusing Carranza of allowing Mexico to be invaded by filibusterers. On two separate occasions, Villa captured Chihuahua City, the capital of Chihuahua, but by the time Pershing's troops arrived, Villa once again had melted into the vast desert of northern Mexico. Pershing kept up his chase for a year and a half, at a cost of some 130 million dollars, before he and his troops finally were recalled for bigger and better wars in Europe.

The Villa forces continued their raids and occasional kidnappings of United States citizens for ransom until after the assassination of Carranza and the assumption of power by Provisional President de la Huerta. It was under Huerta that Villa agreed to go into retirement. As part of the package, he was given a large hacienda at Parral where, on July 20, 1923, he was assassinated, presumably at the order of Huerta's successor, Plutarco Elias Calles.

McManus continued as warden of the New Mexico State Penitentiary in Santa Fe, active in the state's Democratic party and in civic affairs in the state capital. In 1925, McManus was interviewed in Albuquerque by a reporter who was writing a story on the Columbus raid. When McManus related in detail his harrowing experience on that night he mentioned that he still could not understand why his life had been spared.

About a week after the story appeared in the Albuquerque newspaper, McManus received a call in his office from a Mexican who, in broken English, said he would like to talk with him about the Pancho Villa raid on Columbus. At first, McManus demurred, replying politely in Spanish that his schedule was rather heavy.

13

"There was one time a man spared your life and you promised him a favor in return," the caller said.

They met in the bar at La Fonda Hotel about two hours later. The man was in his late fifties. He was wearing a suit with a high starched collar and, from the manner in which he wore it, McManus knew that he was unused to it. His name, the man said, was Marino Contreras and he was the brother of Ramón Contreras.

McManus nodded politely. There was nothing familiar about the man or the name.

"It was my brother, Ramón, who took you on the horse from Columbus and twice spared your life," Contreras said casually.

"I have never been on a horse since that time," McManus replied. He decided that as a result of the story, the man was going to "borrow" some money. "I am grateful to your brother," he said aloud. "This must be apparent."

"My brother now is dead."

"I am sorry to hear that." McManus glanced at his watch. "What is it that you want?"

Marino Contreras told the following story. His brother had not been motivated by any feeling of compassion when he spared McManus' life. It was a matter of war and McManus was of the enemy. Ramón, however, had realized that the raid on Columbus quite possibly was a mistake and that quite probably Villa would meet the fate of all other revolutionaries in the long struggle for power in Mexico. When this happened, it would be a profitable venture to collect the thousand-dollar reward that had been offered in Columbus for the head of Pancho Villa. The favor that would be asked of McManus, in return for his life, was that he act as intermediary in collecting this money.

During the ensuing weeks, the plan of Ramón Contreras had been forgotten and then, two-and-one-half years after Villa's assassination, it had been recalled. It was Ramón, Marino said,

14

who had broken into Villa's grave and severed the head from the cadaver. Ramón then had taken the head to Columbus, had buried it there in a well-protected box, and had gone looking for McManus. While he was asking questions in the Columbus station, he had been arrested by the United States border patrol and escorted back across the border.

"He said the town had rebuilt itself very well," Marino said.

McManus smiled. "You want one thousand dollars?" he asked.

Marino shook his head. "I know the location of Villa's head," he replied. "I will take you there and then we will divide the reward, half for you and half for me."

Again McManus smiled. He had not known that Villa's corpse had been decapitated. At the same time, he marveled at the rashness of the man, approaching a state officer with his confidence game. "Do you have papers to be in the United States?" he asked.

Marino gave him a disappointed look. "My brother spared your life," he said.

"Then it is to your brother that I owe the favor."

Marino Contreras said nothing, stood up, and walked out of the hotel. McManus debated whether or not to report the illegal entry to the police, then decided it was not worth the effort. The man probably would be picked up anyway within the next few days.

Some weeks later, at a political gathering, McManus related his experience to Dennis Chavez, who later was to become a United States senator from New Mexico. Chavez chuckled and replied that a reward of one thousand dollars for Villa's head was a rather small amount at that time. "The government spent one hundred thirty million dollars trying to catch Villa," he commented.

It was at this moment that McManus realized that there

had been no reward posted in Columbus. The thousand-dollar figure had only been cried out by the Columbus citizens and the United States soldiers in reply to the bandits' cries of "Viva Villa." The mental picture of his experience swiftly flashed through his head. Only someone who was there could have known of it. Contreras could have been one of the bandits. Or he could have been telling the truth.

John McManus had a friend who was a professor at the University of New Mexico in Albuquerque, a man who was Mexican and an authority on Mexican history. The next time McManus was in Albuquerque, he called upon his friend and turned the subject of the conversation to Villa. The professor became fascinated by the story and, after dinner, the two men spent the evening going through the professor's private library, which dealt primarily with Mexican history.

It had been shortly after seven in the morning when Pancho Villa left the home of his mistress in the Calle Zaragoza in Parral to return to his hacienda in Canutillo. He was driving a Dodge touring car which, in addition to himself, contained five members of his bodyguard and a servant. The bodyguard consisted of Rosalío Rosales, Daniel Tamayo, Rafael Medrano, Claro Hurtado, and a man named Ramón Contreras.

Approximately two blocks distant, at the intersection of the Calle Juarez and the Calle Gabino Barreda, an eight-man band of assassins, led by Melitón Lozoya, were hiding in a two-room house. Each was armed with an automatic pistol and an automatic rifle. Villa would have to turn into the intersection and cross a plaza to get to Canutillo. The lookout for the assassins was a street peddler who mopped his face with a bandanna as Villa approached.

The assassins first fired a fusillade from the windows of the house and then, as the Dodge careened into a tree, they raced out of the building firing pistols. Villa was able to kill one of his attackers before he died. Only one man in the Villa party escaped: Ramón Contreras. Although wounded, he managed to roll into the bottom of a dry riverbed and work his way back to the home of Villa's mistress, where a doctor was summoned to sew up his wounds. That night, he left on horseback for Canutillo.

A few days later, McManus wrote to the *jefe politico* in Chihuahua asking if a picture were available of Ramón Contreras. He wrote also to the widow of Pancho Villa to ask what had happened to Ramón Contreras after his arrival at Canutillo, the day after the assassination.

The *jefe politico* was able to secure a picture of Ramón Contreras. It looked like the same man, but McManus never was sure. The *jefe politico* wrote also that no one apparently knew what had happened to Ramón, but he was believed to be operating a business with his brother Marino in Juarez. The widow of the former bandit did not answer McManus' letter.

McManus asked the police in Juarez to locate Marino Contreras, but they were unable to do so. About ten years later, McManus ran across an old picture of Villa and his wife with an "unidentified" man standing in the background. It was a better picture than that sent by the *jefe politico* of Chihuahua. There was no doubt in McManus' mind but that the picture was that of the man who had pulled him on a horse into Mexico after the Columbus raid.

Once again, McManus started his search for Marino, but he was as unsuccessful as before. The man had vanished as completely as had Ramón.

Today, ironically, the sleepy town of Columbus, New Mexico, has become a monument to Villa's raid. There is a state park which bears his name, most bars display his picture, and many stores sell "genuine souvenirs" of the audacious assault. The widow of the famous bandit has been named an honorary citizen of the community.

There is a strong possibility that the most genuine souvenir of all, the head of Pancho Villa, lies in a well-protected box somewhere within the town limits.

There is no mystery at all, however, as to what happened to the remains of another Western renegade. There are three skulls and heads and skeletons, all belonging to the same man.

THE LOST
REMAINS
OF
MR. QUEJO

Mr. Quejo's first name, if he ever had one, has been lost in history. Half-Indian and half-white, he hated whites and Indians equally and with reasonable justification. His mother was a beautiful Indian lass of the Cocopah tribe and his father was presumed to be a passing prospector who raped her shortly after the turn of the century.

The Cocopahs shared a belief with most Indians in the Southwest that anyone with white blood was bad, even if it was only half white, so shortly after Quejo was born, the tribal priest performed a religious ceremony which absolved the young lass. He then proceeded to throw the infant over the side of a nearby cliff, thus presuming that he had adequately solved a local problem of miscegenation.

That evening, while the village slept, the young mother crept out to the base of the cliff and found to her amazement and joy that the child still lived. She picked him up and fled with him in her arms up the shores of the Colorado River until the steep channel forced her inland to the caves of Pyramid Canyon.

There was no solution to her dilemma. No Cocopah village would accept her with her halfbreed son. She was too far distant from any white settlement to seek aid, and it is unlikely that such a thought occurred to her any more than the idea that she might receive aid from another tribe. She never was able to solve her problem.

Several weeks later, two Paiute Indians found her dead on the desert floor beside a broken barrel-cactus from which she had tried to squeeze water. Still alive and sucking on the dead woman's breast was the infant Quejo. The Paiutes buried the young mother and brought the child back to their camp, where there was no taboo against miscegenation. It was a humanitarian gesture that in the ensuing years was to cost at least twenty-three persons their lives.

Quejo grew up in the Paiute camp, sometimes doing odd jobs for the whites in mining communities along the Colorado River. In some ways he showed a remarkable talent for learning. By the time he was in his early teens, he was an expert horseman, a marksman, and a superb tracker. His English was intelligible and the miners he worked for always remarked that the "halfbreed" was more energetic than most of the local Paiutes. Never, however, did he participate in Indian games with other Paiutes his age, and at night he would withdraw from the others and sit alone. Paiute youths who knew of his background taunted him constantly, usually with insults referring to his being half a white man.

One night, soon after he had turned twenty, he sat alone, as usual, when a Paiute youth with the unlikely name of Bismarck casually referred to him once again as a white man. Quejo slowly rose and went over to the corral where he blanketed and haltered one of the horses. No one paid any attention. Quejo often rode off by himself in the night. This night, however, was different. After he had mounted the horse, Quejo walked the animal close to the fire, raised his rifle and shot Bismarck in the back of the head. Then he raced away.

The startled Paiutes set off in pursuit moments later, but they were unable to find any trace of Quejo. It was to set a pattern. In subsequent years, neither Indian nor white posses ever were able to follow Quejo after one of his murders. He simply melted into the night. No one ever found out where he slept, yet, so far as anyone knew, he was never more than one hundred miles from the Paiute camp where he was raised.

His next two victims were also Paiutes with whom he had grown up. He shot one in the back and the other in the stomach, stealing into their camp at dawn while they were watering the horses. The latter victim was able to identify his assailant before he died. The remaining members of the camp, a poor and desultory band of the once-great Paiutes, swore revenge but when they were unable to pick up his trail after a short chase, they decided that he was hiding out among the whites and they soon forgot their oaths.

Quejo was not to become ignored by the whites, however. An elderly man named Woodward was found by his wife near a woodpile outside of a small homestead in southern Nevada. He had been shot in the back of the head after his assailant had forced him to remove all of his clothes. Before he died, Woodward was able to identify the murderer as Quejo, whom he had once hired to help him clear some land.

While a posse was being formed, word arrived that the

21

operator of the Gold Bug Mill, about five miles distant on the Colorado River, also had been shot and his body stripped of clothing. The posse scouted the area for two weeks before giving up the hunt. Warrants were issued for Quejo's arrest and reward notices were posted that he was wanted dead or alive, but no one could find Quejo.

The most diabolical thing about Quejo's method was the long interval that passed between his murders. He waited until he was almost forgotten, then struck at some isolated farm and with his 30-30 rifle shot another victim in the head. Usually they lived just long enough to identify him. When they didn't, it was Quejo's method of murder and a total lack of motive that pointed the posse in his direction.

On one paradoxical occasion, however, two brothers were riding into Searchlight, Nevada, after an unsuccessful prospecting trip. It was near dusk when they noticed a man on a horse following them at some distance. When the brothers trotted their horses, so did the man behind them trot his. When they walked their horses, he walked his. A few miles beyond the limits of town, the brothers decided to turn into an arroyo that skirted a craggy mountain studded with cholla and pocked with caves. Both of the brothers thought of Quejo and when they heard hoofbeats against the rocks of the arroyo and knew that the stranger was determinedly stalking them, they became certain that he was the notorious renegade.

When they reached a steep draw that ascended the bank of the arroyo, they raced their horses up it and into a crevice in the mountain which, to their consternation, proved to be a cul de sac. It was too late to expose themselves back at its entrance, so they quickly dismounted and waited, with guns drawn. Soon the shadowy outline of the mounted figure appeared at the entrance to the cul de sac. One of the brothers raised his revolver.

"Suppose he is not Quejo," the other one whispered.

One of the brothers called out, "Quejo!"

Still the horseman did not answer, but he backed his mount slowly away until his outline had dropped below the bank. Neither brother could hear a sound after he disappeared.

An hour later both men still were pondering their dilemma. There was no way to tell if the mysterious horseman outside was Quejo. On the other hand, there was no way to tell if he was not Quejo. By his actions, he had proved that he was not a friend, however, and rather than taking the risk of walking into an ambush in the dark, the two men decided to spend the rest of the night in the comparative safety of the cul de sac.

When the sun rose the following morning, the brother who was taking his turn as guard noticed a flash of light on the canyon wall across from him. Then he noticed another and still another, as the sun's rays passed over the jagged outcropping. He awakened his brother and pointed out the phenomenon. The mysterious flashes lasted another few minutes, then disappeared.

A short time later, the brothers saddled their horses and cautiously rode to the entrance of the canyon. A careful search in the area disclosed no signs of the sinister stranger from the previous night. The two brothers then returned for a closer examination of the wall that had reflected the sun's rays. With a sudden surge of elation, they realized that they were rich. Through the wall of the canyon ran a vein of quartz webbed through with wires of pure gold. It was one of the richest strikes to be found in gold-laden Searchlight, Nevada.

In later years, whenever one of the brothers would hear tales of Quejo's murders, he would smile enigmatically and reply only, "Well, he has a good side, too."

In 1919, Quejo committed the unforgivable sin. He murdered a woman, a white one. Mrs. Edward Bacon, the wife of a mine supervisor at El Dorado, was heating water on a wood-burning stove preparatory to washing her dishes, when a stalking figure wearing Levis and with long black hair held in place by a red band around his forehead, entered her open kitchen door. She gave one piercing shriek as he fired his rifle into her breast. At the same time, her husband, who was working at the mine, experienced an unaccountable premonition of fear. He dashed from his office, leaped upon the saddled horse of a friend and raced to his home and discovered his dying wife.

That Quejo had murdered a white woman, a species still rare to the West, hit a new low in depravity. This launched a manhunt that was to continue for twenty-one years. During that time, Quejo murdered sixteen victims, all within a one-hundred-mile radius of Las Vegas.

On one occasion, a posse led by Clark County Deputy Sheriff Frank Wait employed a Paiute, appropriately named Tracker, who was reknown for his tracking abilities. The Indian followed Quejo's trail for four days through the malpais of the Colorado River canyon where Lake Mojave now lies, and northward up the shore of the Overton Arm of present Lake Mead. The men drove their horses unmercifully over the hot red sands of the Valley of Fire and through its steep ravines until, at last, they came upon Quejo's lair, but once again their quarry had disappeared. His hideout was a small cave and in it were the clothes of several of his victims. More ironic, there were supplies of groceries, including a can of peaches from a Las Vegas market. Tracker was unable to find any trace of Quejo's trail leading away from the hideout.

A few days later, a family of four was killed on the Arizona side of the Colorado, but all had died before the shooting was discovered, so it is not certain that this was the work of the renegade Quejo. The last murder directly attributed to him also involved a woman.

In 1930, Mrs. Edward Douglas, who lived on the outskirts of Searchlight, rode into town in the family buckboard, accompanied by her four-year-old son and husband. She dropped her husband off at the assaying office where he worked, then proceeded to the general store where she picked up a week's supply of groceries. About an hour later, she returned to her home and noticed that a horse with its reins trailing on the ground stood near the door. Her first thought was one of relief, that a man was around to help her carry the supplies into the house.

Swinging her son to the ground, she entered the kitchen, then froze in fright. A man dressed in Levis, a blue shirt, and moccasins, was on his hands and knees on the kitchen floor, uttering strange staccato sounds. Incredibly, she realized that the man was pushing her son's red toy automobile around the floor, imitating the exhaust of an automobile engine, in the manner of a child.

At first, the stranger did not appear to notice her, but soon he rose slowly to his feet. It was at this point that she suddenly remembered the warning about Quejo.

The man bent down, picked up the toy and pushed it into his waistband. When he straightened up again she saw the rifle in his hand. She screamed once, before he shot her in the neck. He then turned the rifle toward the frightened boy and hesitated. Looking at the toy car in his waistband, he lowered the rifle and slowly stepped over the screaming woman. At the door he stopped again and considered the boy, while the agonized mother continued to scream. Abruptly he turned and walked from the house.

The woman lived just long enough to tell the story to a passing miner, who had come to the house when he thought it suspicious that her boy should be wandering unattended along the road. An hour later, the posse was in full chase.

No one ever saw Quejo alive again, but it was a long time before any woman in southeastern Nevada felt safe alone in her house, and many a tough man refused to travel through uninhabited country without a companion.

On February 20, 1940, two Las Vegas residents, Arthur

Schroeder and Charles Kenyon, discovered a partially sealed cave along a precipitous trail near Willow Beach on the Arizona side of the Colorado River. Pulling aside the rocks that disguised the entrance, the two men found a clothed, mummified skeleton. In the cave were a rifle, some ammunition, rusted cans of fruit, a belt, and a string of Indian beads. Clutched in the skeletal fingers of the remains was a red toy automobile.

There was no mystery as to why the cave entrance had been blocked. It was an old Indian custom. Caves that held the dead were always sealed in order to keep coyotes and other scavengers from reaching the corpse.

Kenyon and Schroeder reported their discovery to Deputy Sheriff Frank Wait when they returned to Las Vegas. A short time later, Wait and a couple of other deputies went to the cave, picked up the mummy, and took it to an undertaker in Boulder City, a small town adjacent to Hoover Dam, a few miles south of Las Vegas.

For a few days, no one was particularly enthusiastic about either the corpse or the mystery of its grave, although Kenyon did enjoy telling of the skeleton he had found of a grown Indian holding a red toy automobile. Eventually Kenyon heard the story of Quejo and the little red car. He also heard that the Nevada State Legislature had long ago posted a reward for Quejo dead or alive in the amount of ten thousand dollars. Understandably, Kenyon and Schroeder drove out to Boulder City and asked the undertaker for the body they had found.

The undertaker sadly shook his head. He had no legal right, he explained, to release the body to anyone except a law-enforcement officer or a relative, and Kenyon failed to qualify on either count. The mortician indicated also that he had reason to believe that the mummy was that of Quejo, pointing out to Kenyon that if no one appeared to pay the mounting mortuary bills, the remains probably would have to be placed on exhibit to recoup expenses. This apparently gave Kenyon another idea, as he went to the Elks Club of Las Vegas for help.

Every year there is a Chamber of Commerce type of celebration in Las Vegas known as Helldorado, a promotion extensively supported by the Fraternal Order of Elks. Kenyon, an enthusiastic Elk, promised the Order that he would exhibit the remains in a Helldorado booth for a week before taking it to the state capital in Carson City if his Brothers would help him get the corpse away from the undertaker. At the same time, he sued the mortician.

The court ruling was handed down quickly. The only person who had a legal right to Quejo's body was the coroner unless it was proved to the satisfaction of the court that a legal heir existed.

The undertaker was unimpressed. "Either I get paid or I am going to bury it or exhibit it," he declared.

Before he could do either, the heirs began to appear. First on the scene were two Indians, one right after the other, and both claiming to be grand-nephews of Quejo. Each said the other was lying and each claimed the right to obtain the body for exhibition. Court hearings had hardly started on these cases when a third Indian arrived in Las Vegas.

It was true, he said, that both of the other Indians were grand-nephews of Quejo. He, however, was the grandson of Quejo and could testify on this authority that the corpse in possession of the mortician was not that of Quejo the murderer, although, he admitted, it might be that of some other person named Quejo.

The grandson then went on to reveal that he just happened to have the real Quejo's skeleton in his possession and that he would be perfectly willing to exhibit it, if the price was right. His story had barely made the papers when still another grandson showed up with an "authentic" Quejo skeleton.

27

The courts sighed collectively and pigeonholed all of the contenders' claims.

When the courts lost interest, the mortician entombed his cadaver in a casket with a sealed glass lid and exhibited it at county fairs. The owners of the other Indian mummies promptly booked theirs for display also.

All three of Quejo's disputed bodies have now become lost. The most likely exhibit, the one entombed by the mortician in a glass-lidded coffin, spent its last public days in a Las Vegas Strip museum, until the Strip became too crowded with crap tables to tolerate such things as museums. The man who owned the museum then took it out to his ranch in an area now called Paradise Valley. There, the glass-topped coffin remained propped in an abandoned bathtub in the backyard, until a new housing development overgrew the whole area and Quejo's remains disappeared as adroitly as if he had just committed another murder.

If anyone ever does find the skeleton and he can prove it is that of Quejo, he can still take it to Carson City and collect the $10,000 reward. It has never been canceled.

THE LOST LOVER OF PEARL HART

The Arizona Territorial Prison was a Devil's Island of the desert, although penologists of the late nineteenth century described it as an "ideal institution." Instead of being surrounded by impenetrable jungle, it was circled by a bleak desert. Indians were promised a standing reward of fifty dollars for every escaped prisoner they returned, much to the annoyance of many an innocent prospector who found himself bound to a mule and carted off to Yuma just in hopes that the trip might prove profitable to the Indian who affected the capture.

The Yuma prison came equipped with a dungeon, a "snake den," so named because it was a haven for resting transient rattlesnakes and scorpions. There are probably few sites more admirably suited for the location of a penitentiary. It was located on a high granite bluff that formed the junction of the Gila and the Colorado rivers, thus two sides of the jail were protected by natural moats. Across the rivers were only the rolling sands of the Colorado Desert. To the rear of the promontory was the town of Yuma.

The prison yard was surrounded by high granite walls and the cells had been blasted out of the granite block. On the north corner of the wall was a tank stand and on top of this was a sentry with a Gatling gun. Along the tops of the other three walls guards paced back and forth. The Grading gun, a rapid-firing weapon with revolving barrels, was mounted on a two-wheeled carriage in order that it could be pointed in any direction instantly, and it probably was as strong a deterrent to escape as was the surrounding terrain.

Despite all of these hazards, there were many attempted breaks. One of the first superintendents, Thomas Gates, was taken prisoner and stabbed so severely in one of these breaks that he never fully recovered. He was followed by a Captain F. S. Ingalls, whose son was a guard and whose wife was sufficiently trained in the operation of the Gatling gun to break up at least one attempt at mass escape. Occasionally a prisoner would escape. He usually was a trustee who would take a guard as a hostage and a shield from the bullets of the Gatling gun, but these occasions were rare.

The two most remarkable departures from this grim fortress were accomplished separately by lovers, John Boot and Pearl Hart. John Boot simply vanished. One day he was there; and the next day he was not. Pearl followed him a few months later and the manner of her departure was most extraordinary. Pearl was a most extraordinary woman, as can be attested to by the fact that she was one of only three women ever imprisoned in the Yuma jail.

She was a young woman, under twenty-one, with long black hair, full breasts, and a small body, when she first entered the Arizona Territorial Prison with John Boot. She was as trustworthy as an ocelot and could swear "like a well-traveled sailor."

She and her lover had drifted into Arizona from Kansas and shortly after their arrival there began a series of stage holdups in the Territory that at first followed the same pattern. On an isolated section of a trail, a stagecoach driver suddenly would be hailed for help by a disheveled young woman obviously distraught and the victim of foul play. As soon as the stage was stopped, out stepped John Boot with a revolver in each hand. The distraught young woman then would produce her own revolver and relieve the passengers of their possessions, while Boot would take care of the express box and the mail. As soon as word of this *modus operandi* spread through the Territory, Pearl and John resorted to the more familiar pattern of holdup by just stepping out of some place of concealment as the coach approached. There was a rash of murders about the same time, but the killings were always of lone travelers. They started with the stage robberies and they ended when a posse finally caught up with Pearl and Boot and deposited them in the Pinal County Jail at Florence, Arizona.

At Florence, however, there were no accommodations for women, so Pearl was taken to the Pima County Jail in Tucson to await trial. She remained there only overnight. The next day, the turnkey discovered that Pearl had cut a hole through a thin partition and escaped. On the same night, John Boot had, in some mysterious manner, disappeared from his cell in Florence. About a week later, both John and Pearl inadvertently rode into a posse that was looking for some cattle rustlers near Deming, New Mexico.

The lovers were immediately taken back to Florence and tried on the day they arrived. Boot was sentenced to thirty years

31

in the Arizona Territorial Penitentiary, but the judge hesitated when it came to pronouncing sentence upon the eighteen-year-old Pearl.

"What in hell are you waiting for, you silly old bastard?" Pearl asked the judge mildly.

The judge quickly overcame his reluctance. "Five years in the same place," he said.

Ingalls was not happy about having a woman as a prisoner. He had to have six tier bunks ripped out of one cell and boards placed across the cell bars to ensure her the privacy needed by a female. A dressmaker in Yuma was employed to make her a special uniform.

When Pearl and John Boot arrived, however, Pearl was wearing tight jeans, a man's blouse and was smoking a cigarette, all three of which were considered most unladylike at that time. In contrast, Boot was quiet, well spoken, and he seemed to sigh with relief when he was separated from his mistress.

Mrs. Ingalls was on hand to escort Pearl to her new cell and to explain the house rules. "We'd better keep that woman far away from the other inmates," she told her husband. "She'll shock them with her language and corrupt their morals."

Ingalls kept her away from the inmates, but he could not keep Pearl quiet. She cursed constantly. One of her favorite pastimes was to call out through the bars of her cell for some man to come and join her, an invitation which so upset most of the inmates "that they would howl like coyotes all during the night." Ingalls ordered that the only person to be allowed in the cell block where Pearl was residing would be his wife with a guard, or himself.

Boot was a model prisoner. He responded to orders with alacrity. The only thing he volunteered about his background was that his name was not Boot and his accent indicated that he came from somewhere in New England. Then, one day, a little less than two years after he had been admitted, he vanished. He had become so unobtrusive that no one missed him between breakfast and the customary bunk check at night. No one ever saw him again.

Immediately after his disappearance, there was a remarkable transformation in Pearl Hart. Her whole personality changed. She became quiet, soft spoken, and she asked Mrs. Ingalls if she could have a dress and some cosmetics. Shortly after this favor was granted, she asked if she could see a minister. One of Yuma's leading clergymen came to the jail and was closeted with the once-arrogant Pearl Hart for more than an hour.

"She is remorseful over her sins," the cleric told Ingalls. "I think she was still under the influence of this man Boot and now that he has escaped she realizes the error of her ways."

Another six months passed. The minister came to visit her regularly. No longer did Pearl call out lewd invitations to the male prisoners. She asked for books, which Ingalls brought to her, and she began to write poetry. The minister told Ingalls that he thought justice would best be served if Pearl were pardoned and released to the custody of her parents in Kansas City.

"Only the governor can do that," Ingalls explained.

The clergyman wrote to Governor Nathan O. Murphy. About six weeks later, Governor Murphy was in Yuma and he paid a visit to the Arizona Territorial Prison. During his tour, he asked about the prison's female prisoner and Ingalls told him of the remarkable change in Pearl Hart.

"I would like to see her," the governor said.

Ingalls accompanied the governor to the cell. "Let me talk to her alone," Murphy said.

A half hour later, the governor left the prison, telling Ingalls that he would think about a pardon. "I think she was mesmerized by this wretch Boot," the governor said. "She will probably be better off if she is sent back to her family."

Ingalls agreed. So far as he was concerned the prison also would be a lot better off if Pearl Hart were no longer around. He waited for two months for some response from the governor's office, but no word was forthcoming and Ingalls did not feel it would be proper to remind the governor of his previously expressed sentiments.

A guard came to see him while he was pondering the problem. Pearl Hart was ill and would like to see a doctor.

"What's wrong with her?"

The guard shrugged. "She just told me through the bars that she wanted to see a doctor."

Ingalls sent for a nurse from Yuma. "She appears to be pregnant," the nurse told Ingalls a few hours later. "She has all the symptoms."

Ingalls shuddered violently. There were only two keys to Pearl's cell, one in his possession and the other in his wife's. Only two persons had ever been alone with her in the cell: Yuma's leading clergyman and the governor of the Territory.

"How far along is she?" he asked the nurse.

"She has missed twice," the nurse replied delicately.

The superintendent made a command decision. He sent an aide to the railroad station to buy a one-way ticket for Pearl to Kansas City and then, with two guards and a shocked Mrs. Ingalls accompanying him, he went to Pearl's cell. "Your pardon has come through," he said. "You'll be leaving on the train tomorrow." He next went back to his office and wrote a long confidential letter to Governor Murphy and, among other recommendations, he suggested the pardon be dated back a few days.

According to the Yuma *Sentinel*, a large crowd was at the Yuma depot the following day to witness the departure of the "notorious Pearl Hart."

"What are you going to do now, Pearl?" a reporter asked.

"I'm going into vaudeville. I've already got a year-long booking as a real-life ex-con and real-life robber."

"Are you going to meet John Boot?"

"You're a stupid bastard," Pearl said mildly, then she waved to the crowd as the train pulled away.

As near as can be determined, no one ever heard from her again.

A few years after Pearl's departure, in 1909, the notorious Yuma prison was abandoned in favor of more modern facilities at Florence. The buildings gradually became ruins and as the decay advanced, the prison became a haven for hoboes. Eventually the hoboes became such a nuisance that the more solid citizens of Yuma started a drive which successfully turned the prison into a museum.

No one today is quite certain which cell was the one used by Pearl Hart. Before the train carrying her was out of Arizona, Ingalls had restored the original six tier bunks and filled the cell with more reliable inmates of the male species.

THE LOST PAYROLL AT WICKENBURG

Late one Sunday morning, November 5, 1871, a stagecoach with eight persons aboard left the small town of Wickenburg, Arizona, for the continuation of a trip that originated in Prescott, Arizona, and was scheduled to terminate in San Bernardino, California. About nine miles outside of the town, six of the eight persons on board were slain in one of the most puzzling mass murders in the history of the Southwest. Before the case was considered closed, at least one hundred more persons had been killed and any discussion of the case today in the Wickenburg area still is a point of controversy.

What is even more ironic is that the two survivors of the

massacre most probably were the murderers, yet they were acclaimed as heroes. One mysteriously disappeared a few months after the murders and the other most probably met a violent death a year later.

At first glance, it appeared that the stage had driven into an ambush. Stagecoach holdups during this era were not unusual, but the killing of the passengers and the driver was rare. On board the stage were Mollie Shepherd, a beautiful working madam from Prescott; William Kruger, chief clerk cashier of the Army Quartermaster Corps in Arizona; Fred W. Shoholm, a Prescott jeweler; W. D. Salmon and P. M. Hamel, both members of an Arizona military expedition headed by Lieutenant George Wheeler; C. S. Adams, a rich San Francisco businessman; Frederick W. Loring, writer, poet, and journalist for the New York *Tribune*; and "Dutch John" Lentz, the driver, who was making his first trip for the company.

The two survivors were Mollie Shepherd and William Kruger. The latter was on assignment from the Army to carry approximately $100,000 of Army payroll funds from Arizona to San Bernardino, money which was carried in a large iron box in the back of the stage. In addition to being a cashier for the Quartermaster Corps, Kruger also was Mollie's financial adviser and lover. Shortly before leaving Prescott, Mollie had sold her bordello for a reported $40,000 and she carried this money with her in a small "safe box" which she kept between her feet inside the stage.

The descriptions of both Mollie and Willie are vague. Mollie was believed to be in her early thirties; every reference to her describes her as buxom and beautiful and she had a reputation for "being very close with a dollar." No one ever could recall her buying anyone a drink in her palace of pleasure in Prescott. Willie was known to be short and stocky, in his late thirties, and a man with above-average strength.

The stagecoach was "ambushed" in the bottom of a large arroyo. It was not a good location for an ambush. There was only one small tree and three or four small mesquite bushes about a foot tall behind which a killer could hide. There were no rocks that could afford cover. About three quarters of a mile to the south was a small canyon that divided two small foothills. In every other direction was the flat high mesa extending for many miles.

The first to learn of the massacre, other than those aboard the stage, was a young man named Nelson, who was driving a buckboard along the trail several miles to the west when he came upon Mollie and Kruger. Both were disheveled. Mollie was suffering from a bullet burn on her arm and Kruger had a flesh wound in his shoulder. The horrified Nelson did not waste much time to listen to their story. Driving his buckboard into a cover of brush, he told Mollie and Kruger to wait inside it, then unhitched his horse and galloped to the Vulture Mine, about seven miles distant, where he enlisted an armed escort to accompany him into Wickenburg. Here, a twenty-five-man posse was formed which proceeded directly to the ambush site, arriving there shortly before dark.

The lead horse of the stagecoach was dead, but oddly, the other horses still grazed in the area, unhitched from the coach, but still in harness. The bodies of the victims were strewn around the north side of the stage and one, that of P. M. Hamel, had been scalped. All of the trunks and valises had been torn from the coach and smashed open, but no attempt had been made to search them. Wrapped in a shirt in Adams' valise was more than eight thousand dollars. A smaller amount of money and some jewelry were found in Shoholm's suitcase. A sack of mail had been slashed open with a sharp knife and every letter in it which was addressed to the Army Quartermaster Corps had been opened. All of the other mail was sealed and scattered on the ground among the corpses. The stage was riddled with bullet holes on all four sides. No clothing had been taken, no blankets "nor party colored rugs nor gay shawls." All of this puzzled the posse because marauding Indians invariably took horses, harnesses, blankets, and rugs. Missing, however, was the iron box with approximately $100,000 of Quartermaster payroll funds destined for California disbursement. Also missing was the stage shovel.

Because of the encroaching darkness, the posse split up. A dozen made camp near the scene and the remainder went on to rescue Mollie and Kruger from their refuge in the buckboard. It was close to midnight by the time the two survivors were brought back to the posse's camp.

Kruger told a harrowing story. Adams had been riding outside with Lentz. The others rode inside the stage with drawn curtains, "warming themselves with wit, wine, and humor" and playing a game of "freeze-out" on one of Mollie's shawls spread across their knees. Suddenly Dutch John cried out, "Apache," and a split second later the stage was riddled with rifle fire. The volley was fired from the front, the right side and the rear of the stagecoach. Some of the passengers were wounded in the first volley, which accounted for the blood inside the vehicle. Then all but Mollie and Kruger reacted in an incredible manner. They jumped out of the right side of the coach directly into the rifle fire of the attacking Indians and were shot down. Mollie and Kruger however "kept their wits about them." They leaped from the left side of the bullet-riddled stage and ran across the high, flat mesa to the distant canyon.

Their escape did not go undetected. About nine of the savages saw them and set off in pursuit, firing at them with their rifles, but Kruger "kept them at bay by shouting and firing and brandishing my pistol." The Indians chased the two survivors until they reached the sanctuary of the canyon. Here, the Indians fired a few desultory shots after their quarry, then returned to the stage. It was Willie Kruger who told the posse that the Quartermaster payroll funds were missing. Also gone was $40,000, Mollie's life savings that she had garnered from her palace of pleasure in Prescott.

Additionally, Krueger also told a story about W. D. Salmon that so incensed the posse that its members did not consider it worth the effort to bring this corpse into Wickenburg on the following day. A shallow grave was dug on the site for the remains of Salmon.

On Monday, the posse once again divided. Some accompanied the two survivors to Camp Date Creek, several miles to the north, where there was an Apache reservation and a military encampment. The remainder returned to Wickenburg with the bodies of the victims, except for Salmon's, left at the site. A coroner's inquest was held the following morning and after listening to the testimony from some members of the posse, it issued a verdict that the victims died of gunshot wounds "received at the hands of Indians trailed toward their Date Creek Reservation." (One of the members of the jury was Julius Goldwater, owner of the stage and progenitor of Senator Barry Goldwater.)

A couple of days after the inquest, Captain Charles Meinhold arrived in Wickenburg from Fort McDowell. Meinhold served in what was then the equivalent of the Army Intelligence Corps. He was a small man of thin face and curious mind. He had the habit of swinging his gold-rimmed spectacles loosely in his hand whenever he interrogated anyone. He first asked to see the bodies of the victims, but this was impossible. They had all "been given a good Christian funeral" shortly before his arrival and interred in a local cemetery, with the exception of Salmon. Meinhold, who knew Shoholm, wondered how well his Jewish friend would have appreciated the religious ceremony.

The stage had been returned to Wickenburg and

Meinhold found it outside the local blacksmith shop. It was riddled with bullet holes and there was so much blood inside of the coach that he wondered how anyone would have had the strength to leap out. Surely, at least one or two of the passengers would have been mortally wounded by such a fusillade. It was indeed remarkable that anyone could have got out of the stage. There were no bullets left inside the stage. Either they had lodged in the bodies of their victims or passed on through.

There was another odd piece of evidence, also. Bullets had been fired into the coach from the front, the right-hand side and the rear. This would indeed be a hazardous crossfire for Indians to have set up. Those firing from the front quite easily could have hit one of their comrades firing from the rear. At the same time, those firing from the rear could have killed their friends in the front of the stage. Yet it appeared that some of the bullets had entered the front of the stagecoach and splintered in a straight line out of the rear. The same trajectory also was true from the rear of the coach. It did not make sense. If the coach was to be ambushed, "why weren't the Indians shooting from both sides of the trail and why didn't they fire at an angle just before the coach reached them, or immediately after it had passed."

The following day, Meinhold rode out to the scene of the massacre. Here he marveled that so many Indians could have hidden under such sparse cover. True, they could have brought along tumbleweed or mesquite for camouflage, but it was unlikely that they would have carried the weeds away after the massacre. Here the trail followed a dry river bottom in the center of a high mesa. To the south, the ground rose slowly for about three quarters of a mile, where there was a small range of mountains. It was across this long open stretch that Willie Kruger and Mollie Shepherd had fled to reach the sanctuary of the small canyon. Armed with a revolver, Kruger had held back nine

Apaches carrying rifles. Any reasonable marksman with a rifle could have safely picked off a man armed with a short-range revolver in such open country.

Meinhold slowly began to walk in a spiral from the scene of the ambush. About three hundred yards to the north of the site, he found the stagecoach shovel wedged between two rocks. He looked closely for any signs of digging, but the ground was hard clay and could find none. A half-mile to the south of the site, he came across some human feces which contained beans. Beans were a staple diet of reservation Indians, as they were also of Mexicans and most prospectors. He had no way of telling how long the feces had been there. A half-mile from here, the ground became sandy and he found a pack of playing cards similar to those used by both Indians and Mexicans. There were some moccasin tracks. Finally, after he could find nothing more of interest, he rode on to Camp Date Creek, taking the cards and the shovel with him.

Willie Kruger and Mollie Shepherd were resting in separate rooms in the military hospital. Their wounds were far less serious than Meinhold had been led to believe. Mollie was suffering from a bullet burn across the bicep of her right arm. Kruger's left shoulder had been furrowed by a bullet.

Meinhold interviewed them separately. Basically their stories were the same as told to the posse, but there were a few variances.

"How were the Apaches dressed?" he asked Kruger.

"In the blue denim pants and shirts they are given in the reservation," Kruger replied.

He asked the same question of Mollie.

"They were wearing those long Army greatcoats they give them on the reservation," Mollie said.

"Who jumped out of the stage first, you or Mr. Kruger?"

"Mr. Kruger jumped out, then lifted me down."

Meinhold went back to Kruger. "We both jumped out together," Kruger said.

The intelligence officer suggested to the commanding officer of the hospital that the two survivors were not to be released prematurely and then returned to Fort McDowell, where he wrote a report on the results of his investigation to his superior officer, Colonel Nathan Dudley. The colonel added a few notes to Meinhold's report, pointing out the evidential conflicts, and forwarded this on to the bucolic General George Crook, the Commanding General of the Army in the Territory.

There was a peculiar political situation existing in Arizona at this time. When the white settlers first came to Arizona, they were welcomed by the Apaches, but this friendliness was not of long duration. Pioneers appropriated land that the Apaches felt belonged to them and the Indians retaliated by murdering the whites and burning down their farms. The pioneers then called upon the Army for protection and, as anywhere, when the military forces were escalated in Arizona, the hostilities increased in direct proportion. Maintenance of the military also proved profitable to merchants, freight haulers, and contractors.

The slaughter on both sides eventually reached such proportions that a strong reaction swept through the East and Washington for some alternative measure to the problem, other than the ineffectual military pacification policy of extermination. The pressure finally became great enough on the White House to cause President Ulysses S. Grant to send Vincent Colyar, of the Bureau of Indian Affairs, to Arizona as his personal representative and with a directive to come up with a solution to the problem.

Colyar was an Indian partisan and despite the vitriolic protests in the Arizona press, he halted Crook's policy of extermination and successfully brought the Apaches into reservations where the government fed and clothed them. The white settlers bitterly fought the Colyar program, contending that the Apaches constantly slipped away from the reservations to pillage and loot. Camp Grant, one of the Apache reservations, was attacked by a group of whites and every Apache man, woman, and child within its confines was slaughtered. Many younger women were raped before they were shot. Despite this massacre, however, the Colyar policy continued. A few weeks before the Wickenburg ambush, Colyar thought his program had progressed to such a point that it was safe for him to return to Washington for a personal report to President Grant.

Crook still agreed with the white settlers that Colyar's policy was nonsensical. When he received Meinhold's and Dudley's reports on the ambush, he instantly attributed the "dastardly deed" to the Apaches. He was enough of a political general, however, not to over-react and for a while he did nothing.

Oddly, the press of the Arizona Territory at first was not as convinced that the Apaches were to blame as was General Crook. The Prescott *Miner*, which was the leading newspaper of the day in the Territory, suggested the assassins could have been Apaches, or Mexicans, or Americans disguised as Apaches.

Two months after the attack, Willie Kruger and Mollie Shepherd left the hospital at Date Creek Camp. Both had fully recovered from their wounds, but had remained at the military post "in case their presence was required during the process of the investigation of this tragic incident." Early in January, the couple once again boarded the stage at Wickenburg. Some days later they were accorded a hero's welcome in Los Angeles. The most minute details of their ordeal were printed in the Los Angeles press in the colorful prose of the day. There was no doubt in Willie's and Mollie's minds that the attackers were Apaches. Kruger went into great detail recounting his arduous running gun battle with the bloodthirsty savages as he carried Mollie to the haven of the canyon.

On the East coast, the newspapers were less concerned with Kruger's miraculous escape than they were with continued lawlessness in the Arizona Territory. The New York *Tribune*, which earlier had supported the Colyar policy, now furiously opposed it because of the wanton murder of one of its star reporters, Fred Loring. Another newspaper quoted Crook as saying the ambush would never have occurred "had not my hands been tied" in his campaign to rid the Territory of the Apache menace. Other newspapers picked up the cry. When Colyar's report on the success of his mission was made public, it was greeted with derision by the press and with highly proclaimed skepticism by the politically sensitive bureaucrats in Washington.

During this period, Meinhold had been continuing his investigation of the Wickenburg Massacre, on the orders of Colonel Dudley. He found a prostitute in Prescott who had worked for Mollie up until the sale of the brothel. She reported that Kruger had met with some Mexicans in the brothel a couple of days before the stage departed. Still another friend of Mollie's said that she had been told not to take "that stage on that particular day."

Shortly after Willie and Mollie had departed for Los Angeles, Salmon's body was removed from its burial spot at the massacre site and brought to Wickenburg by the members of the posse who originally had buried it.

The Prescott *Miner* reported: "This humane and benevolent act was done at the insistence of James Grant, mail contractor, and under the direction of Dr. J. Pierson. The bodies of the six murdered men now rest side by side at Wickenburg."

A few weeks later, Kruger was scathingly attacked by the *Miner* for misrepresenting the facts of the burial of Salmon after the Wickenburg Massacre. The paper referred to Willie Kruger as Mollie Shepherd's paramour. It was discussed openly that Kruger had set up the raid with the help of some Mexican bandits.

General Crook angrily disagreed. He announced that there was no doubt but what the assassins were Apaches. At the same time, he released a copy of a letter to President Grant which was a scathing attack upon the Colyar Report. According to some sources, the Crook attack was printed in the New York *Tribune* two days before the original letter reached the White House. Although almost three months had passed since the mass murders had taken place and although they had been under constant investigation by the Army, Crook told a *Tribune* reporter, "The Army will immediately conduct an investigation of the murders in an attempt to hunt down the Apaches responsible for this horrendous deed."

In San Diego, the *Union* printed a story which stated that Mexican raiders were bragging about committing the massacre, "relating detail so accurately that those hearing it had no doubt that it was true. Their boast was corroborated by the fact that they left Sonora with clothes to scarcely cover themselves and returned well-clothed and with plenty of money."

This story was picked up by the Los Angeles *News* and elaborated upon. One of the Mexican participants, the newspaper said, was a Ramón Cordova who presently was a prisoner in jail at Phoenix, Arizona. The following night, a band of vigilantes swooped down on the Phoenix jail, kidnapped Cordova and hanged him from the nearest tree.

Again General Crook issued a statement that the Apaches were solely responsible, chiding the Western press for not agreeing and not rallying public support to combat the Apache menace, as their fellow journalists were doing in the Eastern part of the nation. He implied again, also, that if he were not held back by Washington, he could solve the problem within the matter of a few weeks.

Colonel Nathan Dudley disagreed. As the white settlers began to follow General Crook's cue, Dudley wrote to the Bureau of Indian Affairs: "I do not believe there was an Apache near the scene of the murder. All honest men have the same opinion, if they dared express it."

Reporters in San Francisco found Willie Kruger living in a suite at the Barbary Hotel and asked him to comment on the controversy. "It was Apaches," Willie insisted. "There can be no doubt about it. I saw them and I battled them for hours."

"Are you still in the Army?"

"No, I have been discharged honorably."

"How are you living?"

"From my investments."

"Where is Mollie Shepherd?"

Willie brushed a tear from his eye and the reporter noted that he appeared to have difficulty in answering. Then he raised his head. "She died in Los Angeles a month ago from the wounds inflicted upon her by the savages."

One of the reporters wanted to know why no one had heard of the death before this.

"She asked for a quiet funeral," Willie said. "Of course, I respected her dying wish."

Word of Mollie's death reached the East and no one questioned Willie's version of the passing of his loved one. A San Francisco reporter, however, did, and asked a Los Angeles colleague to get the details. When no record of her death could be found, the reporter went back to the Barbary Hotel. Willie Kruger had moved out. He left no forwarding address.

The New York *Tribune*, still incensed over the death of Loring, continued its attack on the policies of Colyar and the Bureau of Indian Affairs. It demanded in a constant barrage that law and order be restored in the Arizona Territory, asserting that the only way this could be accomplished was to rid the country of Apaches "at once and for all." The outcry was continued by most of the other major newspapers along the northeastern seaboard.

President Grant gave in. He overruled the pacification

policy of the Bureau of Indian Affairs that was instituted by Colyar and ordered General Crook to march against the Apaches.

On September 8, 1872, almost a year after the Wickenburg Massacre, Crook personally led a detachment of troops to the Date Creek Reservation "to arrest those responsible for this foul deed." There has been no explanation ever offered as to why he did not refer the matter to the military detachment which was encamped permanently in an area adjacent to the reservation, nor is there any explanation as to why it did not take part in the ensuing battle.

It was a costly fight. Crook lost a large number of his own men and was almost killed himself, but the toll among the Apaches gathered on the reservation was high, about sixty warriors. A band of fifty Apache warriors escaped.

On September 25, units of the Fifth Cavalry, guided by Hualpai scouts, surprised the band on the Santa Maria River. Forty of the Apaches and a few more soldiers were slain here. After this battle, General Crook announced that the Indians responsible for the Wickenburg Massacre had been found among the dead. "The account is closed," he reported to Washington and the press.

In December of 1872, a short, stocky man, dressed like a prospector, entered a small bar in Phoenix, Arizona, and ordered a straight whiskey. Just as he was about to raise the glass to his lips a gunfight broke out in another part of the room. Two men were killed, one the loser of the altercation and the other, the short stocky man who had just entered the bar.

An investigation, held immediately, disclosed that the winner of the gun battle had acted in self-defense. The prospector had been killed by a stray shot from the other man's revolver. The sheriff went through the stocky man's pockets and found only a few dollars and the key to a nearby hotel room. The man had registered under the name of William Kruger of San Francisco. He had told the clerk he was planning "a little prospecting" and would be there only one night. There was nothing in his room but some toilet articles and a .38 revolver.

In a nearby livery stable, the sheriff found a mule and horse, purchased the day before by William Kruger, and stored in the stable were camping supplies of the type usually used by a prospector.

No relatives came forward. On the following day, this William Kruger was buried in a common grave. Apparently no one thought to ask if he was the sole survivor of the Wickenburg Massacre.

The $100,000 of federal payroll money in the iron box never has been found and today no one is even certain where the massacre occurred, other than that it is about nine miles west of Wickenburg. No one knows where the old stagecoach trail passed. There is a plaque on Highway 60–70 which runs a few miles south of the old trail which states "somewhere near here is located the Wickenburg Massacre site" and the plaque attributes the murders to the Apaches.

The graves of the victims have become lost. If there ever were any markers placed upon them, they have long since disappeared. There are several dude ranches in the area, including the famed Remuda Ranch. Occasionally a rider from the Remuda will pause near the banks of a dry stream on a high mesa and gaze curiously at a mound of rocks which support a crudely made cross and if, upon his return, he asks its significance, he will be told by Dana Burden, the ranch owner, that it marks the site of Salmon's grave. But Burden will wryly admit that the grave was constructed more than three-quarters of a century after the attack. He will not, however, accept any theory other than that the Apaches were responsible for the murders.

Nevertheless, there was no evidence of any rich Indians around the reservation. If Mexican bandits had strayed that far north of the border, they certainly would not have tarried to bury an empty iron box. But if someone was planning to return to pick up his loot, he would have taken the shovel from the stage and buried the box with its $100,000.

If Willie Kruger was the villain in the Wickenburg Massacre, his plan to get rich cost the lives of some one hundred persons. If the Willie Kruger who was killed in Phoenix was the only survivor of the massacre, then there probably still lies buried $100,000 in one box and about $40,000 of Mollie Shepherd's money in another. It will be somewhere on a high dry mesa, near a dry riverbed, about three quarters of a mile from a small canyon, and about nine miles due west of Wickenburg.

CALIFORNIA'S LOST DIAMONDS

Almost fifty million dollars' worth of raw gold was grubbed from the famed Cherokee Mine of California a few miles north of Oroville. In the late 1870's, the Cherokee was the largest hydraulic gold mine operation in the United States. Under the hydraulic method, huge nozzles called monitors shot high-pressure streams of water against the earth, pulverizing and washing hundreds of tons of it an hour through vast sluice boxes where the heavier gold was separated from the gravel.

The remains of Cherokee today barely accommodate its ghosts, but when the gold mine was in operation, the town contained some seven thousand persons, all of whom were more in-

51

terested in gold than in diamonds. The first known diamond discovery was made by a gentleman named Mike Maher, who found a perfect blue specimen in 1863. It was considered a freak of nature and no attention was paid to it and the same disinterest prevailed a short time later when John Moore came across a six-carat stone.

The attention of the miners, the merchants, and the prostitutes was focused solely upon gold until 1893, when the California legislature passed an anti-hydraulic mining law which made it impossible for the Cherokee owners to continue operating at a profit. The town died quickly, but itinerant prospectors continued to pick over the tailings.

One of these itinerants was a lean-faced, whiskered gentleman by the name of Jerome Hulsey. Shortly after the turn of the century, Hulsey appeared in a San Francisco bank carrying three large diamonds which he asked to have appraised and placed in a safety deposit vault. This was precisely the opening step that had been taken by Asbury Harpending a few years earlier when he perpetrated the great diamond hoax by salting a field in Colorado with worthless diamonds.

A representative of the bank replied coldly that the bank was not in the business of appraising diamonds and suggested that he take them to a jeweler for appraisal. The bank would be willing to rent Hulsey a safe deposit box, however, and the be-whiskered prospector thought this was a reasonable attitude for the bank to take. He left, saying that he would be back "if these little agates are worth anything."

An hour later he was back with two of the diamonds and a check from a prominent San Francisco jeweler that paid Hulsey $8000. The prospector placed two diamonds in the safe deposit box and insisted upon taking the money for the check in cash. Hulsey immediately rented a suite at the city's finest hotel, the Palace, where he slept during most of the daylight hours. His evenings were spent whooping it up on the Barbary Coast. In less than a month, he had run through his first $8000.

He returned to the bank, canceled his safe-deposit rental and presumably sold his other two "little agates," but to whom and for how much is unknown. He raised enough money, however, to keep him going for approximately three months at the same standard of living he had enjoyed during the first.

Sometime during the fourth month he was evicted from the Palace for nonpayment of his bill. At about the same time, he approached a San Francisco merchant named Abraham Stein for a grubstake, telling Stein that he knew where several more diamonds could be found. Stein gave Hulsey three hundred dollars which he lost the same evening in a Barbary Coast gambling hall. He went back to Stein, told him what he had done, and asked for another grubstake. This time he told Stein that he had found the diamonds in the area of the old Cherokee Mine, but Stein was unimpressed and turned down Hulsey's invitation to advance another grubstake. Hulsey drifted on and, as near as can be determined, was never seen around San Francisco or Cherokee again.

Several years later, Stein was introduced to William Cooney, a South African diamond expert who was visiting San Francisco. During the ensuing conversation, Stein mentioned his experience with Hulsey. Cooney immediately became interested, so much so that he went to Cherokee. He found that the area abounded in kimberlite, a blue volcanic clay contingent with diamonds. He was so impressed that upon his return to San Francisco, he prevailed upon Stein and three other locally prominent financiers to incorporate the United States Diamond Company under the laws of Arizona, with a capitalization of 2.5 million dollars. The stock sold for one dollar a share, with half offered for public sale and the balance reserved for the five founders of the corporation.

Cooney had a flair for publicity. Two days after the stock

was offered for sale, a woman near Cherokee found a two-carat diamond in the craw of the turkey she was cleaning. The stock doubled its value. The corporation took an option on forty acres of land near Cherokee. Three more diamonds were found in the area by Henry Vail, a vice-president of the corporation.

The pattern was closely following the Harpending scandal and one San Francisco newspaper reprinted the story of the great diamond hoax. The price of the stock dropped from three and one half dollars to seventy-five cents, but Stein sold out before it reached its low point and discovered that he had made about three hundred dollars on the deal, which repaid the grubstake he had advanced to Hulsey.

Cooney suddenly became reticent. He shunned reporters, and the United States Diamond Corporation issued no more press releases. When another newspaper hinted broadly that Cooney and Harpending had much in common, Cooney replied tersely that he "didn't give a damn whether anyone bought or sold the stock." He moved his offices from San Francisco to Oroville, although he continued to maintain a luxurious apartment on San Francisco's Nob Hill. Cooney's three remaining partners, including Vail, became nervous and gradually began to unload their holdings in the open market, eventually driving the price down to three cents a share. Visits to San Francisco by Cooney became less frequent.

The city assessor of Chico, California, was a man named Harold Sweetman, who, because of his friendship with Vail, had bought a few thousand shares of the company. One day Sweetman was visited by a smooth-shaven, well-dressed stranger in his forties who spoke English with the same accent as Cooney. The stranger first asked several questions about the tax structure in Chico, implying that he was thinking of building a small manufacturing plant within the city. He then casually brought the subject around to diamonds. Presently he offered to buy Sweetman's shares in the United States Diamond Company. Sweetman said he would think it over and that night he wrote to Vail asking his advice. Vail suggested that he sell, saying that 3 per cent recovery factor was better than nothing. Sweetman followed his advice and sold to the man, who was temporarily living in Oroville.

A couple of weeks later, Vail received another letter, this time from an old friend named Lorbeer who lived in Oroville. Lorbeer told him of a strange happening at the old Cherokee Mine. Two prospectors who had been picking at the tailings of the mine had galloped into Oroville in a state of high excitement. They carried with them a hatful of diamonds encrusted with blue clay—or what they thought were diamonds. The stones had been given to Cooney for appraisal, and Cooney had sent them on to San Francisco for analysis.

Vail sighed, remembering the turkey with the diamond in its craw, and wrote back that Cooney probably was just trying to put some value on worthless stock. Less than a week later, he received another letter from Lorbeer. Another South African was staying with Cooney, and, Lorbeer added, Cooney had announced that the diamonds the miners found were worthless; nothing but shiny rocks. The two miners had objected when Cooney told them he had thrown the rocks away while in San Francisco and Cooney had apologized and given them five-hundred dollars to atone for his oversight. It was at this point that Vail suddenly became suspicious. He recalled the letter from Sweetman and he knew that there were few prospectors who would be able to tell a shiny rock from a diamond when they saw one.

He contacted all of the original partners and discovered that all had sold their stock on the open market. A few days later, he learned that Cooney held almost 90 per cent of the stock in the United States Diamond Company. Furious, Vail went to Oroville to confront the debonair South African.

Cooney readily admitted that he had purchased all of the stock. "It was a humanitarian gesture," he explained. "I felt it was an obligation upon my part to see that these people got back a little something on their investment. After all, it was because of my mistakes that they did make their investment."

"I would like to see the old mine shaft where these so-called rocks were found," Vail demanded.

Cooney shook his head sadly. "It has been boarded up," he explained. "After all, there is no sense in having other people go through the same disappointment."

Vail was nonplussed. He checked before he returned to San Francisco and found that Cooney had, indeed, closed the old mine. But why, if there were diamonds, would Cooney shut down a mine? Conversely, if there were no diamonds, why had Cooney bought up all the stock?

About a month after Vail's visit, Cooney closed up the offices of the United States Diamond Company in Oroville and moved back to San Francisco. Vail was obsessed with finding the answer to the riddle. The more he investigated, the more curious he became. Cooney had exercised the corporation's options on the acreage around the mine. He had paid the taxes on the property, and, if his manner of living in San Francisco was any indication, he was much wealthier than when he had first arrived.

A year went by and Cooney once again paid the taxes on the property. In the spring of the following year, a flash flood after a heavy rain swept through the denuded area.

In the fall of the same year, Vail was in Chico and he stopped in to see his old friend, the city assessor. Inevitably, the subject turned to Cooney and his peculiar behavior.

Sweetman had been paid for his stock in cash. Not once during the two conversations Sweetman had with the purchaser, did the man volunteer his name. He definitely was a foreigner and he spoke English fluently, but with the same accent as Cooney. A few days after the transaction, Sweetman had been in Oroville and he had seen Cooney and the stranger in the dining room of the Oroville Hotel.

On his way back to San Francisco, Vail detoured by way of the Cherokee Mine. The land was denuded, both from the flood and the hydraulic mining. It was now covered with gravel and debris, and there was nothing resembling the magic blue kimberlite clay. He went to the Oroville Hotel and talked to some of the employees. All remembered the stranger. He had dined on many occasions in the hotel dining room with Cooney during his visit, which was understandable, as he was a guest of the hotel. His name was Schuyler.

Vail asked if he could see the registration ledger.

"Of course," the desk clerk replied.

Jan Schuyler from Johannesburg, South Africa, had been a guest of the hostelry for three weeks. Vail made a note of the address. A few days later, back in San Francisco, he wrote to the mysterious Schuyler.

"Dear Sir," he wrote. "It has come to my attention that you are interested in purchasing stock of the United States Diamond Company. I still have in my possession a few thousand shares of this company which I would be willing to sell to you at a reasonable figure.

"I am aware that you quite probably have not returned to South Africa from California, but I am presuming that your secretary will forward this missive to your present address which, unfortunately, I have misplaced.

"I would be delighted to meet with you anywhere at our mutual convenience to discuss the aforementioned matter."

A little more than two months later, Vail received a reply written on the stationery of the DeBeers Syndicate of Johannesburg. It said that Mr. Schuyler presently was in New York in the United States and that Vail's letter had been forwarded to him.

Vail made a few more inquiries and discovered that the DeBeers Syndicate reportedly controlled 88 per cent of the world's diamond production and that it kept a reserve fund of approximately half a billion dollars, from which it could finance purchase of newly discovered diamond mines throughout the world.

Vail never received a reply from Schuyler. A subsequent letter sent to the DeBeers Syndicate also went unanswered.

For several years after the closing of the mine, Cooney lived as a millionaire in San Francisco. In later years, he lived more conservatively and, in 1922, he moved to Salem, Oregon. Then in 1929, the stock market crash apparently hurt him severely because during the Depression he lived very modestly in Salem. When he died in 1942, at the age of ninety, he was almost a pauper.

The area in which the old mine shaft was located is well known. Cherokee still is carried on California maps, but no one seems to know who, if anyone, has title to the old mine.

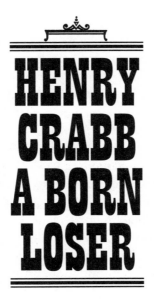

HENRY CRABB A BORN LOSER

The popularity of the filibusterers during the mid-nineteenth century was indeed great in San Francisco. It was here that William Walker raised money and troops for a hapless expedition into Baja California that ended in ignominy when he commandeered some stolen cattle from a Mexican bandit. Because of this, Walker was run back into the United States with his only possession the suit of underwear he was wearing.

Natives of San Francisco spent money as lavishly as a Pentagon general when a filibustering expedition was involved, raising the funds effortlessly on the presumption that the filibusterer was going to liberate the Mexicans. No one ever did quite understand why the Mexicans never gave a damn about being liberated.

After William Walker came a gentleman by the name of Gaston Rausset de Boulbon, who said he was a French count, but who was definitely one of the finest French chefs of the city by the Golden Gate. Boulbon replaced his tall white hat with a duck-billed cap one day in 1852 and declared himself the governor-general and military dictator of the Mexican State of Sonora.

Generous San Franciscans quickly raised enough money to buy Boulbon a brig named the *Challenge*, with enough left over to finance and supply an army of three hundred. A few weeks later, the *Challenge* dropped anchor at the harbor of Guaymas. The first detachment to land was greeted by an army of four hundred Mexican soldiers, under command of a General Yañez. Forty-eight of the count's army were killed and seventy-eight were wounded. The count was brought before a Mexican military court that convened on the beach, found guilty of filibustering, and executed. The remainder of his army, still on board the *Challenge*, decided to return to San Francisco. They were only a few miles out of the harbor, however, when the ship was capsized by an extraordinarily large tidal bore sweeping up the Gulf of California, which effectively wiped out the remainder of the Boulbon liberation expedition.

Five years passed before the next attempt was made to liberate Sonora. Unlike the others, the idea for this expedition was originated in Sonora by experts in the art of chicanery. They picked their victim well: a handsome and fairly young dilettante from San Francisco who was thoroughly fed up with the illiterate masses in California and the so-called democratic procedures in the United States.

His name was Henry A. Crabb. He was the son of a rich Southern farmer who had made a fortune dealing in slave traffic. Shortly after achieving majority, Crabb moved to San Francisco.

With the help of his father, he financed a half-dozen small businesses in San Francisco, none of which took much of his time, but all of which proved successful. He liked to entertain and to deliver polemics on the role of the Negro in the new society of the United States so it was natural that he would gravitate to politics. He served one term in the California State Assembly, but was defeated when he ran for reelection. He next ran for the United States Senate as a candidate for the Know-Nothing Party. Again, he was defeated. It was after this that he began to complain seriously about the emergence of the lower classes in the United States as a political force.

Shortly after his arrival in San Francisco, Crabb had married a beautiful young Mexican aristocrat named Filomena Ainsa, a direct descendant of the well-known Spanish explorer, Juan Bautista de Anza. Her father was Don Manuel Ainsa, who, although he was eminently successful in business in San Francisco, was a very bitter man because all of his holdings in Sonora had been confiscated. He, too, objected to the emergence of the lower classes as a political power, not only in the United States, but in Mexico as well.

When Don Manuel was very young, Augustine de Iturbide had proclaimed himself Emperor of Mexico. Iturbide had the support of the Ainsas, along with most of the rest of the Mexican aristocracy. Very shortly after he assumed power, however, the regime was challenged by a revolutionary named Vincente Guerrero and Guerrero won the support of the state government officials in Sonora. The mine-owners shut down their mines in protest. The landowners let their land lie fallow. In retaliation, the state government confiscated all of the Ainsa properties as a warning to other aristocrats. Manuel Ainsa fled to the United States with his parents.

The other members of the aristocracy in Sonora fought back by financing a local revolution against the state government, a revolution which they won. They then declared their support of the distant Emperor Iturbide. The Ainsas returned to Sonora, happily, to reclaim their property; then left sadly when they discovered their former friends had divided it among themselves because the Ainsas had not remained to help in the revolt. Eventually, Iturbide was overthrown, but the new federal government did not think it worth the effort to replace the conservative state government in isolated Sonora and this conservative element still ruled the state when Boulbon and Walker made their abortive attempts to "liberate" it.

Manuel Ainsa had a close friend in Sonora named Hilario Gabilondo. Like Ainsa, Gabilondo came from a proper family, and like Ainsa, his family had lost considerable holdings to the state government which was controlled by Governor Jesus Gandera. There was still another man who had felt the confiscatory hand of Gandera. His name was Ignacio Pesqueira and he had fled to the hills to attempt the organization of a peasant army which would overthrow Gandera. Unfortunately, Pesqueira had no arms, no money, and such a small handful of followers that Gandera did not think it important enough to send General Yañez after him.

The voyage from Sonora to San Francisco is not a long one and Hilario Gabilondo made frequent trips to the California city. Usually, he was either a house guest of Crabb's or Ainsa's. On his trip in December, 1856, he was the guest of Ainsa. It was on this trip that he proposed to his host that Ainsa and Crabb finance a shipment of arms to Pesqueira and also lend him a sufficient amount of money to overthrow the corrupt government of Gandera. In return for this relatively minor investment, Gabilondo proposed, Ainsa would have all of his former holdings restored. Crabb would be given a large grant of land and, additionally, the authority to operate some of the more productive mines in the area.

"But Pesqueira is nothing more than a peasant," Ainsa protested.

"He can be handled all the more easily," Gabilondo replied. "Once he is in power, we will make him feel like an aristocrat and he will do as we want."

The following day, Gabilondo and Ainsa went to see Crabb. The frustrated politician was indeed interested. He told Gabilondo how disgusted he was with the stupidity of the California electorate. The idea of the good life of a Mexican aristocrat in Sonora appealed to him. An agreement was drawn up and signed by Crabb and by Gabilondo, the latter identifying himself as a bona fide agent of Pesqueira. In return for a shipload of rifles and ammunition and $10,000 of United States currency, Crabb was to be given 400,000 acres of good farmland and a franchise to operate at least two of the more productive silver mines for a period of ninety-nine years. As soon as Pesqueira was in power, Crabb would come to Sonora.

In addition, Crabb wanted the agreement signed by Pesqueira so that there would be no misunderstanding. Gabilondo protested, but Crabb was insistent.

Two months later, Gabilondo was back in San Francisco. Pesqueira had signed the contract and as soon as Pesqueira was in control of the government, Crabb would be given a royal welcome on his arrival in Sonora.

A few weeks after this, a ship anchored offshore somewhere between Guaymas and Hermosillo to unload a large shipment of arms and ammunition for Pesqueira. Presumably, the $10,000 in cash also was given to Pesqueira through Gabilondo, to allow him to finance the recruitment of an army of his own. The revolution that overthrew Gandera and sent him and General Yañez to refuge in Mexico City was extremely short. The federal government in the Mexican capital was pleased over the outcome because it wiped out the last pocket of Iturbide supporters. If anyone in the capital wondered where Pesqueira acquired his strength, the question was not raised publicly.

As soon as word of Pesqueira's success reached San Francisco, a jubilant Crabb mapped his plans for his foray into Mexico. Ninety men were recruited immediately for an overland trip to Sonora. General John D. Cosby was retained to raise another thousand "volunteers," who would then proceed by ship to Port Lobos on the Sonoran coast and rendezvous with Crabb's advance party in the vicinity of Altar, Mexico. Some of these men would be placed in government positions; others would have managerial positions on the hacienda or at the mines. All would become rich. Crabb made no mention publicly of the concessions he had been granted by Pesqueira and the San Francisco newspapers gleefully reported the expedition as another filibustering foray. The Mexican consul general, Don Luis del Valle, forwarded copies of the newspapers to Mexico City. Others wound up in the possession of Jesus Gandera and General Yañez in Mexico City. Before Crabb departed from San Francisco in January of 1857, Mexican newspapers in the capital, Guadalajara, and Vera Cruz were angrily denouncing the start of still another filibuster by American bandits. The Mexican federal government sent a courier to Hermosillo to see if Pesqueira was adequately equipped to withstand the expected invasion. The courier reported back that Pesqueira had a force of more than twenty-five hundred men equipped with the latest American rifles, plus ammunition, and even three mobile cannons. His army, the courier said, was better equipped than the best troops in the federal forces.

Crabb assumed the title of general, bid farewell to his wife and four-year-old son, Augustin, and sailed with a division of ninety men from San Francisco to Los Angeles. Among the ninety was Jesus Ainsa, his brother-in-law, who was to act as interpreter. The advance contingent paused in El Monte, a suburb of Los Angeles, to outfit the expedition, then headed overland toward the arduous Camino del Diablo to Mexico. Why Crabb chose this tortuous overland route in place of a quicker and more comfortable sea voyage is a mystery that never has been explained, other than that Crabb was destined to be as poor a gen-

eral as he was a politician. The expedition was plagued with trouble even before it had completed the comparatively easy stage of
the journey between El Monte and Yuma. Men became sick from
drinking bad water. Others were injured in accidents. One of the
covered wagons that had been purchased collapsed a little more
than fifty miles out and had to be abandoned along with supplies
for which there was no room in the other wagons.

In San Francisco, General Cosby suddenly lost all interest
in the expedition. He made no attempt to recruit the additional
thousand men, nor to buy the ship and supplies. Men who did
apply to join the task force were turned away. One report tells
that the general moved into more luxurious quarters on Nob Hill
and invested heavily and successfully in the stockmarket.

In Mexico City, Gandera and General Yañez managed to
get copies of the report made by the federal government courier
and both speculated publicly that Pesqueira had received his arms
from Crabb and that he planned to turn the State of Sonora over
to the filibusterers as part of the deal. Pesqueira was incensed.
There was not a bit of truth to the charge, he cried. To prove it,
he issued a manifesto calling upon all Sonorans to take up arms in
defense of their homeland and drive out the filibusterers.

In the latter part of March, Crabb reached the small border town of Sonoita. His forces of ninety had dwindled to sixty-
nine. The casualties had been left behind in small towns to
recover and of the sixty-nine, twenty-nine were in such poor
health that Crabb decided to leave them behind to rest and follow
the main expedition at a more leisurely pace. It was in Sonoita
that Crabb learned for the first time that all was not going well in
Sonora. While camped just across the border, he was greeted by
an emissary of Don Jose Maria Redondo's, the prefect of Altar, a
city a few miles into Mexico, who stated that if Crabb entered the
State of Sonora he would be annihilated by the armed forces of
the state.

Now Crabb was incensed. He wrote a stinging letter to

65

Redondo, pointing out that he was coming at the invitation of some of the most influential persons in the state and warning Redondo that if any blood was shed, Redondo would have to bear the full blame. He told the messenger, also, that he would be glad to receive Redondo and explain the situation to him when he arrived in Caborca, where he was to rendezvous with nine hundred other men arriving by sea. Then, with forty men at his side, General Henry Crabb marched into Mexico.

In Hermosillo, Pesqueira greeted the news of the invasion by issuing another manifesto urging his fellow Sonorans to "rise and repulse the pirates." He then appointed Hilario Gabilondo as commander-in-chief of the Sonoran forces and Gabilondo dispatched a military detachment of 250 soldiers to Caborca with orders to ambush Crabb. The detachment consisted of one officer, Captain Lorenzo Rodriguez, and 249 enlisted men. Few, including Rodriguez, had ever been in a fight.

Rodriguez chose Caborca as the site of the ambush. He lined up his men in the cover of a large wheat field immediately outside of the old city's limits. On the morning of April 1, General Crabb and his army of forty men arrived in the outskirts of Caborca. When the first fusillade failed to bring down any of the enemy, Captain Rodriguez suddenly realized that he had positioned his men too far distant from the invaders to ensure any accurate fire. Standing up, he led his men in a charge, but as soon as he got within range of the Crabb forces, he was shot and killed. His detachment immediately retreated into the city.

There was a slight skirmish as Crabb entered the city, but within a very short time, the Mexican detachment took refuge in the Catholic church and the invaders requisitioned a large adobe house across the plaza from the church. For the rest of the day, the battle was a Mexican standoff, both sides firing in a desultory fashion at the other, but with no casualties inflicted.

The following day, Crabb decided to attack the convent

that abutted the church. Fifteen men, including Crabb, made the dash across the plaza. Eleven of them reached their objective. Once the convent was captured, Crabb decided to blow down the main connecting door to the church. A keg of powder was placed against the base of the door, but the "slow match" was damp and the powder could not be exploded. Crabb then wrote a note to the remaining men in the adobe house on the other side of the plaza asking that they send over another "slow match." A small Mexican girl who had been hiding in the convent was asked to take the note across. She agreed to undertake the chore, but apparently after leaving the convent she forgot her mission, for a new "slow match" never arrived.

For the next two days, nothing happened, other than that one Mexican soldier was shot while attempting to raise a Mexican flag over the belfry of the church. Then early in the morning of the next day, Crabb heard a commotion in the plaza, with cries of "Viva Don Hilario Gabilondo." General Crabb sighed with relief. One of his influential friends had arrived and apparently had the confidence of the Caborca citizenry. General Crabb raised a white flag of truce. Accompanied by one of his men, he stepped out of the convent.

J. Y. Ainsa tells of the next sequence of events in a small, privately published pamphlet printed in Phoenix, Arizona, in 1951.

As the two invaders came out of the convent, armed men began appearing in the plaza, although none came near and no one spoke. Crabb and Byven, one of his aides, walked down the street toward where they could hear the hails for Gabilondo and finally, after wending their way through several narrow streets, came out onto a large corral containing approximately one hundred saddled horses. Adjacent to the corral was an adobe building with a long veranda, crowded with armed men. At the end of the veranda, speaking to the men, was General Crabb's

67

friend, Gabilondo. Joyfully, Crabb pushed his way toward him.

"Don Hilario, my friend," he said holding out his hand. "It is a pleasure to see you."

Gabilondo gave no sign of recognition. "Who are you?" he asked harshly.

Crabb looked at him in amazement. "You do not know me?" he asked. "You do not know the man to whom you granted all the concessions and whose money you have taken?"

Gabilondo waited for no more. Lifting a sword from a table, he swung it in an arc. Before Crabb could realize what was happening, his head was partially severed from his body. Gabilondo then ordered that the unconscious General Crabb be dragged from the porch and the decapitation completed. Byven was taken prisoner and upon orders of someone other than Gabilondo, was immediately taken away by a six-man detachment to Altar.

In the plaza, meanwhile, the nine men left in the convent slowly came out into the open, following the example of their general. Two of the armed Mexicans in the square drifted behind them, looked inside the convent, saw that it was empty, and then one of them signaled. The nine men were instantly shot where they stood. Many of the assailants then were cut down by a fusillade of bullets from the opposite side of the plaza by the remainder of Crabb's forces.

The fight was about over, however. Within the next couple of hours, the Gabilondo army successfully set fire to the thatched roof of the adobe house. The defenders attempted unsuccessfully to put out the fire by blowing up gunpowder. By dusk, they had to choose between surrender or incineration; they chose the former, but their lives were prolonged by only a matter of minutes. After all had surrendered their arms, they were marched over to the corral and all but one were shot. The exception was a sixteen-year-old youth named Charles Edward

Evans, who was imprisoned for about six months, then sent back to the United States.

A few days later, a Gabilondo patrol intercepted the second contingent of Crabb's forces, a twenty-man group, and killed them all. The patrol then went on to Sonoita, crossed the border and killed the ill and the sick who had been left there, with one exception, Jesus Ainsa, who was taken prisoner. Ainsa, Evans, and Byven all were released and returned to the United States. Jesus Ainsa, however, returned very shortly to Sonora where he was granted land and mining concessions, only to have them expropriated some years later when still another revolution resulted in a new party in control of the government.

In Guaymas today, there is a statue of General Yañez, who defeated the filibusterer Boulbon. In Caborca, the date that marked the death of Crabb is celebrated as an annual holiday because he is thought of in Mexico as a hated filibusterer, rather than as a vain and rather foolish man who was the victim of a most elaborate swindle. Pesqueira governed for many years in Sonora and Gabilondo died a wealthy and respected man, as did General Cosby in San Francisco.

The head of General Crabb was displayed in a large bottle of mescal in Caborca for many years, then it, too, became lost.

A LOST CHORD IN TIJUANA BRASS

Telegrams come and telegrams
   go
Over the wires to Mexico
Ferris the bold, is keeping them
   hot
But Diaz the diplomat answers
   not
                —*San Francisco Chronicle*

The decimation of Henry Crabb's party proved a successful deterrent to other would-be filibusterers and Mexico was left pretty much alone by North American invaders, until the start of the twenty-four-year-long revolution in Mexico that followed the ouster of the Dictator Porfirio Diaz in 1912. General John Pershing spent 130 million dollars in his futile chase of Pancho Villa around the desolate deserts of Chihuahua, after Villa raided

Columbus, New Mexico. At about the same time there was an incursion into Baja California by a peculiar assortment of Wobblies—soldiers of fortune, dedicated and mercenary Mexicans loosely united under the banner of a Mexican presidential contender named Ricardo Flores Magon. For several years, this ragtail army of Magon's lived in the northern part of Baja California in a state of utter confusion because of Magon's reluctance to leave his Los Angeles hideout and, even more, because of the antics of a California press agent and promoter known as Ferris the Bold.

Richard Wells Ferris made his first public appearance as an actor in Washington, D.C. He moved to Los Angeles in 1867 where he continued as an actor. He married a well-known actress named Florence Stone and for several years they appeared in popular plays together, both in San Francisco and in Los Angeles. By 1910, he had become expert enough in fooling the public that he decided he was well qualified for politics. He ran, as a Democrat, for the lieutenant-governorship of California. Out of the 100,000 votes cast, Ferris lost by only 6,000. Immediately after the election, he had plans for running for public office again and decided that it would improve his image if he temporarily gave up his acting career. Through political friends, he was appointed director of publicity for the Panama-California Exposition, a year-long fiesta to be held in San Diego's sprawling Balboa Park.

"You can count on me to dream up some live publicity stunts which will hold the public's attention indefinitely," he promised the Exposition's commissioners. The commissioners nodded in approval, although it is unlikely that any of them knew what Ferris had in mind. Certainly Ricardo Flores Magon had no idea that the revolution he was setting up in Baja was due to become demoralized because of the activities of a San Diego press agent.

Magon's role in fomenting dissent against the Diaz regime has been well chronicled by historians. An avowed anarchist, he had been fighting Diaz since 1900, when he founded the newspaper *La Regeneratión* in Mexico City. Forced to flee to the United States, he continued to publish the paper, first in San Antonio, Texas, then in St. Louis, Missouri, and finally in Los Angeles. It was in St. Louis in 1906 that he planned the first unsuccessful rebellion against Diaz in Chihuahua and Sonora. He tried again in 1908 and failed. Members of his Liberal party were arrested by the thousands in Mexico, despite Diaz' assertion to James Creelman, a reporter for *Pearson's Magazine*, that he would welcome the formation of an opposition party.

By 1911, when Ferris the Bold was hired as publicity director for the Panama-California Exposition, Diaz had a more powerful enemy in the person of Francisco I. Madero, who had formed the Anti-Reelectionist party and whose army had taken possession of the City of Juarez, across from the United States city of El Paso. Magon believed the Maderistas should be subservient to the Liberal party if for no other reason than Magon's seniority in fighting Diaz and thus, in Los Angeles, Magon mapped his plans for the invasion of Baja California. This, he believed, would give him a Mexican base from which he could eventually assume his proper role in the Mexican government. The target for the invasion was Mexicali.

Four Magonistas were contacted in the border city and ordered to recruit supporters, a task that was rather difficult to carry out, as most of the fervid Magonistas were in jail. On the United States side, the assignment of raising a guerrilla army was given to two Mexicans, Jose Maria Leyva and Simon Berthold. Both were active members in the Industrial Workers of the World, better known as Wobblies, who had spent most of their time in Los Angeles exhorting against the labor policies of General Harrison Oris of the Los Angeles *Times*. These two men paused at the Wobblies headquarters in Holtville, picked up four men there, then crossed the border to collect a dozen men who had been recruited there. The sixteen-man army captured Mexicali easily. The only casualty in the early morning raid was the town's jailer, who was shot accidentally while the Magonistas were being released from prison.

When word of the invasion reached the Baja California capital in Enseñada, it was treated casually by the territorial governor, one Colonel Celso Vega. Vega had been appointed by Diaz, but apparently he was of sufficient political bent to wait out the situation calmly until he could determine how the revolution was proceeding on the mainland. Many Mexicans apparently had similar inclinations because there was no immediate uproar in Mexicali over the change in the municipal government. The city's capture, however, did stir up a furor in the United States.

The Wobblies immediately gave their support to Magon and, as most of them were out of work, it was not difficult to expand the army of occupation to approximately 150 men. The army was divided into about even thirds of Wobblies, Mexicans, and Cocopah Indians, and later was augmented by a scattering of mercenaries. It was financed by taxes placed on the merchants and collections made by appeals through Magon's newspaper and money raised by the Wobblies in southern California.

Vega finally decided to run the invaders back across the border. He enlisted an army of 100 volunteers and six regulars and marched toward Mexicali. A few more volunteers arrived from Tijuana and in the town of Tecate, Vega paused for drill practice. Unexpectedly heavy rains slowed the practice sessions and many of the volunteers quietly slipped away. Nevertheless, Vega was able to dislodge a small contingent of Magonistas from Picacho Pass and by mid-February, he set out for Mexicali once again. When his army was passing through a ranch owned by an American named Louis Little, it was ambushed by the

Magonistas. Several more of the Vega "volunteers" resigned immediately and Vega was wounded. After a few minutes of fighting, Vega headed back toward Ensenada and, peculiarly, the Magonistas went back to Mexicali.

It was at this point that Ferris the Bold began to take an interest publicly in Baja California. He called a press conference in San Francisco and announced that because Baja California was so close to San Diego, where the Panama-California Exposition was to be held, and because so many visitors would be coming to San Diego, it would be in everyone's best interests if Diaz would sell Baja California to a group of American multimillionaires. He followed this up quickly with a series of announcements that J. P. Morgan and James Hill were interested in the project. The new state would be named the Republic of Diaz and after a brief period of independence, it would be sold to the United States for "a neat profit to the sponsors of the transaction." Ferris then called upon Dr. Plutarco Ornelas, the Mexican consul in San Francisco, with a demand that the proposal be forwarded at once to Diaz for consideration.

A few days later, Ferris announced that if Diaz refused to sell, he would be faced by a Ferris-led filibuster. No sooner did this announcement come out, than ads appeared in the New York *American*, the *World*, and the *Herald* seeking more than one thousand men with a solid military background to join General Dick Ferris. The ads promised to pay all expenses for those found to be qualified.

The Los Angeles *Herald* reported that Ferris planned to operate a sporting republic beyond the border with gambling and the pursuit of pleasure.

Magon paid little attention, nor did his ragtail army, which was still carousing in Mexicali with occasional shootouts and "elections" of commanding officers. The Mexican merchants and professional strata were finally becoming annoyed. The Calexico

74

Chronicle referred to the Magonistas as "predatory marauders" and the resentment against the enforced tribute to support the band grew daily. Peter B. Kyne, the western novelist, interviewed Rhys Pryce, after he had been elected general, at the commandeered Little Ranch and was told that money collected on the Mexican side of the border had been sent on to Magon in Los Angeles to purchase more arms and ammunition and enlist more men. Magon, according to Pryce, used the money for propaganda, and thus his triumphant army was restricted to a membership of 150 and confined to the Mexicali area. From Los Angeles Magon issued orders which were ignored. He, in turn, ignored repeated suggestions that he come back to Mexico and assume command of his troops, whose mission was to seize control of the entire nation.

During this hiatus, Ferris the Bold was rather inactive in his drive for a separate state in Baja California, probably because he had taken an additional job as press agent for the San Francisco Native Sons Fiesta. As soon as this project was completed, however, Ferris returned to San Diego, picked up a reporter from the *Tribune*, and journeyed to Mexicali to meet with General Rhys Pryce.

"We discussed matters of mutual concern," Ferris said. "It would be premature to disclose the details of the conversation at this time."

Even this meeting prompted only a minor reaction from Magon. He kissed him off with the following comment in his newspaper. "Ferris, the Ferocious Filibuster, is still making a wee noise like a sporting republic for Baja California. But that noise has become very wee indeed, scarcely more than the feeble peep of a newborn chick."

The Mexican segment of the Magon army in Mexicali began to dwindle. Most of the Mexicans were patriots who had long followed Magon's leadership, but when Magon still refused to return to Mexico, these soldiers switched their allegiance to the more courageous Madero who, on the mainland, was winning his battle against Diaz. Because of these defections, Magon's army now consisted primarily of a group of thugs and Wobblies. Among its officers were Marshall Brooks, a cattle rustler from Campo; Sam Barron, a professional train robber; James Dunham, who had murdered his wife and several of her relatives with an ax in Los Gatos; and Mojave Red, who was reputed to have beaten at least a half-dozen men to death with his huge fists. With additions such as these, Magon's army had increased to about 250 men. Shortly after the visit to Pryce by Ferris the Bold, Pryce took his army on the march. A small segment moved to the south and captured the tiny fishing village of San Quintín without a shot. The main force of the army moved on to Tijuana, about sixteen miles south from the center of San Diego. Neither the defenders nor the attackers of Tijuana had much ammunition. Pryce had been promised a cache of 20,000 rounds from Magon, but once again, Magon had found a more important purpose for the money which had been sent to pay for it. The defenders of Tijuana numbered about 150 and Colonel Vega had failed to send sufficient ammunition to beat back the attack.

Ferris was well aware of the pending battle and from San Diego he proclaimed that the fight would be a safe one for tourists and residents to watch, as there was a notable lack of ammunition on both sides. Visitors thronged by the hundreds to the border and extra United States troops had to be called out to prevent many of the tourists from crossing over into the battle zone. One indignant tourist slugged an American soldier with a bottle of whiskey and was carted off to jail.

Despite the scarcity of ammunition, 32 persons were killed and 24 wounded before Magon's army of the Liberal party captured Tijuana, sending the defenders fleeing either to Enseñada or across the border into political exile in the United States.

There was little for the disgruntled tourists to see, although they could hear occasional rifle shots in the border city.

When the fight was over, Magon claimed the twin victories of Tijuana and San Quintín as outstanding for the Liberal army. Fund-raising rallies were held in Los Angeles to carry on the struggle against the capitalistic robbers in Mexico and one of them was addressed by no less a person than Emma Goldman, the fiery American anarchist. Ferris also approved. He predicted that Tijuana would become the sporting capital of the new republic and that visitors to the Panama-California Exposition would find a side trip to this fun-loving city a delightful experience.

Magon sent an administrator, Antonio de Pio Araujo, to Tijuana to handle civilian affairs and formulate policy for the Liberal party. Pryce and his second in command, Jack Moseby, welcomed Araujo, but ignored his recommendations. Ferris also arrived in Tijuana, accompanied by a reporter from the San Diego *Union*. Again, Ferris and Pryce met secretly, then came out to talk to the newsman. When the reporter asked Pryce if he was working for the Liberal party, Pryce nodded that he was.

Ferris shook his head. "Rhys is too nice a fellow to be mixed up with that bunch," he replied.

Pryce did not bother to contradict Ferris the Bold, and the reporter and promoter once again returned to San Diego. Immediately after their departures, Pryce initiated some civil measures of his own. All tourists coming to Tijuana were to be charged a twenty-five-cent admission fee. Southern California gamblers who wished to provide their own venture capital could open up their own gambling casinos, providing they were agreeable to paying 25 per cent of their gross receipts to the Liberal army of occupation. Faro and poker palaces started immediately and work was begun on an elaborate gambling casino that "will rival Monte Carlo in its grandeur." Within a week the "take" for Pryce's army of occupation was running into hundreds upon hundreds of dollars daily. On two occasions, Pryce sent couriers north to Los Angeles carrying money to Magon. One shipment was for $300, the other for half of this amount. Magon, the great liberal and anarchist, accepted the money and said nothing about Pryce's treatment of Araujo.

In Mexico City, Madero successfully toppled the government of Porfirio Diaz, and the aging dictator fled into exile. Magon accused Madero of offering to sell out to Diaz for 20 million pesos and vowed to continue the struggle, but he still remained in Los Angeles. In Tijuana, Pryce's army grew numerically, but few of its members were Mexicans. There was a steady influx of Wobblies and one, who joined briefly, was the famed IWW troubadour, Joe Hill. Fifty Italian anarchists arrived en masse from the Pacific Northwest and were immediately enlisted. The army's casualty rate was high, not from battle, but from constant fighting among its members. A senior officer named Hopkins found a war chest containing $8,000. He decided upon immediate retirement and crossed the border, taking the money with him. He was last seen boarding the "Owl" train for Los Angeles.

The new government in Mexico City denounced the occupation of Mexicali, San Quintín, and Tijuana as filibustering. Ferris immediately replied that the army of occupation was a genuine republican force and that elections soon would be held to prove that the people of Baja California wanted an independent nation and that any attempt to destroy this new and glorious state would be met valiantly by its united citizens. Pryce went to San Diego for a meeting with Ferris, leaving the town in charge of an "acting general named Tamelyn."

What transpired at this meeting is unknown, but on the following day, Pryce went on to Los Angeles and Ferris went to Tijuana, where he met with Tamelyn and Moseby. After this meeting, the troops that could be found were summoned for an assembly.

"You've got to haul down the red flag," Ferris orated to the group. "While that might mean the symbol of the Liberal party in Mexico, it means anarchy in America. You've got to get that out of sight of every American who passes this border. You've got to cut out socialism, anarchism, and every other ism you've got into." He added that a government would have to be established that would appeal to the American press and "the better class of Mexicans" and by doing this they could get more American money and sympathy.

When the speech was finished, Ferris returned to his Exposition offices in San Diego. A few hours later, the troops once again were assembled by an officer named Louis James. Unfortunately, his rank was not high enough to command the presence of more than seventy-five soldiers and they were anxious to get back to the faro games. They listened to approximately the same exhortation from James as had been given by Ferris a few hours earlier. One of the soldiers walked over to a flagpole and cut the halyards with his machete, then kicked the fallen flag to one side. James then nominated Ferris for president and called for an immediate vote. The count was "seventy-five aye; none for nay." Ferris the Bold had won his second bid for public office overwhelmingly.

James left immediately for San Diego to convey the news to Ferris. "You have just been elected president of Baja California," he announced. "Your people are awaiting you in Tijuana."

"I'm busy today," Ferris replied.

"Well, we need a new flag," James said. "We cut down the old one."

Ferris did have time to design a new flag, one with two horizontal bars across a field of blue with a white star in the center, which he sent to a tailor with orders to have it ready by the following morning. He then called a press conference to announce his election and to say that he was seriously considering acceptance of the office. The new state now would be known as the Republic of Madero, rather than the Republic of Diaz, as originally proposed. He would see that Madero was notified of this new development, Ferris announced, and he would see also that the Mexican government was paid 15 million dollars to cover their costs for the revolution in Lower California.

"What happens if Madero doesn't like it?" a reporter asked.

"He will just have to accept it," Ferris replied.

"What about Flores Magon?"

"We are severing all connections with this junta."

Meanwhile, the Wobblies in the army, who had not bothered to attend the earlier election, held an assembly of their own. During this meeting, Hopkins and Pryce were court-martialed in absentia, the halyards repaired on the flagpole, and the red flag was flown once again over Tijuana. The Wobblies then proceeded to hold an election for a new general, and Jack Moseby defeated his competitor, Paul Schmidt, by twenty votes. Schmidt immediately resigned and left for the United States, where he was arrested for trying to smuggle a Mexican horse across the border. Moseby then sent word to the San Diego *Union* that "Dick Ferris has absolutely nothing to do with the revolutionary movement and his presence in Tijuana is not desired."

Ferris, meanwhile, had gone to Los Angeles with James where, with some friends, they were celebrating his election at a dinner in the plush Alexandria Hotel. While here, he received word that the Wobblies had deposed him as president and elected Moseby as their governing general. Ferris then announced that in order to make his position legal, he would return to Tijuana and run against Moseby in still another election.

James accompanied Ferris as far as San Diego, on his return trip. Here Ferris hired a chauffeur-driven car which, with the flag of the new Republic of Madero flying from a standard on its mudguard and Ferris in the rear seat, set out on its trip to Tijuana from in front of the Exposition offices in San Diego. A short time later, the car sped through customs and into downtown Tijuana. Here it was stopped by the Wobblies, who ripped off the offensive flag, pulled Ferris from the seat, and sent him running for his life back to the border. The following day, the beautiful Mrs. Ferris, accompanied by three friends, arrived in Tijuana as an intermediary between her husband and Moseby, but she found Moseby unsympathetic. He sent her bouncing back across the border without even refunding the dollar admission charge she had been forced to pay when she entered. When she related this unseemly conduct to her husband, he responded by issuing another lengthy statement resigning his presidency. He found that his duties with the Panama-California Exposition were too demanding to participate in the founding of the new republic.

With General Jack Moseby in charge of the occupation army, there was no relationship with Flores Magon and the attempt to justify the invasion as a part of an internal revolution was ludicrous. Moseby put on a Wild West show to attract tourists, but he did not know how to publicize it and no one came. The gambling patronage fell off. He then threatened to blow up a small railroad owned by Adolf Spreckels and a canal works that irrigated property owned by General Harrison Otis unless he was paid approximately $100,000. At the same time, Madero had sufficiently consolidated his position in the Mexican capital to pay some attention to the filibusters on the Baja Peninsula.

With the help of the powerful General Harrison Otis, Madero reached an agreement with President Taft under which

Mexican troops could be transported to Baja California over United States territory. The troops were to be unarmed while in the United States, but the agreement stated that arms could be carried in baggage cars. When word of this reached Colonel Vega in Enseñada, he no longer remained aloof to the problem in Mexicali and Tijuana. He organized an army of almost 600 and marched on Tijuana. Moseby sobered up his Wobblies and outlaws and went out on a train to meet the Vega forces. Moseby was outnumbered almost six to one and his army of wenching faro players was no match for the Vega forces. Several of his men were killed after a brief fight a few miles south of Tijuana. Those who survived fled back to the United States and were promptly arrested as they crossed the border. At the same time, in Mexicali, a group of Mexican vigilantes quickly rounded up the remnants of Moseby's forces in that city. Some were killed; the rest pushed back across the United States border where they, too, were delivered to the United States Army. The last filibuster in Mexico was ended. It was ended before the arrival of the federal troops from Mexico.

There was a Congressional hearing over the invasion, but, as is generally the case, little came of it. Flores Magon, who never did return to Mexico alive was jailed for violation of the United States neutrality laws. After completing his sentence at McNeil Island in Washington, he later was convicted of an espionage charge and sentenced to Leavenworth, where he died on November 21, 1922. In 1945, his body was taken to Mexico City where his remains were interred in the Rotunda of Illustrious Men. He is a subject of controversy in Baja, but throughout most of the rest of Mexico, his reputation is assured.

Moseby, after his return to the United States, was arrested for desertion from the United States Marine Corps. After conviction of the charge, he was sentenced to jail and en route was shot and killed while attempting to escape. Pryce is believed to have died in San Francisco's skid row.

Immediately after Moseby's defeat, Ferris the Bold went back to the stage with his wife, where he played to packed houses as the lead man in a production named *Man From Mexico*. He became interested in aviation and promoted several air races successfully. In 1921, he formed the Yellow Cab Company in Los Angeles and from then on lived quietly until his death in 1933.

To his death, he was convinced that he was the man responsible for keeping the revolution going as long as it did. "That was a lost cause before it started," he once confided to a friend. "They all would have been run out of Mexico within twenty-four hours if I hadn't showed them how to keep it going."

Ricardo Castillo, a prominent Tijuana restaurateur and historian, disagrees. "Magon was a hero to many Mexicans," he says. "At the time, the whole nation was lost and there were many loyalties. Many believed in Magon as deeply as others believed in Madero or Diaz. It was the interference from this press agent, Ferris, that kept the Mexican supporters away from Magon. Without that, Bajans possibly would have rallied behind the so-called Magon Army and have gained control of the entire Baja Peninsula as well as Sonora. Ferris was a man of pure brass. It is quite possible that he may have lost Magon the war."

There is a strange sidelight to the antics of Ferris the Bold and his press agentry in Baja California. The banquet room in which he held his dinner party to celebrate his "election" as provisional president of the newly formed Republic of Madero was never used again.

At one time, the Alexandria Hotel was among the most popular in Los Angeles and its suites have been occupied by Presidents Taft, Wilson, and Theodore Roosevelt, along with many of the world's famous personalities. Because of Ferris the Bold, however, it became half the hotel it once was.

Today, no one knows who made the reservation for the banquet room where the Ferris celebration dinner was held.

Thus, no one knows who was responsible financially for puncturing an oil painting that was hanging in the room. The painting was on loan from a local artist, uninsured, and the price that the owner placed on the damage to his work was termed exorbitant by one partner in the hotel, a Mr. Kreedman, and reasonable by the other, a Mr. Roddee.

The disagreement triggered a lifelong feud between the two partners. Roddee wrote out a check to pay for the painting from hotel funds and then gave the artist his work to take back to his studio to repair. When Kreedman brought up the matter to Roddee, he suggested that since the hotel had paid such an exorbitant price for the painting, it was the property of the hotel and therefore should be returned to the hotel as soon as possible and remain permanently in its possession. Roddee demurred. The painter was a close friend of Mrs. Roddee's and the check had been paid to cover the damage to the painting, not for the painting itself. Unfortunately for the painter, who had two other works on display in the same room, the argument became very heated and unresolved. Eventually Roddee stormed out of the hotel and went to his home, leaving his partner Kreedman brooding in his office.

A short time later, Kreedman came up with a possible solution to the dilemma. He could not remove the paintings and take possession of them because that would be theft. There was, however, nothing to prevent them from being shown publicly. Subsequently, before he left the hotel, he ordered his maintenance department to put a new lock on the door to the room and give him all of the keys to it.

The following day, Roddee learned of his partner's behavior and understandably was upset. Again, there was a heated argument with Kreedman. Before this one was over the two men had decided to dissolve their partnership. Neither of the partners wished to buy the other out, however, as both wished to remain in the hotel business. A compromise was reached. The hotel would be divided into two equal parts and a toss of the coin would determine who would build the new entrance. Roddee lost the toss. Kreedman kept the name of the Alexandria and the existing lobby.

The very next morning, work was started on the division of the hostelry. The corridors on each of the eight floors were sealed off by brick walls. The partnership was legally dissolved. At the same time, Roddee started work on a new lobby and a new entrance to the portion he had retained. Construction had gone on for several weeks before Roddee made a terrible discovery. There were neither stairs nor an elevator leading up from the first floor of his half of the building, nor was there any practical way that a stairwell or elevator shaft could be installed. Even a fire escape could not be installed unless it descended the face of the hotel and marred its appearance. Roddee took down his awnings, boarded up the entrance, and went home to figure out an answer to his problem. He never did.

Up through World War II, the Alexandria remained one of the more popular spots in the city. Its dining room was considered one of the best. Name bands played nightly in its ballroom, but few, if any, of the patrons realized that it was only half the hotel it used to be. Both Kreedman and Roddee had passed on. The Alexandria still exists, patronized during the day by lawyers and bankers who have their offices nearby. At night, its patrons are basically businessmen from out of town who wish an address convenient to the offices of the banks and attorneys.

Until 1967, the sealed-off portion of the hotel remained intact, with more than 130 rooms still furnished and still inaccessible. A passerby, if he had the inclination, could still peek through the boards to the partially finished lobby that never saw a guest. Until this year, Miss Lee Roddee, then seventy, still paid the taxes and insurance on the building, but then, after a tax hike, she decided to have it razed to make room for a parking lot.

The banquet room where Ferris the Bold had made his presidential acceptance speech was in the Roddee portion of the hotel. When the wreckers started their work, the daughter of the artist whose painting had been punctured more than a half-century earlier, Mrs. Roberta Ullman, was present. Workmen helped her up a ladder to the second floor, where the room was located, and broke down the still-locked door. The dust was three quarters of an inch thick. No one possibly could have been in the room for years.

There were no paintings on the wall.

A COUPLE
OF LOST
SQUADRONS

The United States Navy has always prided itself on the caliber of its officers, with particular reference to their ability to follow orders. A good example of this discipline can be found to this day upon a rocky section of the Pacific Coast some twenty-five miles north of Santa Barbara. On the evening of September 9, 1923, a squadron of seven destroyers was heading south a few miles off the shore. The weather was a little foggy, but the flotilla was proceeding in close formation and at full speed. The captain of the lead destroyer absentmindedly made a left-hand turn and the whole flotilla sailed at full speed into the rocky shore. The destroyers were upended like plastic boats in a bathtub, but miraculously, although the injured list was long, only twenty-two sailors were drowned.

The committees investigating the disaster could understand how one commanding officer, a skipper, could inadvertently run his ship at full steam into the shore, but they found it odd that the six other skippers would blindly follow him to destruction, until someone explained that in the Navy, officers were taught to follow orders and that this was a prime example of disciplinary responsibility.

In view of this prime example of the Navy's sense of duty and discipline, it is rather difficult to explain how the Navy ever came to commission one Thomas Ap Catesby Jones as a commodore some three quarters of a century earlier. Possibly it was because of Jones that the Navy no longer boasts the rank of commodore. In the historical annals of the United States Navy, the adventures of Commodore Jones are conveniently overlooked and one can easily understand why, if he understands the Navy's sensitivity toward discipline.

Jones came from a proper New England family and was appointed to the Naval Academy, where he was graduated without an indication that he might be inclined to erratic behavior. It took him fifteen years to rise in rank from ensign to commodore, which was about average, and he had to wait an additional two years before he was given a command of his own.

On December 4, 1841, the Secretary of the Navy, Abel Upshur, announced that because of the unsettled conditions in the Northern Hemisphere, he was increasing the size of the United States naval force in the Pacific Ocean by one squadron. The squadron consisted of six ships and was placed under the command of Commodore Thomas Ap Catesby Jones. The commodore took his fleet on a leisurely voyage around the Horn and eventually reached the California coast. California at this time was owned by Mexico.

For several weeks, the fleet tarried in San Diego as guests of the Mexican government, then slowly proceeded up the coast, eventually reaching the Mexican capital of California at Monterey. At this time, the United States was at peace with Mexico, but as Jones said several years later, he had no way of knowing this because communications were extraordinarily poor between the fleet in the Pacific and the Navy headquarters in Washington. As a result, on a warm spring day in 1842, Commodore Jones sailed his fleet into the harbor of Monterey and proceeded to capture it. The capture was not a difficult feat. His warships lobbed a few cannonballs into the hills in back of the town. He sent a landing party ashore to arrest Governor Micheltorena and a few other assorted government officials. He then granted liberty to most of his men to celebrate the occasion.

The citizens of the community did not seem particularly upset over this turn of events, but the capture of a state capital of a friendly nation was not received in good favor by either the United States or Mexico when the news eventually reached these heads of government. The United States Secretary of State, Daniel Webster, personally apologized to the ambassador from Mexico in Washington. The American ambassador was ordered to convey his regrets to the government of Mexico in Mexico City. It took several days to get word to Commodore Jones that he was to turn Governor Micheltorena loose along with his assistants and to get his sailors out of Monterey and back on the ships.

Reluctantly, Commodore Jones complied, but he kept his squadron in the Monterey Harbor "in case hostilities did break out" and because there had been no orders issued for him to resume cruising. Once again, the Mexican government protested and once again the heads of state apologized to each other. Commodore Jones was to get out of Monterey Harbor and, additionally, he was to be relieved of his command as soon as

Commodore Dallas could arrive to take over. Jones was ordered to return to Washington "in such mode as be most convenient and agreeable" to himself. With typical military efficiency, the Navy also forgot to mention a spot where Jones could meet Dallas.

The phraseology of the orders apparently was the custom of the time in correspondence between officers and gentlemen, but it is unlikely that anyone in Washington had any idea as to how Commodore Jones would interpret his instructions. He found it most convenient and agreeable to sail with his fleet from Monterey to Hawaii, an area with which Washington found it even more difficult to maintain communications than Monterey.

Several months later, word was received in the nation's capital that its missing squadron was anchored off the shores of Honolulu. A few weeks after this, word was passed to Commodore Dallas as to where he could make his rendezvous. Dallas was sent across the Pacific in the frigate *Erie* to take over his command and to explain to Commodore Jones that a detour via Hawaii was not what the Navy had in mind when it told him to return in the "mode most convenient and agreeable to himself."

When Dallas arrived in Honolulu, however, he found no squadron and he learned from some other sailors and natives that the squadron had sailed a few weeks earlier for an unknown destination in the South Pacific. How long Dallas waited in Hawaii before he learned that the missing squadron of Commodore Jones was anchored in Tahiti is not on record.

Once again Dallas took off in pursuit only to discover, when he arrived in Papeete, that Commodore Jones again had set sail, with his next stop scheduled at Valparaiso in Chile. Weeks later, Dallas arrived in Valparaiso where he learned that Commodore Jones had sailed north the day after the first cold snap of winter had struck the city. Well aware of Commodore Jones's preference for a balmy tropical climate, Dallas immediately sailed north, but still he could find no trace of the missing fleet. Dallas never did. He died in Callao, ironically, some three weeks before Commodore Jones sailed into the same port for refueling and reprovisioning.

It was here that the cruise of Commodore Jones took a more definite turn. Daniel Webster had secured orders from the Navy which were more explicit in ordering the wandering commodore to return to his base, and copies had been given to every consul-general or his representative at every port where Jones might put in for reprovisioning. In Callao, the consul-general boarded Jones's flagship almost before it dropped anchor and personally ordered Jones to go home immediately and in the most direct manner possible.

A good Navy man, Commodore Jones did not disobey his new orders. Once again he sailed south for the trip around the Horn. He paused at Valparaiso for supplies and while his ships were being provisioned, another U.S. Navy ship sailed into the bay. On board this ship was Commodore John Drake Sloat. He had been sent out to pick up the chase from the late Commodore Dallas and was overjoyed at running into the elusive Catesby Jones so early in the game.

Jones welcomed Sloat aboard and studied Sloat's orders carefully. He noted that although they had come from the Navy Department, they bore an earlier date than the instructions he had received in Callao and he presumed, therefore, they must be void. He refused to give up his command and, with the new commodore along as his guest, he sailed the squadron back to Washington, arriving there shortly after the inauguration of President James Knox Polk in 1845, more than three years after his departure.

The Navy Department apparently was most understanding. It agreed that there was some confusion over the orders that Sloat carried, but this was straightened out with a minimum of difficulty. Commodore Sloat was put in command of the squadron after Jones was relieved of command and once again the flotilla was sent around the Horn to patrol the California coast.

No action ever was taken against Catesby Jones. Relations with Mexico at this time no longer were friendly and Commodore Jones was lauded by President Polk for his "elevated principles of duty." Neither Polk nor anyone else ever asked how the Navy could lose an entire squadron of ships for three years.

Catesby Jones was given a new assignment, but it was on shore. Never again was he given the opportunity to command a ship.

A few months after Commodore Sloat arrived in California, he sailed his squadron into Monterey Bay, lobbed a few cannonballs over the town into the hills, then sent a landing party ashore to take possession of the town. This time there was no problem. The United States was at war with Mexico.

A statue still stands in Monterey commemorating Commodore Sloat's capture of the city. There's not even a plaque to Catesby Jones.

THE LOST WOMAN OF SAN NICOLAS

Lying some seventy-six miles out to sea from Los Angeles Harbor is the island of San Nicolas. Shaped somewhat like a prehistoric fish, it is approximately nine miles long and three and one half miles wide. For many centuries prior to the arrival of the Europeans, it was the home of an aboriginal tribe of Indians whose population fluctuated between five hundred and a thousand. They lived from the sea and from the birds and bore no similarities to the Indian tribes of the California coast.

San Nicolas also is the home of many hundreds of sea lions, seals, and walrus and for many thousands of birds such as ravens, cormorants, sea gulls, blue herons, canaries, larks, robins,

93

and bald eagles. Like most of the other channel islands, San Nicolas has been bombarded with a continuing barrage by the United States Navy, but surprisingly, the birds and the pinnipeds have survived the assault. With one exception, however, the Indians showed no such tenacity to survive in their island home.

The Indians had lived on this small blot of an island for many hundreds of centuries before it was "discovered" in 1602 by the Spanish explorer Sebastian Vizcaino, who was searching for safe harbors where Manila treasure galleons could find shelter in case of trouble. He named the island La Isla de San Nicolas in honor of a patron saint of sailors. He sent a small boat ashore and was welcomed by Indians "living naked in the manner of savages and accustomed to public licentious practice." He marked it on the maps as a possible galleon haven and moved on.

For the next century and a half, San Nicolas went largely unnoticed and the Indian inhabitants remained in isolation. They had no boats, no nomadic inclinations, and they lived comfortably off the sea and bird life which abounded on the island. Before the island started to erode, anthropologists located some sixty-eight village sites and estimated the population had remained static at around one thousand persons.

In the early nineteenth century, San Nicolas was discovered to be a haven for otters and seals. Ships carrying hunters of these choice fur-bearing mammals descended upon the island with the regularity of a ferry boat. With this onslaught, the Indian population of San Nicolas began to decline. There are unconfirmed reports that some of the hunters killed the otters and the seals for profit and the Indians for sport. Many of the women were kidnapped and taken to Los Angeles for sport of a different nature. By 1835, the Indian population of San Nicolas had dwindled from an estimated thousand to slightly more than forty men and women.

It was at this time that some padres in a Franciscan mission decided that the remaining San Nicolas Indians would lead a happier life if they were brought to the mainland to work under the guidance of the good fathers. Accordingly, the padres chartered a schooner named *Peor Es Nada*, under the command of Captain Charles Hubbard, to sail out to San Nicolas and return to Los Angeles with the Indians. There are two versions as to how Captain Hubbard accomplished his assignment.

One story relates that Hubbard called all of the Indians together and explained to them that they would get much more to eat at the mission and find life much more enjoyable by avoiding the constant encounters with the seal and otter hunters. The Indians agreed that this was indeed true, and after gathering up their meager possessions, climbed on board the schooner. The supporters of this version have failed to explain how Hubbard was able to communicate with the Indians, who spoke a dialect unknown on the mainland.

The other version is less kind to the captain of the *Peor Es Nada*. It states that Hubbard drove the remaining Indians at musket point to the shore from where they were ferried by longboat to the waiting schooner. Those who would not come quietly were shot.

Both stories, however, concur in what happened next. A young Indian woman cried out that her child, or her baby brother, still was on the island and, as the schooner got underway, she leaped from its deck into the water and swam back to San Nicolas. Captain Hubbard did not bother to send a boat after her. He had a charter waiting to carry a group of otter hunters to Santa Rosa Island, and following this he was committed for another charter up the California coast to San Francisco.

The schooner was met at Los Angeles Harbor by Franciscan monks and before they set off for the San Gabriel Mission with their future Indian converts, Hubbard told them of the young Indian woman who had escaped. No one thought she could live for long alone on the island and apparently no one thought it worth another seventy-six-mile voyage to capture her.

The last of the San Nicolas Indians soon were assimilated by the agrarian Indians working for the mission and after they had learned to speak Spanish, they reported that the young woman who had swum back to the island was the daughter of a chief who had been killed by the otter hunters and that it was true, indeed, that she had left behind a child whom she had hidden from Hubbard's raiders. By this time, several years had passed. Hubbard was dead. He had gone down with his schooner, which had floundered off the Golden Gate during a storm. The woman surely had not lived more than a few weeks and the island was left to the birds and the pinnipeds and the occasional forays of the otter hunters. The hunting expeditions now were few. There were so few otters left that trips to the outlying island were unprofitable.

On one of these rare expeditions, however, more than fifteen years later, two hunters named Thomas Jeffries and George Nidever, accompanied by some Indian helpers, spent two months on San Nicolas, shooting a cargo of seal and otter. Near the end of their expedition, on a warm summer night, one of the Indians in the party mentioned that he had seen a naked woman running across the ridge of a hill near where they were shooting the seals.

Nidever laughed and later back in Los Angeles he related the story as an example of how an Indian caught "squaw fever" after being separated from the opposite sex for a few weeks. His companion, Carl Detman, had heard the story of the missing daughter of the San Nicolas chief and of her escape from Hubbard and after telling Nidever of the legend, the two men became fascinated with the idea that the Indian might really have been a woman running across the ridge of the hill and that she could be the last of the San Nicolas tribe.

Three years later, in 1853, Nidever, accompanied by

96

Detman, went back to San Nicolas on another otter hunting expedition, but this time they left the hunting to the Indians and undertook an exhaustive search of the island for some sign of the missing woman. It was Detman who found the first clue, some small footprints in soft earth near a fresh water spring.

The otter hunt was abandoned and the Indian hunters were pressed into the search. Three weeks later Detman found her. Accompanied by two Indians, he came up the eastern side of one of the peaks near the north end of the island. She was sitting in a camouflaged grass shelter, looking down on a beach where Nidever and another group of Indians were searching for her tracks. So well hidden was her lair that Detman would have passed it but for the low growl of a dog. When the woman saw Detman, she put her hand to the dog's neck to smooth his hackles, then slowly stood up and faced Detman with no expression on her face. From neck to knees she was encased in a dress made of green cormorant feathers and the sheen of the feathers was reflected in the sun. She showed no signs of fear.

Detman spoke to her softly and she replied in a language he could not understand. A moment later, when he motioned for her to come with him, she nodded slightly, then walked by his side down the hill where they joined the startled Nidever. A short time later, when she was invited by a gesture of the hands to step into the longboat that would take her to the anchored schooner, she did as she was asked. Her dog attempted to get in the boat, but she spoke to him softly and the animal went back to the beach and sat down on his haunches. When the schooner sailed for Santa Barbara the following morning, the dog was still on the beach.

Again there is a conflict in stories as to where she lived when she arrived in Santa Barbara. Some reports indicate she was placed in a convent near the Santa Barbara Mission where she was, in effect a ward of a Father Gonzales. A more accepted version is that she lived in the home of Nidever where his wife cared for her. No one could understand her, nor did she have the ability of other members of her tribe to learn even primary words in either English or Spanish. The monks at the Santa Barbara Mission attempted to locate one of the San Nicolas Indians who had been taken to San Gabriel, but all who had known her had either disappeared or died. A couple of second-generation members of her tribe were located, but they knew nothing of the native tongue of their parents.

The woman, who had been in perfect physical condition when she arrived in Santa Barbara, could not adjust to her new environment. Her cormorant dress, taken from her and replaced by "garments of a more decorous nature," was sent by the padres as a gift to the Pope and it presently can be seen in the Vatican Museum. She could not conform to a "proper diet." She was accustomed only to raw abalone and fish. She could not eat.

Within a month, she was too weak to walk. Within less than three months after her departure from San Nicolas, she died. Shortly before her death, she was baptized by a Santa Barbara priest who gave her the name of Juana Maria, and she was buried in the graveyard of the Santa Barbara Mission under that name. In 1928, the Santa Barbara Chapter of the Daughters of the American Revolution placed a plaque over her grave. The plaque refers to her only as an Indian woman who had been abandoned on San Nicolas for eighteen years.

The lost woman of San Nicolas was the last survivor of her tribe. For many years historians thought that the island was settled by Indians some six hundred years ago, but recent Carbon-14 tests of Indian artifacts on San Nicolas indicate that Indians lived there as far back as 2000 B.C. They left behind exquisitely carved creatures of the land, the sea, and the air, and they bear such a strong likeness to the artifacts of the Ghalas-at tribe of Alaska that there must be a relationship.

In the not too distant geological future, San Nicolas itself probably will become lost. After Nidever took home the last of its original inhabitants, sheep were introduced onto the island and within a few decades they had eaten the green to the sand and the rock. During World War II the Navy used it as a practice bombing range and then in 1946, the Navy turned it into a secret guided missile testing site. Today, the island has eroded into little more than a nine-mile stretch of lava rock and sand. The prevailing winds average between thirty-five and fifty miles per hour and often the sand is whipped into such a swirling mass that from a distance it appears as fog in the lee of the hills with waves gnawing at its feet. It is a mystery that the thousands of birds do exist in such a bleak and barren area. No longer could a young woman, or even a strong man, survive alone for eighteen years on San Nicolas.

San Nicolas will become lost, as did its inhabitants of some four thousand years ago.

LOST ARTS

The art and petroglyphs of the lost San Nicolas Indians puzzle archaeologists no less than do the relatively recent discovery of intaglio art scraped into the floor of the Southwestern deserts of the United States and the common use of the amazing Minoan maze as a design by certain Indian craftsmen. There has been no reasonable answer advanced to explain the intaglios and the only possible answer to the riddle of the Minoan maze is that it was brought to the Southwest by descendants of the ancient Scythians.

In the fall of 1930, George Palmer, a Nevada airport operator, took off from Las Vegas to visit relatives who lived in a small community along the Colorado River near Blythe, California.

After Palmer had crossed the Riverside Range and headed south, and while flying over the flat mesa country, he noticed a string of horse tracks spread out along the ground. A moment after this thought registered, he wondered how he could possibly see hoof-prints from an altitude of more than 5000 feet. He looked again. The hoofmarks were still there. He shook his head. A horse that could leave tracks which could be seen from almost a mile in the sky would have to have hooves between three and four feet long and this, indeed, he thought would be one hell of a big horse. While he was speculating on this thought, he was even more as-tonished to see the outline of a crudely drawn man stretched on his back on top of a mesa. He banked and dropped down to about 2000 feet for a closer look. Not only was there the outline of a man, but next to it someone had delineated an extraordinarily im-mense horse and a coiled snake. The area was desolate. No one lived within miles and, he decided, it would be virtually impossi-ble for anyone to scrape out a figure so huge without losing the proportions. Nevertheless, someone had.

When he landed at Blythe a short time later, he delayed the visit to his relatives and called upon some pioneer residents of the community to ask about the strange figures. Many of them had traveled the area on prospecting trips, but none could recall seeing any such figures. He was looked upon in much the same manner as a man who has just seen a flying saucer.

Upon his return to Las Vegas, Palmer made it a point to fly over the area once again, convinced that he had suffered some form of temporary aberration and that the figures would be non-existent. They were still there. He flew over them for about a half hour, carefully marking their location on his air map. When he returned to Las Vegas, he made a crude sketch of his discovery, wrote a detailed report of what he had seen and sent it and the air map to the Southwest Museum in Los Angeles.

The Museum made a record of the contribution, but because there were no roads going into the area and because it was the start of the Depression and no money was available to finance an investigation of the discovery, the matter rested in the files until 1952.

During World War II, the intaglios were once again "discovered," this time by military pilots on air maneuvers over the desert. It was on the basis of these reports, plus the Palmer sightings, that the National Geographic Society and the Smithsonian Institution sent archaeologists into the field who not only confirmed the Palmer sightings, but found additional intaglios on the opposite side of the Colorado River, in Arizona.

The largest of the Blythe figures was a woman 171 feet long with outflung arms spanning a distance of 158 feet. There were three other figures in this group. One was a male measuring 95 feet, and the other consisted of an animal and a coiled snake. The technique for making the intaglios had been rather simple. The artist, or artists, had merely removed a layer of desert-varnished rocks to expose the lighter colored earth beneath. Like the artifacts found on San Nicolas, the scientists estimated they were etched some time before the birth of Christ, which, incidentally, punches another hole in the oft-repeated story that the Spaniards introduced the horse to the New World.

Twelve years after the Blythe site had been explored, another set of giant effigies, also judged by experts to predate Christ, were discovered on a similar desert plateau in Peru. These intaglios were etched into yellow subsoil and outlined with dark stones. The Peruvian figures, located near Nazca, included a spider, a bird with an elongated beak, a killer whale, a 262-foot monkey and the site's largest figure, a bird measuring 787 feet. Whether or not the Peru artists were related to those of the Colorado desert has never been determined.

A cluster of other giant intaglios then was discovered from the air in a remote area of Imperial County, California, adjacent to the Baja California border. Here the immense figures appear to represent matters of fertility, with huge phallic and womb symbols. Dr. Emma Lou Davis of the University of California at Los Angeles made a special study of them and estimated the age of these figures at 1500 years.

A peculiarity of all of these sites is that the figures are spread out on mesas over which there is no higher vantage point to observe the completed work. Because of their immense size, they are not recognizable from the ground and at the time they were made could be seen only by God and birds.

During the winter of 1966, some amateur archaeologists from Blythe discovered an ancient Indian village which Carbon-14 tests date back to approximately 8500 B.C. The village is in the same general area as the giant effigies discovered by Palmer. Ancient trails led to and from the village. When Dr. Davis surveyed the site, she determined that the trails were made by three different cultures. In many areas, the trails ran conspicuously parallel. No one has come up with a valid answer as to why later cultures refused to tread on a trail so firmly established that it still is clearly defined approximately 10,000 years after it first came into existence. Nor is there any speculation as to why the second trail was abandoned, in turn, by later inhabitants of the village. So rigid was the taboo against using the older trails that wherever they crossed, stone bridges were built to let the pedestrian pass safely.

Despite Palmer's report in 1930, it was not until 1967 that the huge horse tracks discovered by the pioneer aviator were studied scientifically from the ground. The exploration team was led by Dr. Davis, who found that the tracks closely approximated Palmer's calculations from the air. There are ten groups of prints, each shaped like a horseshoe with circular impressions measuring a little more than three feet across at the widest point. Flanking these ten prints are two straight rows of similar impressions and near each of these, are ten rock piles, a point which might indicate that these ancient and superstitious Indians preferred the decimal system. Indians who lived during the colonization era favored the numbers three, four, and seven, in both legend and religion.

On the same large plateau, and comparatively near the huge horse tracks, is a perfectly preserved dance circle, which also provides an element of mystery. On the arid Mojave desert, dance circles usually were small because, due to the dearth of food, desert Indians traveled and lived in small bands. When they danced, as is the custom today, they wanted to be somewhere within hailing distance of their fellow dancers. The mysterious dancing circle is immense. It would have taken hundreds upon hundreds of Indians to have created it.

It is a reasonable assumption that the giant horse prints, the dance circle, and the huge intaglios all spring from some cult that lived in the area eons ago and that all quite probably had a religious significance. Not so easily explained is the Minoan maze.

The Minoan maze is of circular design, so unique in appearance and intricate in structure that authorities on prehistoric rock art, such as Campbell Grant, have stated that it is a "million to one shot" that the symbol could have arisen independently in both the New World and the Old. At first glance, it looks like a partially melted heating unit from an electric stove, but it is a maze in the truest sense. To the superstitious, it could well be a symbol of bad luck because so many races that have used it have now become extinct. There is little mystery as to its antiquity.

Early representations of the Minoan maze are on coins struck more than 4,000 years ago in the Knossos Palace in Crete. Some sources contend that it symbolized the legend in which Ariadne gave her lover, Theseus, a spool of thread to guide himself out of the labyrinth he had entered to slay the Minotaur. The Minoan period, from which the maze gets its identity, dates from 2700 B.C. to 1100 B.C. when it came to an abrupt end because of a devastating earthquake. As far as is known, the Cretans had no written language. About a century before the earthquake, the Cretans were infiltrated by Scythians, who had been driven away by the Assyrians from their home in Eurasia. It is possible that the Scythians introduced the peculiar design into the Minoan culture, although most historians believe that the Scythians picked up the maze from the Cretans.

The Scythians moved on to the West and probably were responsible for introducing the distinctive maze into Etruscan art. An excellent example was found on an Etruscan vase dated about 700 B.C. Although the Etruscans could write, no scholar has been able to decipher their language, so if any ancient Etruscan ever bothered to chronicle the origin of this peculiar symbol, there is no one around who can read it.

It is known that the Scythian tribes migrated slowly to the north, and examples of the Minoan maze have been found etched in glacial rocks in the Camonica Valley of the Italian Alps. The Scythians then continued north to that part of England now known as Wales and generally are considered to be the forebears of the Welsh. Others moved on to Ireland, recording their presence by engraving still another Minoan maze into a massive block of granite in the Irish Wicklow Mountains where, for some unknown reason, it now is referred to as "The Hollywood Stone." Across the St. George Channel from Wicklow, on a ledge in Rocky Valley in Cornwall, England, are engraved two other Minoan mazes.

It was not until recently that scholars realized the Minoan maze had made the long leap to the New World many hundreds of years ago and thus provided a clue to one of the great mysteries of the Southwest: the identity of a lost civilization that was in existence before the fall of Babylon.

This civilization is referred to today as the Hohokam, which literally means nothing, as it is a word taken from the Pima tribes meaning the "unknown ones." At the peak of their period, their culture embraced more than two hundred and fifty cities with a capital in what is now known as Casa Grande. The date it was founded is unknown to archaeologists. An agrarian race, they developed a highly complicated and efficient irrigation system which ran off the Gila, the Salt, and the Santa Cruz rivers. One canal was more than a half-mile wide and extended for more than seventeen miles.

So well engineered were their canals that in many areas, they had devised a system whereby the water ran uphill, a feat which most historians believe was first devised by the ancient Minoans. Like the Minoans also, the Hohokams were fond of leisure and sports. They built special floors and marked them in the manner of a modern tennis court and near one, the remnants of a rubber ball have been found encased in caliche.

The New York of the nation was a large city, its name unknown, but whose ruins were named by the Spaniards as Casa Grande, or "large house." The area now is a national park.

Etched into a second-floor wall of this prehistoric palace is a huge Minoan maze. It has long been recognized as such by scholars and one explanation that was accepted until recently is that the design was carved on the wall by a passing Spanish soldier. This theory was discarded, however, when archaeologists determined that the second floor of the ancient palace collapsed some years before Columbus set sail on his voyage of discovery and the only way any Spaniard could have etched the design was for him to have built a complicated scaffolding system that would enable him to get that high above the floor.

Then another Minoan maze design was found carved into a wall near Oraibi in northeastern Arizona and shortly after this discovery, four more were found in the same area. Scholars found another in a nearby Hopi Indian village and then still another in the Galisteo Basin in New Mexico.

Diggers then began to unearth pottery shards with portions of the Minoan maze inscribed upon them when another discovery was made belatedly. Pima Indians, who live in the area, many of whom are fair-skinned and blue-eyed, still were using the design in pottery they were making. When asked if there was any significance to this choice of design, they replied with a shrug and indicated that it had been passed down for years.

The archaeologists have been able to determine that the mysterious Hohokams were in the area about 300 B.C. and apparently reached the peak of their empire around 1300 when, like the Mayans far to the south, most of them suddenly vanished. Why they abandoned their cities is unknown.

The ruins of many Hohokam cities still can be found around Arizona, but the most accessible probably are the Casa Grande north of Tucson and the Pueblo Grande near Phoenix.

There is a legend that the Romans lost an expedition near Tucson and that the Phoenicians once sailed up the Rio Puerco in New Mexico, as related by these writers in *The Mysterious West*. There is a strong possibility that the Scythians moved on from Wales to Arizona. How else can one explain the irrigation expertise and the appearance of the ubiquitous Minoan maze?

A FEW LOST LADIES

Other than in a few religious circles, there has always been a fondness for the lost ladies who have strolled the primrose path in the West. They never were referred to contemptuously as prostitutes, but rather by their names, which ranged from French Rosarita to Tugboat Annie. Prostitution still is legal in the State of Nevada, except in Clark County where it has been banned at the request of casino operators who want nothing to distract the attendance from the gaming tables. (The law here requires that even the swimming pools in the hotels must close down at 6 P.M. in order to get the sunbathers back to the crap tables.) Houses still operate in most of the Northwestern states in a semi-legal manner, except for Oregon, where an attorney-general named Robert Y. Thornton closed them down in the mid-fifties, apparently as a concession to the Methodist vote. They started closing in California somewhat earlier, except for one holdout in Jackson in the center of the state in what is known as the Mother Lode Country. This town was not forced to turn its girls out into the street until 1956, when California Attorney-General Edmund G. (Pat) Brown followed the Thornton syndrome.

Brown did not have an easy time carrying out his crusade in Jackson. Sid Smith, one of the Mother Lode's better-known chroniclers, recalls that Brown first sent plainclothesmen from his office into Jackson in 1951 to check on reports that bordellos were operating openly.

"They didn't have much trouble in finding the action," Smith recalls. "They asked directions from a local cop. Brown then complained to the chief-of-police, who shut them down. The next day, the city council fired the chief and replaced him with a new one, so the houses only lost one day of business."

Complaints from Brown to the new chief evoked a reply that he had "looked around and couldn't find anything like that going on."

In the spring of 1956, Brown sent in some state officers who dropped into the four operating houses and arrested approximately fifty persons. This effectively shut down a local industry that had been operating in the community for more than a century, when the town first became an entity known as Botilleas because of the empty whiskey bottles abandoned by miners.

About a decade later, a group of Jackson businessmen were discussing the numerous plaques that had been erected around the Mother Lode Country as historical markers for the edification of passing tourists. One of them lamented the fact that no recognition ever had been given to the last of the California whorehouses in Jackson. It was an oversight that the group decided to rectify.

Immediately they banded into a committee known as the Environmental Resources Enabling Committee to Investigate Our Necessary Services, with its objective to place a bronze historical marker in front of the old bordellos.

The mayor thought the idea an excellent one, as did the chief of police. The plaque was cast, encased in cement and unveiled a few weeks later before television cameras brought from as far as Los Angeles and San Francisco. The plaque was built in the shape of a heart. In the upper left-hand section was a red lantern and balancing it on the right was a dollar sign. The inscription read:

BOTILLEAS BORDELLOS

———

WORLD'S OLDEST PROFESSION
FLOURISHED 50 YDS. EAST OF
THIS PLAQUE FOR MANY YEARS
UNTIL THIS MOST PERFECT
EXAMPLE OF FREE ENTERPRISE
WAS PADLOCKED BY
UNSYMPATHETIC
POLITICIANS

———

E.R.E.C.T.I.O.N.S.

The plaque was installed on a Valentine's Day. The attack on the commemorative plaque was started the following Sunday by Reverend Wayne Long of Jackson's Methodist Church, who charged the installation was a crack in the door to bring back prostitution. This was followed by a plethora of anonymous calls from elderly ladies demanding that the offending plaque be removed. The city council refused. Wax casts were made of the inscription and smaller replicas appeared in the bars around

Jackson. Reverend Long increased the tempo of his crusade and the number of anonymous telephone calls from indignant ladies increased. Three or four days later, someone dumped a bucket of red paint over the inscription. Sometime during the dark hours of the sixth day following the unveiling, someone dug the plaque from the cement. No one knows where it was taken. The anonymous telephone calls dwindled and then ceased.

"It was the women," says Smith. "Most of them are pretty unreasonable when it comes to whoring. Why, when Julia Bullette was buried, there wasn't one woman who attended her funeral just because she ran a pleasure palace, yet if it hadn't been for Julie, the North might have lost the Civil War."

Julia Bullette was a dark-eyed, black-haired beauty of unknown origin. There are some reports which say she came to Virginia City, Nevada, directly from London. Others report she was a Creole who followed Horace Greeley's advice when she became tired of working in the French Quarter of New Orleans. No one in Nevada particularly cared. The women hated her and all men but one loved her, not only in a professional sense, but for what she did for Virginia City.

If an epidemic swept through the city, Julia closed the doors to her palace at the corner of Union and D streets and spent days helping the sick. She was one of the town's heaviest contributors to the Sanitation Fund, a forerunner of the Red Cross and, upon one occasion, when the community was attacked by Paiutes, Julia was the only woman who refused to seek safety, preferring instead to stay with the men and bandage their wounds. She was the only woman ever to be elected an honorary member of Virginia City Engine Company Number One. Whenever there was a parade, she rode on the engine and whenever her company answered a fire call, Julia Bullette was on hand with coffee and refreshments for the firefighters.

Her palace was a gourmet's delight. Before anyone reached

a satin-covered bed, he was engaged in "good conversation," and offered skillfully prepared French dishes and the finest wines and champagne. It can be presumed that the fee for a dalliance with Julia was far more costly than in some other houses of pleasure around Virginia City. One of the Comstock Mines was named the "Julia" in her honor and the best club car of the Virginia and Truckee Railroad bore the gold-plated name "Julia Bullette." When newly elected Governor Nye came to Virginia City, it was Julia who entertained him and other state functionaries at dinner, while the "good women" of the town gnashed their teeth behind closed curtains.

She ran her own poverty program, available for almost any legitimate touch; yet she retained enough to earn the reputation of being the best-dressed woman between San Francisco and Chicago. On most of her appearances in public, she was accompanied by her favorite lover, Tom Peasley, who incidentally also was chief of Engine Company Number One. At the Opera House, she kept her own loge and during summer productions she would be seen wearing an opera hood of white silk and the latest fashionable dress. In the winter, she often appeared wearing her prized sable cape and muff.

In Virginia City, as in other towns of the West, a killing was not uncommon. Most attracted no more than a passing comment, but when Julia Bullette was found murdered, every male but one was shocked.

Her body was found on the morning of January 20, 1867, a Sunday, by a friendly competitor named Gertrude Holmes, who had entered Julia's palace through the back door to share breakfast. After receiving no answer to her call, Gertrude discreetly tiptoed up the stairs to see if Julia was engaged with a client of means, left over from the preceding night. She was lying naked on the bed. Her clothes, in an untidy pile, were on the floor and it was obvious to Gertrude that Julia had died suddenly and not from natural causes. Her legs were partially over the edge of the bed, as if in the last seconds of life, she had started to get up, before being struck over the head with a club.

Two doctors were called and both agreed that Julia had been dead for approximately eight hours, that she had been hit over the head by a heavy stick, which was found in the room, and that she had been strangled while unconscious. The outraged males of Virginia City scoured the town looking for a satisfactory suspect to lynch, but none could be found. Early in the afternoon, one hapless visitor from San Francisco was collared, but he escaped the noose when he was able to prove that he had spent the night with one of Gertrude's girls.

By evening, the city was in mourning. Most of the men, from mayor to miner, spent the night outside the funeral home containing Julia's coffin. The only evidence that had been gathered was the statement of a newsboy who had heard a scream about five in the morning. The motive apparently had been robbery, for Tom Peasley could not find many pieces of Julia's jewelry. The following day, every business in Virginia City from casino to haberdashery was shut down. The Olympic Road Company canceled its appearance at the Opera House, but none of the cast dared leave the city for fear that suspicion might be directed toward one of them.

The funeral for Julia Bullette took place on Tuesday and it was the grandest ever to be held in the city. Her body was placed in a special silver-handled coffin which was borne in a black-plumed, glass-walled hearse. It was preceded in the procession to the graveyard by an eighteen-piece band and the marching men of the Virginia City Engine Company Number One. It was followed by more than two thousand mourners, all men. The wives, who would have no part in the services, pointedly drew their shades, or shuttered their windows, as the cortège passed. On the way to the cemetery, the band played funeral dirges, but on its return it turned to more festive tunes, such as "The Girl I Left Behind Me" and "When the Saints Come Marching In."

Approximately three months after the murder, the sheriff arrested one of the most avid mourners and charged him with killing Julia Bullette. His name was John Millain. He was recognized first by Martha Camp, another prominent madam, as a man she had surprised in her room a few nights earlier. He had made an attempt to stab her with a knife, but had fled when her screams attracted some of her clients. While he was being held in jail, a Gold Hill matron indignantly reported that Millain had sold her a dress pattern which originally had been sold "to that Bullette woman." Then the sheriff found that Millain had sold some of Julia's diamonds to a local jeweler and then, it was discovered, a trunk which Millain had left with a friend contained most of Julia's furs, including her sable cape, a large amount of her clothes, her jewelry, and a few silver bricks with her name engraved upon them.

The men of Virginia City wanted a quick trial and a hanging. The good women were opposed. They not only doubted the guilt of such a charming Frenchman, but argued that even if he were guilty, he had only rid the community of a harlot. They came in droves to Millain's cell, bringing him wines, hand-knit sweaters and socks and pâté de foie gras that had been brought overland from San Francisco. They circulated petitions, one calling for his immediate release and another, after he was convicted, demanding that his sentence be commuted to life imprisonment.

The trial was not a long one. There was no need for it to be, as the jury was all male and wanted to get on with the hanging.

The trial lasted one day. In his summation, District Attorney Bishop said: "Although this community has, in times past, seen blood run like water, in most cases there has been some cause brought forward in justification of the deed, some pretext.

114

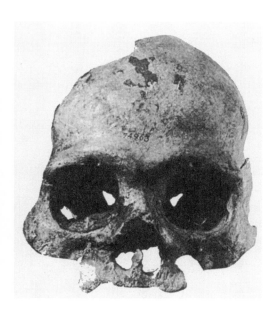

The skull found in Calavaras County, California, in 1866 and pronounced by some experts to be more than a million years old. *Peabody Museum, Harvard University*

Francisco "Pancho" Villa with his wife. Between them is Ramon Contreras, one of Pancho's bodyguards. *Westways Magazine*

The remains of the mass murderer Quejo. The half-Cocopah Indian did away with more than twice as many victims as Billy the Kid.

The Arizona Territorial Prison at Yuma.
Westways Magazine

Captain F. S. Ingalls, superintendent of the Arizona
Territorial Prison.
Westways Magazine

The cell blocks were primitive in the Arizona Territorial Prison at Yuma. The few prisoners who were able to escape were captured by Indians and returned for a fifty-dollar reward.

Westways Magazine

This grave supposedly marks the site where W. D. Salmon, one of the victims of the mysterious Wickenburg Massacre, was buried. No one today is sure where the ambush occurred.
Dana Purden

Jack Mosby (left), the "soldier" most often elected general by the filibusterers when they held Tijuana.
Historical collection, Title Insurance and Trust Company, San Diego, California

Sand bags, placed around the Customs House at Tijuana during the invasion taken over by Ferris the Bold, were used to create an illusion of a military zone for North American tourists who were charged admission to enter the city.

Historical collection, Title Insurance and Trust Company, San Diego, California

Sentries, such as this, were rare. The soldiers that invaded Tijuana were not the best disciplined troops. *Historical collection, Title Insurance and Trust Company, San Diego, California*

When a Mexican Army eventually marched from Ensenada against the filibusterers holding Tijuana, the invaders were rounded up from the bars, put on a commandeered train, and sent out to meet the Federalists.

The filibusterers at San Ysidro, where they were taken into custody by United States troops.

Historical collection, Title Insurance and Trust Company, San Diego, California

The smashup of seven U.S. Navy destroyers on the California coast five miles north of Santa Barbara on September 9, 1923. *Los Angeles Times*

Ruins of the Casa Grande in Arizona.
National Park Service

A view of the mysterious Minoan Maze carved on a high wall of the Casa Grande.
National Park Service

Julia Bullette; this portrait hangs in
Virginia City's Bucket of Blood Saloon.
Golden West

The grave of Julia Bullette with Virginia City in the background.

The cornerstone of the old Presbyterian mission long abandoned in the New Mexico ghost town of Trementina.
Woodfin Camp

The towers from which Charles Hatfield the rainmaker sent his magic potions pouring into the sky, and brought down the waters in San Diego, California.
Historical collection, Title Insurance and Trust Company, San Diego, California

One of the first dams to collapse, as a result of Hatfield the rainmaker, was the Sweetwater Dam.
Historical collection, Title Insurance and Trust Company, San Diego, California

Another bridge washed out through the powers of Hatfield the rainmaker in the older section of the City of San Diego.

Charles Hatfield looks over newspaper accounts of his powers. The city never paid him.
Historical collection, Title Insurance and Trust Company, San Diego, California

Treasures ranging from Spanish gold to Confederate money have been found in the rugged lava flow from Mount Taylor in central New Mexico.
H. L. James

This baby sea serpent was caught by Al Dixon off Newport Beach, California. Another one about ten times as long got away.
G. T. Peabody, courtesy of Westways Magazine

This prehistoric minnow was caught by a fisherman in Lake Mojave.

This rare photo of a "Big Foot" was taken by Roger Patterson of Yakima, Washington. Patterson, who has been trailing the elusive creatures for more than a decade, managed to get within camera range in a remote northern California valley. Anthropologists have labeled the tracks left by the Big Foot as "mysterious" and "authentic."

However, on the morning of the twentieth of January last, this community, so hardened by previous deeds of blood, was struck dumb with horror by a deed which carried dread to the heart of everyone . . . a deed more fiendish, more horrible than ever perpetrated on this side of the snowy Sierra. Julia Bullette was found lying dead in her bed, foully murdered, and stiff and cold in her clotted gore. True, she was a woman of easy virtue. Yet hundreds in this city have had cause to bless her name for her many acts of charity . . . and the nation, indeed, is indebted. But for her, the Union might not have been preserved."

The hanging of John Millain attracted even more people than the funeral of Julia Bullette. Virginia City took on a festive air. The gallows were erected in a natural amphitheater about a mile from the city, where at least five thousand persons could see the execution. Unlike Julia's funeral, which attracted only males, this audience brought out the good women of Virginia City, who wept as they scolded their happy husbands. Millain's last statement was to thank the good ladies of Virginia City for their concern over his welfare and for the delicacies they had brought to him in prison.

According to legend in Virginia City, every married man in the community, except for the preachers, spent the night of the hanging away from his connubial bed, and the girls in the palaces of pleasure were so exhausted by daylight that all of the bordellos were closed down for three days.

Another legend that still persists is that without Julia's help, the North might have lost the Civil War. This is based upon the fact that most of the miners who worked the rich silver mines were from the South and their sympathies naturally were with the Confederacy. The mine operators, the politicians, and the hierarchy of Virginia City were sympathetic to the Union. According to the legend, at one time during the war, when the Union was in desperate need of money, an incredibly large shipment of silver bricks to New York from the fabulously rich Comstock Lode was scheduled to go out by wagon train from Virginia City.

From a miner, Julia learned that the entire shipment was to be hijacked and diverted to the South. Julia put on her finest silks and rode out of Virginia City with the wagon train. The diversion was avoided because not a miner placed his sympathy for the South above his love for Julia.

Julia's sympathies obviously were with the North. She was a black.

A COUPLE OF LOST TOWNS

Most of the ghost towns of the West tell the same tale. They came into being because of a mine and when the mine was played out, so did the town play out, except for a few hangers-on who were charter members of the community's booster committee. Such towns are all over the West, but few have much history worth relating.

An exception, perhaps, is the California ghost town of Columbia, in the Mother Lode Country not far from Jackson, where the plaque dedicated to the oldest example of free enterprise raised such a furor.

Columbia was one of the latest cities to come into being

117

during the California gold rush, and it was born because of some loose talk by a group of Mexican prospectors. Some three or four members of the Mexican group let it drop in Botilleas one night that they had found a rich one. As a result, they were followed back to their claim by a group of American prospectors headed by a Thaddeus Hildreth. The Hildreth party ran off the Mexicans when the yield was discovered to be between fifteen and twenty pounds of gold daily. Imaginatively, they named their claim Hildreth's Diggings.

A few days later, some of Hildreth's party drifted back to Botilleas and after a few drinks made the same mistake as the Mexicans. Within three months the population of the area had grown to five thousand and the name of the town was changed to American Camp. Within three years, the population was up to some thirty thousand, the name of the town had been changed to Columbia, and it had a chamber of commerce and a daily newspaper, *The Star*.

By 1853, it was the second largest city in California and some members of the Columbia Boosters Club decided that the town should become the state capital of California. The capital at that time was located in Benecia, a coastal community a few miles north of San Francisco. Had it not been for the activities of a resourceful young attorney named Horace Bull, Columbia quite probably would not have lost its bid to become the seat of the state capital.

The Columbia Boosters Club drew up a petition for the state legislature which was signed by more than ten thousand of the local citizens, requesting that the capital be moved to Columbia. While awaiting the appointment of a committee to carry the petition to Benecia, the document was placed in a Columbia bank vault for safekeeping.

While the petition was in circulation, there had been an incident in one of Columbia's saloons over the favors of one of the barmaids. As a result, a gentleman named Peter Nichols of Saw Mill Flat fatally stabbed one John Peroit of Pine Log. Because of the Booster Club influence, an instant trial and subsequent hanging were not in vogue in Columbia, so the bar patrons merely took Nichols down to the jail and turned him over to the sheriff. Nichols was allowed to hire an attorney, Horace Bull, and the case did not go to trial until six days after the murder.

Despite the efforts of Mr. Bull, Nichols was found guilty and sentenced to be hanged. Mr. Bull promptly served notice that he would appeal. Approval for this was granted, provided he got the whole matter straightened out within ten days in order that the hanging could be carried out. Mr. Bull appealed the case in a most unorthodox manner.

He went to the Boosters Club and explained that inasmuch as he had to go to Benecia to file his appeal, he would be glad to take along the petition. The Boosters Club thought this to be a practical suggestion and turned the petition over to Bull. The attorney then scissored off the portion of the petition pertaining to the proposed shift in the state capital and pasted over the ten thousand signatures a request for Governor John Bigler to spare the life of, and grant a pardon to, Peter Nichols.

When the governor saw the petition and realized the popularity of the defendant, he commuted the sentence immediately. Bull had successfully appealed the case and Columbia had lost its bid to become the state capital.

Understandably, Nichols disappeared as soon as his pardon came through and eventually the Columbia Boosters Club discovered Bull's perfidy. The resourceful Bull, however, offered to make up for his delinquency by giving the town a new fire engine, an offer which was accepted. In fact, he promised the city the finest fire engine in California and with a delivery date of about two weeks.

Waiting on the San Francisco docks was a new fire engine

built for King Kamehameha III of Hawaii. The Hawaiian monarch never received his fire engine. No one apparently knows just how it was done, but the fire engine was delivered in Columbia by Bull within a week. In appreciation for his donation, Bull was elected chief of the Columbia Fire Company Number One.

There is another ghost town in the Southwest: Trementina, New Mexico, that may hold the secret to the whereabouts of the long lost mine of Father La Rue in Los Organos Mountains.

Father La Rue was the adopted name of the son of a rich French farmer. According to legend, he joined a monastery when his father refused him permission to marry his sweetheart because of an insufficient dowry. When his studies were finished, he was sent to Mexico and assigned to clerical duties in a small village north of Durango. For a few years he taught and converted the Indians to Catholicism and tended to the wants of soldiers traveling between New Mexico and Mexico City.

Father La Rue was not a man of mercy. One version of his learning of the rich gold mine in Los Organos contends that he rifled the bags of an aging soldier who was spending the night in the village and that, after discovering a map which would guide him to the mine site, he dispatched the soldier with a quick thrust of a dirk. Another version says that the soldier told the priest of the mine shortly before he died.

It is known that Father La Rue suddenly decided that life in a village north of Durango was rather dull. He picked up several members of his flock and took off for Los Organos, where he did find the mine near what is now St. Augustine Pass on Soledad Canyon between Espiritu Santo Springs and La Cueva de las Vegas, overlooking the Mesilla Valley.

He built a small fortified village around the colony and not only proceeded to mine the rich ore, but built an underground smelter which refined the ore into gold bricks. Whenever an

120

Indian chanced by the site he was either sent on his way or killed by colony guards.

Supplies were brought in from Mesilla and paid for with gold dust, which was the preferred tender of the times.

After La Rue had been mining and smelting for a couple of years, the head of the diocese in Mexico City realized that it had been a long time, indeed, since they had heard from their station north of Durango. They assigned an investigator by the name of Maximiliano to look into the matter. The villagers reported only that the padre, accompanied by some fifty of his hand-picked parishioners, had gone north. Maximiliano trailed the party to Parral and learned from residents of this community that the missing priest had still been heading north when he passed through.

Several months later, the persistent Maximiliano had followed the trail as far as Mesilla. As first the merchants, aware of their good customer and wishing to keep him, reported that the party had traveled through, still headed north, but when Maximiliano could find no trace of them north of Mesilla, he returned to that community. By chance, he was present when Father La Rue's supply wagon came in for provisions. It wasn't much of a problem for such a persistent detective to trail the wagon back to the La Rue colony. Nor did it require much observation to determine what was going on.

Maximiliano confronted La Rue and demanded that all of the gold in the mine be turned over to Maximiliano as a custodian of the church, a proposal which Father La Rue regarded with disfavor on the grounds that the gold belonged to the colony and not to the church. Maximiliano left, promising to return with an army to seize it.

As soon as the investigator had departed, Father La Rue ordered all of the gold bricks placed in the mine and the shaft sealed. When Maximiliano returned a few weeks later with a detachment of soldiers from Santa Fe, he was met with resistance. When the colony finally was overrun, nothing was found but a few stoic adults, including La Rue, who refused to show the stubborn detective or the soldiers the location of the shaft. After a few days of torture, an exasperated Maximiliano killed the priest in a fit of pique and eventually returned to Mexico City.

Shortly before the turn of the nineteenth century, a young man in Durango named Santiago Blea was married to Juanita Sanchez in the Catholic Church in Durango, Mexico. In appreciation for the ceremony, he presented the priest with a brick of gold weighing about ten pounds. Such a gift aroused the priest's curiosity. Blea was cooperative. He was descended from one of the men who had accompanied Father La Rue to the north, a man who had escaped and had left behind instructions as to how to reach the storeroom where the gold bricks were located. Santiago had been gone for several weeks and had come back with six of the bars, all that he could carry practically.

The priest explained to Santiago that the gold was the property of the church, a point which Santiago did not approve any more than had Father La Rue. His bride, however, insisted that the gold be turned over to the church. Whether or not Santiago succumbed to her wishes is not known.

According to the legend, however, both Santiago and Juanita fell into such disfavor with the priest that they left Durango. Years later, when Santiago died, Juanita used some of the gold to build a church "far north of Durango," in order to assuage any hard feelings that may have lingered over their use of the treasure which may have belonged to the Church. The legend says that the remaining gold bricks were buried at the site of the new church.

Some seventy miles to the north of Fort Sumner, New Mexico, is the mysterious ghost town of Trementina. The word means "turpentine" in Spanish and there are many piñon trees in the area, which could have furnished a source for turpentine, although there are no signs of this industry in the ruins of the town. Unlike other ghost towns in the West, there is no indication of mining anywhere in the area. Shortly before the town was abandoned, it was chosen as the site for a Presbyterian mission, but this was never successful and it was closed down in the early 1930's. What makes the town worthy of mention, however, is the cornerstone for the Presbyterian mission, which was built at the start of the twentieth century. Chiseled into this large rock slab are words, in Spanish, which say, "Erected to the memory of Santiago Blea and Juana T. de Blea, 1912 s." Miss Alice Blake, the Presbyterian medical missionary who lived in the town, says the Presbyterian mission was built about 1912. There is no one around who can remember where the cornerstone was found or who has any idea why a Presbyterian church would use such a dedication stone. No one can recall anyone named Blea.

There is an intriguing aftermath to the legend of the La Rue Mine. In 1937, a Dr. Milton E. Noss, a chiropodist from Hot Springs, New Mexico, was deer hunting in the Los Organos Mountains when he stumbled upon a nearly vertical shaft on the slopes of a Mount Victorio. He climbed into the shaft and when he emerged a short time later, he had forgotten all about his hunting expedition. He went directly to his home and told his wife, Ova, that he had found an immense underground cave in which gold bars were stacked like cordwood. They weighed between fifty and seventy pounds each. He had two in his possession and told his wife he had removed eighty-six others before he had dynamited the cave entrance to hide it from other passing deer hunters. Apparently Noss lived from the proceeds of his find very well until after World War II. By that time, he had divorced Ova and she had remarried.

After the war, Noss entered into a partnership with Charles Ryan of Alice, Texas, to go back to the cave and reopen the entrance. When he applied for a prospecting permit in the area, he discovered that his former wife had been issued an exclusive prospecting permit for a portion of the area by the New Mexico Land Office. Noss and Ryan, however, were granted another permit to prospect an area of Los Organos adjacent to the section reserved for Ova.

In the spring of 1949, Noss and Ryan set out for the cache, arranging for provisions and supplies to be air-dropped after their arrival. The plane bringing in the supplies was piloted by Curtis E. Noble of Albuquerque. The initial drop was scheduled for March 4, 1949, but as the plane neared the rugged mountain area for the rendezvous, it crashed. Noss pulled Noble and Marvin Beckwith, who was Noss' stepson, from the wreckage, placed them on mattresses in the back of the pickup truck and took them to a hospital in El Paso, where Noble was pronounced dead on arrival. Beckwith was seriously injured, but survived.

The next day, Noss met Ryan in Hatch, New Mexico, which is about halfway between El Paso and Hot Springs. The two men suddenly became embroiled in a furious argument, which ended when Ryan shot and killed Noss. Ryan was arrested and then released under $25,000 bond. During his preliminary hearing, Ryan said only that the argument arose over what he termed "illegal" use of Ryan's trucks. Ryan later was acquitted of the murder charges on the grounds that the killing was done in self-defense. He returned to Texas and, so far as is known, never returned to the area in which the cave is located.

Apparently Noss died keeping the exact location of the shaft a secret. Also kept secret was the location of the eighty-six gold bars he had hidden near the site before he dynamited the entrance. One of the bars he had taken to his home and the other, somehow, wound up in the possession of James Hurst, a United States Secret Service agent based in Albuquerque.

Mrs. Ova Noss still holds the prospecting rights in the

area, although a second Mrs. Noss has claimed that the treasure, if found, rightfully belongs to her. The prospecting rights are not doing Ova Noss much good, however, as the permit covers lands now embraced by the White Sands Proving Grounds and the military will allow no one to prospect in the area.

(The town of Hot Springs no longer is on the map. It was renamed Truth or Consequences after the producer of a radio quiz program by the same name agreed to originate the show there if the city council would change the name of the community.)

There is, however, no problem in searching around Trementina for the bars of gold that Juanita buried there near a church that later was used as a Presbyterian mission. The last inhabitant of Trementina departed in 1955.

A
METEORIC
LOSS

The thinly populated community of Port Orford, which lies astride a scenic coastal highway in southern Oregon, lends its name to a puzzling meteorological mystery. Few persons outside of Oregon ever have heard of this tiny community, yet any competent astronomer in any nation on this earth will nod knowingly when someone mentions the lost Port Orford Meteorite.

This is no ordinary rock from outer space. It is believed to be a portion of the huge Pallus Meteorite which fell into what now is Siberia a few thousand years ago. It has physical components unknown to present-day science and which have been discussed in innumerable scientific tracts. All over the Pacific

Northwest there are stories that large rewards have been posted for its discovery. Although no one seems to know who is putting up the money, many searchers have spent months looking for this meteorite on the assumption that "Approximately one hundred tons of it lies above the ground in a timberless, grassy spot near Bald Mountain."

There is no question as to its existence. A fragment of it was chipped off in 1856 by Dr. John Evans, a government geologist, who was then exploring the little-known Oregon Territory. It was discovered by Evans on either the second or third night out from a trip which originated in Port Orford, and was scheduled to terminate either in an area which now is known as Gold Hill or in Roseberg.

On the night of the discovery, Evans made camp a little earlier in the afternoon than he had planned because of an unusual queasiness that he attributed to a mild form of indigestion. He next noticed that his compass was gyrating wildly and, then, a couple of members of his party were staggering as if they had been imbibing more than was good for them. None, however, would admit to drinking. Then others began to complain of stomach disorder. Shortly before dusk, one member of the exploration party walked away from the campsite about two hundred yards, stumbled and fell. He managed to get to his feet and stagger back to the camp where he felt somewhat better. A few minutes later, he went back toward the huge rock where he had fallen and once again he lost his balance and tumbled to the ground. This time Evans went to help him. As he neared the man, he was seized by an acute dizziness and felt himself stumbling around in a most unusual manner.

He helped the man back to the camp and as they moved away, their equilibrium was restored. There was no odor of a gas that could be affecting them, nor were they in a high enough altitude to be suffering from oxygen intoxication. They were in a large meadow, grassy but dry, that was ringed by timber. Off in the distance was a moderate-sized peak encrusted by snow that Evans had marked on his map as a Mount Baldy. The huge boulder rested in approximately the center of the meadow.

The men broke camp and moved back to the edge of the meadow, where presently they again felt normal. The following morning, Evans once again hiked toward the boulder. The closer he came to it, the more difficult he found it to control his movements. "It had the most strange effect upon the equilibrium," he wrote in his journal. Evans, however, managed to chip off a large portion of the boulder which he placed on one of the pack animals before resuming his journey.

Upon his return to Washington, several months later, Evans shipped the rock sample to the National Academy of Science in New York, headed by Dr. Charles T. Jackson, with a report of his strange experience. It was Jackson who made the discovery that the sample contained identical components, some unidentifiable, to the famed Pallus Meteorite of Russia. Jackson split the sample into two portions, kept one, and sent the other to the Academy of Science in Vienna, where his findings were confirmed. There appears to be no disagreement among scientists that this huge meteorite broke apart high over the Pacific, one portion falling in Oregon, the other in Siberia.

Because of its mysterious components, the Congress of the United States appropriated funds to finance another expedition to Oregon to relocate the meteorite. The expedition was to be headed by Jackson and Evans. At the time of the appropriation, however, Evans was in Central America on another exploration, where he died of "quick consumption" before the campaign could be launched.

Immediately before his death, he wrote to the National Academy of Science, "There cannot be the least difficulty in finding the meteorite. The western face of Bald Mountain, where it is, as its name indicates, bare of timber, is a grassy slope without projecting rock in the immediate vicinity of the meteorite. The mountain is a prominent landmark and can be seen from a long distance, as it is higher than any of the surrounding mountains."

Evans' death postponed the start of the expedition. Then it was delayed further by the outbreak of the Civil War. After the conclusion of this conflict, the Academy again appealed for federal funds to finance the expedition to Port Orford, but despite their pleas, the necessary money never was appropriated. No one has ever knowingly come across the meteorite since.

Richard Evans, a descendant of Dr. Evans, who lives in Washington, D.C., still has the daily journal kept by his great-grandfather during his exploration of the Oregon Territory. In it, there is a reference to "an oddly shaped tree with a huge boil on its trunk near where I camped and took a sampling of the strange rock."

About a three-day journey by horseback to the east of Port Orford and a short distance to the south is a tiny community known as Gold Hill. Many years ago there was a small gold mine there, but today Gold Hill is known for a curious phenomenon that exists a short distance beyond the town's limits. People going into this area outside of Gold Hill lose their equilibrium. Some have a slightly dizzy feeling and others stagger like drunks. Compasses spin wildly and watches lose all sense of time. Objects fall at an angle rather than straight down.

There are three mountains in the area, any one of which could qualify for the title of Mount Baldy, but it is unknown whether or not any tree that has a boil on its trunk exists in the area.

What is even more strange is the fact that apparently no one has ever wondered if Gold Hill is located on the lost Port Orford Meteorite. One possible answer for this is that no astronomer has ever visited Gold Hill and that no tourist who has visited Gold Hill ever has heard of the lost Port Orford Meteorite.

Other huge meteors have fallen in the West in Arizona and Nevada. What now is known as Big Soda Lake, five miles west of Fallon, Nevada, was created by a mile-long meteorite that slammed into the earth many years ago. If any meteorite ever struck near a populated area, the devastation probably would be total within fifteen miles, but the odds of such a happening are rather remote. The odds of such a bombardment from outer space striking a ship at sea are even more remote, yet many sailors believe this is what happened to the *Asiatic Prince* in the Pacific. It is one of the most mysterious disappearances in modern sea annals.

Built in 1926 for the Prince Line, the *Asiatic Prince* was a modern freighter under the command of a Captain Duncan. She carried a crew of forty-eight plus four apprentices. On March 16, 1928, she sailed from Los Angeles Harbor in late afternoon for Yokohama, Japan, and reportedly its cargo manifest listed a very large shipment of gold bullion and some arms and ammunition.

Shortly after dusk on the same evening, a man named Gordon Paynter happened to be on the west side of Santa Catalina Island when he saw a huge fireball in the sky. At first it appeared as a bright star, then it rapidly grew larger and larger, "a gigantic shooting star" that came right down into the sea, "rather than disappearing over the horizon or burning up as most do."

Other residents of the mainland in southern California, twenty-six miles to the east, also saw the shooting star and were impressed by the length of its voyage through the earth's atmosphere.

After the sighting of the "shooting star," the *Asiatic Prince* vanished. There was no radio contact either with shore or passing ship. The weather was good and the seas were relatively calm. It was the habit of Captain Duncan to maintain radio communications with land when he was at sea. Two days later, on March 18, agents for the Prince Line attempted to contact the freighter, but were unsuccessful.

At first it was thought that the ship's radio had failed and that Captain Duncan would put in at Honolulu to have it repaired.

Eight days later, a garbled SOS message was picked up from an unknown ship a few hundred miles west of Honolulu. Because the *Asiatic Prince* was known to be missing, it was thought that the message came from her, despite the fact that the call signs were not those of the missing ship. A futile search was launched in this area. More than a month later, a ship somewhere in the China Sea radioed that it was under attack by pirates and, probably because of the gold cargo, there were some who claimed that this was a distress call from the *Asiatic Prince*.

Lloyd's of London records indicate that the ship probably went down somewhere west of Hawaii, but there are few sailors who believe it. A fireball fell into the sea and from that moment on, the ship was never heard from again. There is another strange aspect to the disappearance of the *Asiatic Prince*.

It was a new ship of modern design. Many lives were lost. An exceptionally valuable cargo was lost. Yet there never was a formal investigation held as to the cause of its disappearance.

THE LOST TREASURE OF CUCAMONGA

The village of Cucamonga had been around for a long time before the coming of the white man, and it had survived without a curse or disappearing treasure. The land around the village was fertile, and the Cucamonga Indians lived an agrarian life, although they had their own efficient defense plans, so efficient that other tribes of marauding Indians never raided the Cucamongas.

When the padres came to the Mission San Gabriel, they reported that the Cucamongas "were unusually intelligent and industrious and were not easily managed."

The Cucamongas were not reluctant to learn from the padres. Within a short time after the Mission San Gabriel was opened, the Cucamongas were raising cattle and horses in addition to corn and melons. They tolerated the priests, but did not contribute as much to the establishment of the clerical hierarchy as did some of the other Indian tribes in the southern California area.

The tolerance lasted until 1839. In January of this year, Tiburcio Tapia, described as one of the leading citizens of Los Angeles, petitioned for a grant to the Cucamonga lands as an award for his devoted service. The grant was made on April 16 of the same year. The Cucamongas were not averse to being paid for building Don Tiburcio a huge adobe fortress on top of the highest hill in Cucamonga. When Don Tiburcio, however, indicated that the entire Cucamonga area was his domain and that henceforth the Cucamongas would be raising their crops and cattle for him, the Indians showed their displeasure by attacking the fortress they had built.

Don Tiburcio, anticipating this reaction, had brought in troops from Los Angeles and the Cucamongas were driven off their lands into the nearby foothills and canyons, where, for a number of years they continued to raid the fortress with such regularity that they virtually decimated themselves. The few that survived drifted away and more passive Indians were brought in to work the huge fields that Don Tiburcio gradually turned into vineyards running for miles in all directions from his fortress.

The suppression of the Cucamongas, however, did not herald a long era of peace and prosperity for Don Tiburcio. Less than five years after his grant had been awarded, Don Tiburcio realized that he faced an even more formidable enemy than the Cucamongas. This was the United States, which had made most clear its designs on Alta California. One of the precautions he took was to convert his Los Angeles holdings into gold coins and to hoard the earnings of his vineyards. Two large chests full of coins were kept hidden in the fortress and then, as the outbreak of war appeared inevitable, one of these chests was buried "somewhere near the west wing" of the mansion.

As happens on many occasions with hoarders, word of the

treasure spread around the countryside and eventually reached the attention of a Cucamonga Indian who decided that the money rightfully was his. His plan to acquire it was relatively simple. He applied for a job as a servant, was hired, and a couple of nights later was able to slip into Don Tiburcio's bedroom where he promptly slit Don Tiburcio's throat. While he was searching for the chests, he was surprised by the majordomo of the vineyard, who promptly shot him.

Don Tiburcio had one daughter, Maria Merced Tapia, who knew that another Indian in her father's employ actually had dug the hole where the chest was buried. The Indian agreed that he had indeed helped bury the chest, but he explained that Don Tiburcio had told him that he would die instantly if he revealed its location. The Indian had no intention of dying before his allotted time and no amount of persuasion could convince him that Don Tiburcio's curse was no longer any good. In exasperation, Maria Tapia had the servant thrown out of the fortress, fearful that he might overcome his fear of the curse and dig up the chest.

A few years later, Maria married a Leon V. Prudhomme, who moved into the fort. For the bridal chamber, they used the same room in which Don Tiburcio had been murdered. According to legend, on her wedding night Maria saw a small circle of light move across one of the adobe walls of the bedroom and rest on a particular spot. Her husband thrust a knife into the wall over the light and, quite to his surprise, found a small cavity in which was a purse of coins and a piece of paper so yellowed with age that no one could decipher the writing upon it. The few lines that were visible indicated that the paper was a crudely drawn map.

Maria and her husband lived in the fortress for approximately fifteen years, spending most of the time looking for the fortune her father had hidden. It was her inheritance and her dowry. Prudhomme apparently was no rancher and the couple lived by selling off portions of the land grant periodically to more capable ranchers. By 1858, they were down to less than two hundred acres, which they sold to John and Mercedes Rains, then they moved to Los Angeles.

Rains was an efficient businessman. He purchased more acreage which had been sold by Maria. He moved out of the old adobe mansion built by Don Tiburcio into a large brick house that he had built on a nearby hill. The fortress was allowed to crumble. He also raised cattle, built his own winery, and in short order was considered one of the wealthiest men east of Los Angeles in southern California. Rumors began to spread that Rains occasionally would display an old gold coin that was a part of Don Tiburcio's hoard. Word of this eventually reached the attention of Patrico Gonyllas, whose mother had been a Cucamonga Indian.

On the night of November 17, 1862, Gonyllas and his two sons paid a visit to John Rains and explained to him that the treasure rightfully was theirs. When Rains refused to divulge its location, the three of them dispatched Rains in the same manner as another Cucamonga Indian had disposed of the late Don Tiburcio.

This time there was no majordomo around to extract vengeance, but during the uproar, Mrs. Rains had disappeared, so the three murderers departed hastily. Two days later Gonyllas and his two sons slipped across the border into Baja California. No one knows where Gonyllas hid while he was in Baja California other than that it was somewhere in the vicinity of El Rosario.

Lewis Rawson, a descendant of early Californians, who presently owns a large ranch in Temecula, is the nephew of a woman who lived in El Rosario. Gonyllas came to her home on three or four different occasions to buy supplies and each time he paid for them with a "canteen full of mercury," telling her that he had discovered a large pond of the quicksilver near his camp.

Today, mercury is becoming very scarce, thus expensive, and a pond of mercury would result in a fortune to its finder. It is found in cinnabar and is processed by a simple retort system. Rawson still has some of the mercury that was given to his aunt by the fugitive Gonyllas, and it is pure. In Baja California during the hot desert summer, the sun can vaporize the mercury on the cinnabar and when it cools, it can form in pools.

Gonyllas and his sons came back to the United States several months later. They were arrested when they crossed the border and all were hanged a short time later for the murder of John Rains. During his trial, which was brief, Gonyllas suggested that he would exchange the location of the mercury pond in return for a prison term for himself and his two sons. The offer was rejected. Mercury was only used in thermometers then, and there was plenty of it around.

Mercedes Rains married Jose C. Carrillo a few months after her husband's death. A short time later she sold the ranch. The old adobe winery built by Rains has been restored and is open for business. It is the oldest winery in California. The house where Rains was murdered now is a residence at 7869 Vineyard Avenue in Cucamonga. On the top of the adjacent hill is the site of the old fortress where Don Tiburcio was slain. The old fortress has disappeared and is now covered by homes and a portion of a golf course.

If the legend is correct, somewhere under one of those homes, or possibly under the eighteenth hole, is a fortune in gold coins.

THE LOST SAINTS

Up until 1966, it was well established that there were twenty-one missions along the famed El Camino Real of the West and those who said there had been more were merely passing along myths. Then, in December of that year, the long-lost Santa Gertrudis Mission was found and now it is well established that there were twenty-two missions built along El Camino Real.

For years, there had been legends that there was a Santa Gertrudis Mission and explorers had hunted for it from the middle of Baja California to the outskirts of San Francisco. Historians and archivists, however, who had found obscure references to the missing mission believed that, if indeed, such a mission ever had existed, it lay buried in the Canada Larga, not far from the area where the Union Oil Company had brought in California's first oil gusher in 1888 on an 8000-acre ranch owned by Mrs. Mary Louise Canet.

There were no treasure tales connected with the Santa Gertrudis and thus the search for it had been conducted in a rather academic manner by scholars and in a haphazard manner by amateur archaeologists. In mid-1966, the California Highway Department disclosed plans to build still another superhighway between Los Angeles and Ventura, a portion of which would cut across the Canet Ranch.

About the same time Brother Henry, an archivist for the Christian Brothers Monastery in Napa, California, came across an early mission log from the San Buenaventura Mission, in Ventura, which referred to the Santa Gertrudis Mission.

"The governor has advised everyone in this mission (Santa Buenaventura) to retire to Santa Gertrudis because it is feared two ships carrying Peruvian insurgents are about to attack the community. We have packed everything that time will allow us to take along."

The report was written by a Father John Senan in 1818 and it described Santa Gertrudis Mission as being located about three leagues inland.

The two announcements were noticed by Roberta S. Greenwood, a southern California archaeologist, who also noticed that the new freeway would pass about three leagues east of the Santa Buenaventura Mission. With an associate, Robert O. Browne, of Ventura, she paid a call on the ninety-three-year-old owner of the ranch.

Mrs. Canet knew nothing about a lost Santa Gertrudis Mission. "I remember, however, there used to be a foundation and some walls standing out there in the bean field," she replied. She also recalled that one of the farmhands had found a large pot filled with old coins when he was plowing in the area.

138

The two archaeologists immediately set to work. Aided by a state grant, they managed to uncover the ruins of Santa Gertrudis along with a few assorted crucifixes and candlestick holders, before the freeway bulldozers arrived. The site presently is under about eighteen feet of gravel, asphalt, and cement.

The Santa Gertrudis Mission, which was found so soon before it was to become lost forever, was built by the Franciscans and the Franciscans apparently were less inclined to acquire treasures than were their brothers, the Jesuits.

It is the lost Jesuit missions around which the legends circulate, as they are believed to contain caches of incredible amounts of bullion, jeweled gold-and-silver icons. Recorded in the files of the Catholic Archdiocese of Mexico and on several old maps, crudely drawn but still in existence, are the names of several Jesuit missions that have become lost. One of the most famous is the Santa Isabel Mission, which was photographed as recently as 1922 in the Pajarito Mountains of Arizona and which is known to be a repository for Jesuit treasure which was hidden there shortly after the order was expelled from the New World by the king of Spain.

Another example is the lost Mission of San Dionysius. Its location is clearly marked, near Yuma, Arizona, on the banks of the Colorado River, by the cartographer Father Eusebio Francisco Chino, the mysterious Jesuit who is better known as Father Kino. One of Father Kino's diaries tells of his visit to this mission, yet today no one has been able to find any evidence of Mission San Dionysius.

The early missions of the West and Mexico were founded by the Jesuits and the archivists of the diocese also were Jesuits. In the mid-eighteenth century, this order found itself embroiled in a political situation when the king of Spain became suspicious of its increasing power and ordered all Jesuits expelled and replaced by the more docile Franciscans. Thus, it is understandable that the Jesuits, wishing to keep some of their more valuable possessions, hid them in missions such as the Santa Isabel and destroyed the records telling of their existence.

The Franciscans were more agrarian than clerical and, as in the case of the Santa Gertrudis Mission, their missions became lost primarily because no Franciscan padre ever bothered to note, except casually, that they had been built.

Still a different situation arises with the Dominicans. After the Mexicans passed the Secularization Act in 1833, the Dominicans were expelled because they were Spanish and most of them refused to take an oath of allegiance to the newly independent nation of Mexico. Most of the Dominicans unroofed their missions and departed as ordered. Their leaving was least lamented in Baja California. Here the priests had become so corrupt and greedy and powerful that they successfully defied the Dominican Order on the Mexican mainland.

The records of the Catholic Diocese in Mexico contain countless reports of brutal conduct by the maverick Baja Dominican friars against the Indians, of carousing, wenching, and theft. In 1803, the Dominican Order requested soldiers to forcibly remove and exile the superior of the Baja California mission for misconduct, along with some priests at the Loreto Mission. Shortly before the Mexican revolution the Dominican Order heard that their Baja California brothers were operating a gold mine and smelter with slave labor, that the mine was called the Santa Clara Mission and that the gold was being shipped out through the harbor now known as Scammons Lagoon. Once again they asked for military help, but this time none was forthcoming because of the emergency attending the revolution. The alleged mission was described as being west of San Ignacio and north of Bahia Ballenas. There was a church near the mine, the report stated, that "bore no cross on its peak" but could be recognized by the statues of five monks set in niches along the face of the building.

It took many months for word of the expulsion order to

reach the carousing Dominicans at Santa Clara. When the message did arrive, it came only a week before the soldiers were scheduled to arrive at the various Baja California missions to escort them out. The priests, with their slave labor, worked desperately, but efficiently. Hundreds upon hundreds of gold bars were buried a short distance from the secreted church. Not so easily hidden, however, were several hundred pounds of gold dust. It could not be buried loosely. There were no containers available that would not rot in the ground very quickly. According to the legend, however, this group of maverick priests had prepared for such an emergency. Each of the five monks in the niches of the church was a hollow statue and each one was filled with several hundred pounds of valuable gold dust. The Indians then were told to take the statues to their villages, to keep them in a place of honor and to treat each statue as a saint, as a symbol of their faith, until the Dominicans returned. Anyone who did not treat these saints in a most reverent manner would incur the full wrath of the Lord.

When this was accomplished, the friars dismantled the smelter, covered up the entrance to the mine, deroofed the church and departed for their respective missions to await the soldiers. Several years later, one of these maverick priests apparently regretted his evil ways in Baja California and made a full report of the incident to his superiors in Spain. A copy of the report made its way back across the Atlantic to the diocese in Mexico City, where it was filed and forgotten because no record of a Santa Clara Mission could be found in the church library. Many years later, a La Paz priest wrote to ask the location of the "lost Santa Clara Mission" which he had been told was somewhere on the Baja California Peninsula. This request apparently was filed and unanswered.

Early in 1900, two North American adventurers and prospectors named Ulysses Andreson and William Williams rode into a small ranch some miles southwest of San Ignacio in a mountain range known as the Santa Claras. Five statues, each about six feet tall, were lined up in the yard. One was being painted by a Mexican and Andreson noticed that a woman with Indian features who passed close by them crossed herself as she looked toward the idols. Andreson went closer, then moved back as he sensed a sudden hostility from the Mexican who was doing the painting.

The two North Americans moved out of the village and camped. The next morning, they discovered a rich vein of gold near where they had slept. There is no record of the two men discovering a mine shaft or the ruins of an old mission. Andreson and Williams worked the lode until they had as much ore as they could carry out on burros purchased from the natives. The vein was so worked out that they did not think it worthwhile to return.

A few years later, an expedition from the National Academy of Science, headed by Edward Goldman and Edward Nelson, was exploring the southern Baja California area. Goldman made a side trip into the Santa Clara Mountains searching for antelope and jaguar. In his report, he wrote that on the other side of the Vizcaino Desert, about fifty miles from San Ignacio, he came across a small village with a "fine tank of good water" on the western side of the Santa Clara Mountains. "There is evidence of placer mining in the mountains here," he said. He makes no reference to any saints.

In 1922, a Mexican writer-explorer wrote of a trip he made through the area. He also refers to signs of placer mining and a "deserted village" adjacent to the mine. He advances no theory as to why the village had been abandoned nor does he mention the saints. The next known mention of them occurs about ten years later when a British journalist named Frank Newman arrived in Black Warrior, in Baja California to write a story of the mating of the huge gray whales in Scammons Lagoon, which is nearby.

He wrote of seeing four large statues of priests about six feet tall "so heavy that it requires a half-dozen strong men to lift one. Despite their weight and somewhat grotesque appearance, they travel from one isolated community to another to commemorate some religious fiesta. Their origin is somewhat of a mystery."

They were next noticed by Mrs. Barbara Edwards of Whittier, California, who was visiting Santo Domingo, many miles to the north of Scammons Lagoon. "They are about three feet high," she said, "and require five men to lift each one. Originally there were five, but now there are only four, as one was loaned to a neighboring village for a celebration and never was returned."

According to Mrs. Edwards, the guardian of the saints was the eldest resident of the village, a patriarch who proudly pointed them out to her in a shed in back of his house. Mrs. Edwards disagreed with Newman. "They are perfectly beautiful," she said.

The day before Easter in 1964, the police in Enseñada, Baja California, a tourist city about sixty-five miles below San Diego, were called to a Catholic church. The priest was sad. About a week earlier, some residents of Santa Domingo had, at great expense and hardship, trucked four statues of great weight to the church to be displayed during the religious holidays. They had been in custody of the village for many years and, although somewhat primitive in appearance, they obviously were of great value to the villagers. The men of the village referred to them as saints, the priest said, and they would be returning to pick them up on the day after Easter. Unfortunately, someone had stolen two of them.

The priest pointed out the two remaining ones at the sides of the church doors. All four were alike, he said, and although they were excellent examples of primitive art, they were too heavy to be easily stolen by a gringo souvenir hunter. The two police officers tried to lift one of the statues and agreed with the priest.

The search at first concentrated around Enseñada. No one could be found who had seen them taken. No one around the church had heard anything unusual the night before. The police in Tijuana were notified, and in turn contacted the border patrol station in the United States. A customs officer recalled a pickup truck crossing the border about two in the morning with two statues in the bed of the truck. He was shown a picture and he thought they were similar. He recalled there were three people in the cab of the truck; two men and a young girl with long blond hair. They were United States citizens. The statues, they said, had been purchased for five dollars from a clutter shop in Tijuana.

The Mexican state police in Baja California reported the theft to the U.S. border patrol and the FBI, and it was routinely logged by other law enforcement agencies in southern California.

One of the more popular sports in southern California is dune bugging. A dune bug is a small compact vehicle with exceptionally large tires that will travel like a fast tractor over the sand dunes and the deserts of the area. Addicts will tow their dune bugs from the cities, park by the side of a lonely road and then drive for miles across the desert, exploring, prospecting, or just driving for the thrills of climbing a large sandy dune. There is a law in California that any passenger car towing a trailer cannot exceed a speed limit of fifty-five miles per hour.

Approximately one week after the theft of the saints from the Enseñada church, a California Highway Patrol car gave chase to a sports car towing a dune bug that was traveling about seventy miles per hour on a wide highway between Palm Springs and Indio. Inside the sports car was a young married couple from Los

Angeles. Propped inside the dune bug was an old wooden statue of a saint or a priest.

The patrolman wrote out a speeding ticket to the driver and then, suddenly remembering the report of the stolen saints, went back to look at the statue. The driver of the sports car went with him. "I found it in the sand just off one of the back roads near Palm Desert," he explained.

"Is it heavy?"

"Not very."

The patrolman discovered that he could lift the statue with one hand. The stolen property report described the saints as being extraordinarily heavy. He waved the driver on his way. A few hours later, however, after his return to his station, he reported the incident to the FBI. A day or so later, an FBI agent called upon the couple in their surburban Los Angeles home. The statue was in a patio with a straw hat over its head.

With the hat removed, the statue matched the description of one of the saints stolen, except that the agent could pick it up easily.

"There was another one like it near where we found this," the man volunteered. "It was about fifty yards farther down the road. Apparently there had been a sandstorm and the other one was partially buried in a dune. Besides, we didn't have room to carry it." The man had no objection to turning the statue over to the FBI.

A day after this the FBI found the second statue near Palm Desert. This one also was light and the base of the statue was at right angles to the first one. It was not difficult to guess that they had been thrown into the sand from a passing truck. Unless one stopped, they would appear as a log or a discarded fence post. It also was easy to determine why the statues had lost so much weight. The bases screwed off and the interiors were hollow. Whatever had been inside had been removed.

145

Both statues were dusted for fingerprints, but none were found. A short time later they were taken to the border at Tijuana and turned over to the Mexican state police who, in turn, took them back to the church in Ensenada. The other two statues no longer were on the church steps. The men from Santo Domingo had taken them back to their village.

There is an aftermath to the story that cannot be verified. The priest, who was a wise and understanding man, was concerned over the reaction from the Indians when they discovered that their saints weighed much less when they were returned than when they had been donated for the Easter holidays. Accordingly, he instructed his acolytes to fill them up with sand before they were returned to Santo Domingo.

The location of the four heavy saints now is unknown, except to a few elders of the village of Santo Domingo. When asked, the elders have replied evasively that they have been loaned to another village for a fiesta. But somewhere in northern Baja California are four wooden saints, two of them loaded with sand from the beaches of Ensenada, and two others quite probably loaded with gold dust worth a fortune that was taken from the old Santa Clara Mission mines. In some village, somewhere in that mysterious seven-hundred-mile-long peninsula, quite probably is still another saint, also loaded with gold dust, which really is not dust at all, but pure gold sand.

THE LOST SECRETS OF CHARLES HATFIELD

The late Adolf Spreckels did well in sugar but he was not worth a dam in water. Around the turn of the century, southern California was in the throes of a long drought. The city of San Diego was going through a population boom and there were justifiable fears that if the water shortage lasted much longer, the boom would dry out.

Spreckels, one of the most prominent members of the community, banded together a group of the city's more prosperous businessmen in an effort to solve the problem. Engineers and surveyors were hired and told to find quickly the most practical spot for a dam to be built to hold the water for a new reservoir for the city.

147

Some weeks later, agreement was reached on the site for construction of the Morena Dam. It was located sixty miles east of San Diego in the Cuyamaca Mountains near the Mexican border. From both an engineering and geological point of view, it was an excellent location. It was at the head of a small lake fed by a stream and the dam would fit nicely between the walls of a steep canyon. Funds were raised from private sources to buy the property and finance the major part of the construction costs. Before the first spadeful of earth was turned on the project, title to the dam and the surrounding area was turned over to the city, as a public gesture.

It takes time to build a dam. Long before it was completed, workmen noticed that the lake was getting smaller and that the stream that fed it was getting narrower. Still, there was a general air of optimism. The drought could not possibly last much longer and when it ended, the lake would fill and provide a reservoir that would meet all of San Diego's needs for at least a half-century or more. Two years later, when the completion ceremonies were held, the optimism was less noticeable. The lake was more than one hundred yards from the base of the dam and the stream that fed it was little more than a trickle. A short time after the dedication ceremonies, the lake had turned to a marshy meadow and the stream was nonexistent.

By 1912, the water shortage had become acute. In that year, a real estate agent named F. A. Binney and a delegation from the San Diego Wide Awake Improvement Club approached the city council with the suggestion that it hire Charles M. Hatfield to come down and produce a little rain. Hatfield was a rainmaker of no small reputation, but the city council told Binney and the members of the Wide Awake Improvement Club that it doubted Hatfield's talents were sufficiently advanced to warrant any spending of the taxpayers' money upon such frivolity.

Binney, however, believed in Hatfield as strongly as a

148

flying saucer fan believes in visitors from outer space and he kept returning to the council with his proposal. There was some justification for the council's skepticism, because Hatfield was only a part-time rainmaker. His main source of income came from commissions he made selling sewing machines in California. He and his brother Paul had been born in the Midwest but had been brought by their parents to California when they were children. They had settled near Vista, in San Diego County, at the start of the long drought. With the help of their father, they had built a platform of some twenty feet in the back yard of their farm, placed a windmill on it, then whipped up a batch of chemicals which they blew into the cloudless sky. A short time later, Vista was treated to a light rain, which was the only place it rained that day in southern California.

The skeptics were not convinced, so the Hatfields made up a slightly stronger potion and blew it into the sky on a day when there was not a cloud in sight. This time, Vista got .65 of an inch and no one else got a drop. The Hatfield fan club began to grow.

The Los Angeles Chamber of Commerce offered Hatfield one thousand dollars if he could make it rain in the city. Hatfield built a new tower in the vicinity of Baldwin Hills and blew the fumes from his chemicals into the sky for four months. Los Angeles measured eighteen inches of rain, while San Diego didn't get a drizzle. The chamber finally asked him to quit his operations because the tourists were complaining about the long siege of rain and clouds. The chamber cheerfully paid Hatfield the stipulated fee.

His reputation as a rainmaker spread far and wide. In 1915, the Denver *Post* devoted nearly an entire page to his talents as a rainmaker. He filled a lake in Stanislaus County, California, and a reservoir in Fresno. Still, the parched city council in San Diego steadfastly refused to hire the rainmaker, despite the insistence of the indignant Binney and the Wide Awake Improvement Club.

Early in December of 1915, a delegation from the Wide Awake Improvement Club journeyed to Eagle Rock, a suburb of Los Angeles, and implored Hatfield to turn his attention toward San Diego. Hatfield, apparently, was touched because, on December 8, 1915, the city council received a letter from him in which he offered to produce forty inches of rain around Morena Dam at no expense to the city.

"What have we got to lose?" Binney cried out to the council, after the letter was read.

For the first time the councilmen agreed with Binney. They ordered City Clerk Allen H. Wright to send a telegram to Hatfield asking him to attend a council meeting on the following day.

Hatfield showed up with a written proposition. "I will fill the Morena Reservoir to overflowing between now and next December 20, 1916, for the sum of ten thousand dollars, in default of which I ask no compensation: or I will deliver at Morena Reservoir thirty inches of rain at no charge, you to pay me five hundred dollars per inch from the thirteenth inch to the fiftieth inch—all above fifty-inches to be free, on or before the first of June, 1916. Or I will discharge forty inches during the next twelve months, free of charge, provided you pay me $1000 per inch for all between forty and fifty inches, all above fifty inches free."

The city council told Hatfield to go ahead and fill up the reservoir for a flat fee of $10,000. Binney and the Wide Awake Improvement Club cheered and Hatfield accepted the directive as a contract. A few days later, he and his brother, Paul, started to build their platforms on a high hill near the Morena Dam. This time, they did not use the windmill. Instead, they built in a well-protected brick fireplace on the platform, laid in a huge supply of firewood, and stewed their chemicals over the fire. The first wisp of smoke from the potions rose into the air on Thursday, January 13.

Thirteen days earlier, the famed Agua Caliente Racetrack had opened its doors, just across the United States-Mexico border. The daily attendance averaged around 10,000 fans. Additional thousands of tourists were in San Diego attending an exposition in Balboa Park.

On Friday, January 14, black clouds began to form early in the morning over Morena Dam. By noon, it was pouring so hard that the races at Agua Caliente were called off. The tourists remained away from the exposition. The rivers began to fill. City Attorney T. B. Cosgrove nervously remembered the Hatfields.

"While it obviously is raining hard," he told a San Diego reporter, "and although obviously the runoff is pouring into the Morena Reservoir, no money should be paid until it is determined that this is the direct result of Mr. Hatfield's efforts."

By the following Monday morning, the rain still was falling in sheets. The situation was becoming serious. Part of the Agua Caliente Racetrack washed away. Dry rivers had risen so rapidly that several smaller bridges were washed out. The secondary roads were impassable and rail communication to the north was shut off.

Charles Hatfield called the San Diego city hall to report that he had accumulated 12.78 inches of rain. "I just wanted to tell you that this is only a sprinkle. Within the next few days, 1 expect it to rain right."

Hatfield apparently was very serious. By January 20, it was still pouring. A Sante Fe passenger train was marooned near Oceanside, a few miles north of San Diego, and the passengers finally were removed by a seagoing launch. More than one hundred homes were washed out in Tijuana and the city building department reported that it would cost about three-hundred-thousand dollars just to replace the bridges that had been washed out. An attempt was made to reach Hatfield by telephone, but the lines had been washed out. A party was sent on horseback to the Morena Dam.

The Hatfields were still in their house on top of one of the platforms and the smoke and fumes from their fires still boiled upward into the sky. One member of the party, no one remembers his name, climbed up the ladder and said the city would immediately pay him ten thousand dollars to shut off his machine. Hatfield thought the offer a reasonable one, doused his fires and removed his chemicals. Approximately a half hour later, the rain stopped.

Two days later, a happy and well-groomed Charles Hatfield appeared before the city council and presented it with a bill for ten thousand dollars. Cosgrove shook his head. The man who had made the offer had no authority to speak for the city. Under the deal, Hatfield was to be paid only if he filled the Morena Reservoir to overflowing and, according to witnesses who had gone out to the dam, it was only about half full.

It was an angry Charles Hatfield who left city hall, still carrying his unaccepted bill for services rendered. He was still angry when he got back to his platforms and he apparently was still angry when he mixed up his chemicals once again, for this time he made them stronger than ever.

On January 24, it started to rain again. This time the deluge did, indeed, make the earlier storms appear as mere sprinkles. The ground could hold no more rain. It poured down the sides of the hills and the mountains, flash flooding through canyons into riverbeds that spilled out into the coastal mesas before the ocean. Even the banks of the dry rivers collapsed before the incredible surge of water. The coast road to Los Angeles was washed out, as was the railroad tracking between the two cities. Railroad officials covered one rail bridge with a dozen loaded freight cars on the theory that their weight would prevent the bridge from falling. Both bridge and rail cars were washed out to the shore of the sea. Ships were swept from their moorings in the bays and almost all telephone communication was severed. A dam in Switeear Canyon in back of Balboa Park showed signs of giving away and, for some reason, city engineers decided to help it collapse by setting off a huge charge of dynamite at its base. This wave of water alone took several San Diego homes out to sea. Another large dam, known as Sweetwater, split without warning and still another disastrous wall of water swept down toward the city. A few hours later, a dam holding back a reservoir known as Lower Otay Lake simply vanished under the pressure of the water. In addition to countless homes, this wall of water wiped out a 3000-foot section of track of the San Diego & Arizona Railroad, which was owned largely by Spreckels, who had been responsible for the construction of Morena Dam where the Hatfields were working so diligently.

On January 26, the city council dispatched another delegation to seek peace with the Hatfields, but this group now was unable to get through to the platforms. They did bring back a message from the caretaker at Morena Dam. The water level behind the dam had risen eighteen feet within the past two days.

On the following day, the last of the homes in the Tia Juana River Valley were swept out to sea. The known dead counted more than twenty. United States Marines were alerted to prevent looting from mercantile establishments that still were left standing, although knocked from their foundations. A residential area known as Little Lander was obliterated. Still Hatfield continued sending his chemicals into the storm-swollen skies, and still the incredible deluge continued.

On January 29, the Morena Dam caretaker sent word that the water level at the dam was less than a foot from the top and that he had observed Hatfield studying the top of the dam with a pair of binoculars. Shortly before the following noon, the water began to spill over the top of Morena Dam. An hour later, it was cascading down its face like a waterfall. A short time after this, the caretaker noticed that smoke no longer was rising from the Hatfield platforms. By late afternoon, the rains were over. At Morena Dam, the skies were blue and the few clouds that were in the sky were a puffy white.

The Hatfield brothers climbed down from their platform and went to the caretaker's home to pick up their horses, but the caretaker indignantly refused to return them "because of all the trouble they had caused."

The Hatfields set out on foot for San Diego, approximately sixty miles distant. "We were amazed at the damage," Paul Hatfield later told reporters. "We expected a little flooding, but nothing so much as we saw."

The Hatfields realized, also, that they were not very popular when, on the following morning, they met a group of farmers armed with axes and pitchforks heading up the trail to chop down the platforms and "to spear them damn Hatfields like a forkful of hay." Both Hatfields were invited to join the foray, but they declined, identifying themselves as the Benson brothers who had been wiped out by the floods.

On the morning of February 6, Charles Hatfield met with reporters in the real estate offices of Binney. One reporter said he acted like "a proverbial conquering hero, home from the fray and awaiting a laurel wreath." Hatfield said he was in no manner responsible for the loss of life and damage caused by the storm. "I entered into a contract with the city and it was up to the city to take the necessary precautions."

The city council also was in a rather unfriendly mood. Cosgrove made it most clear that the stipulated $10,000 fee would not be paid. He explained his reasoning behind the refusal.

If the City of San Diego paid Hatfield anything, then it would be assuming liability for all of the damage caused by the floods. The, resulting suits and claims would run into millions. In addition, he added, there was no way that Hatfield could prove that he had been responsible for the rain, a point which was indeed fortunate for Hatfield, otherwise he would be target for the suits and damage claims.

Hatfield did not quite see the matter in the same vein as Cosgrove. The two brothers went back to Eagle Rock, from where they sent repeated demands for payment of the promised fee. In December of 1916, Hatfield sued San Diego for $400,000. In a preliminary hearing, Cosgrove pointed out that no contract had been signed with Hatfield, but that the city was willing to settle for the full amount provided Hatfield would assume responsibility for the 3.5 million dollars in lawsuits that had been filed against the city for hiring the rainmaker.

Hatfield said he would think it over. Six months later he offered to settle the whole affair for $1800, which he said was less than his expenses incurred in the project. Cosgrove was not even interested in this bargain price. Hatfield did not pursue it. He was worried about being sued himself, although as near as can be determined, no suit ever was filed against him. His suit against the city remained on the court docket until 1938, when it was quietly dismissed "as a dead issue."

The San Diego experiment marked the end of the rain-making career of Charles Hatfield, although in the ensuing years he was offered several opportunities to apply his talents in areas ranging from Texas to South America. The deals always fell through when Hatfield asked for a substantial retainer in advance. He died quietly in Los Angeles in 1952 and none of the obituary writers commented on his remarkable talent for producing rain.

His brother, Paul, still lives in a Los Angeles suburb. "Sure he could make rain," he says. "We just stumbled on a secret that someone else will find someday. They already are getting close to the idea by seeding clouds to make rain and seeding clouds to disperse fog.

"They have had a lot of meteorological experts who have studied the San Diego case and have come up with the story that it rained in Oregon and Washington at the same time we brought the rain to San Diego. Hell, it always rains in Oregon and Washington. But don't overlook the fact that it hadn't rained in San Diego for years before we went to work, it didn't rain again for a couple of years after we left."

Paul Hatfield does not know the formula, however. His brother kept that to himself. When he died, the secret potions of Hatfield the Rainmaker were lost forever.

LOST IN LAVA

In the central northwest section of New Mexico there is an extinct volcano known as Mount Taylor that is as treacherous today as it was when it first spewed its molten lava for many miles to the south. It towers more than 11,000 feet into the sky from the high mesa on which it is rooted, and it has been a source of fatal fascination to many an unwary airman because of the heavy downdrafts that sweep down its slopes. The wreckage of many a light plane lies in the deep crevasses of the long lava flow, along with military aircraft from the Second World War. It was on the lava flow from Mount Taylor that the flamboyant motion picture producer Mike Todd met his death in an air crash. Somewhere nearby is believed to be the wreckage of an oil company's courier airplane that crashed during the late thirties while ferrying a reported $100,000 from Los Angeles to New York.

The area is one of the most mysterious in the American Southwest. Nearby dwelt one of the most ancient, and certainly one of the strangest, communities in all of the Americas. Built hundreds of years before Coronado made his trek to the north to search for the seven cities of Cíbola, the town of Acoma rests atop a 400-foot-high mesa that juts as abruptly out of the ground as does a New York skyscraper. Access can be gained only by ladders or by climbing up niches carved out of the face of the cliff, yet on the top of this huge, remote cliff, are terraced adobe homes, some three stories tall, and the largest mission church in New Mexico. Nothing grows in Ácoma. Everything from water to firewood is hauled up the face of the cliff, yet at one time this was the home of more than 6,000 persons.

When Coronado's soldiers first came to Ácoma and scaled the cliffs to enter the town, they were welcomed, but the feeling of camaraderie did not last for long. In 1598, the Ácomans bludgeoned the Spaniards into a state of semiconsciousness, then tossed them over the cliffs to the rocks below. Some years later, after the Franciscans had arrived at the town, the Ácomans once again lost their temper and tossed the padres over the cliffs.

Other Spaniards and other monks came, however, and around 1700, work on the huge mission church was started. The walls are more than 60 feet high and 10 feet thick. The ceiling beams for the edifice are about 40 feet long and 14 inches square and came from mountains more than twenty-five miles distant. All of the materials were carried up by the Indians.

There was reason for the intense Spanish interest in Ácoma. They were convinced that it was indeed one of the seven cities of Cíbola. According to the legend in Mexico City,

Montezuma told Cortes that much of the silver of the Aztecs came from the distant city of Ácoma, a city on a cliff near the black hills where the silver mine was located. If there was a mine in the lava flow, the Spaniards never found it and neither has anyone else.

Not far from Ácoma is the Enchanted Mesa, which is much smaller and rises even higher than Ácoma. The walls are even more sheer here and, again, according to legend, this was at one time the residence for the leaders of the Ácoman society. It is possible to get to the top of the Enchanted Mesa through a "chimney" in approximately the center of the cliff, although it is a most arduous climb. One archaeologist who did make the climb found many artifacts to prove that Ácomans actually did live on the top of the Enchanted Mesa. It was abandoned abruptly, the Ácomans say, after an earthquake, followed by another eruption from Mount Taylor. So quick was the departure that three Ácoman women were left behind. One jumped off and was killed. The other two perished from starvation. For many, many years, it was impossible to get to the top of the Enchanted Mesa, but then there was another earthquake and the chimney was opened.

There are many who believe that the cliff-dwelling Ácomans took to their high perch to avoid the lava flow from Mount Taylor, and that prior to this, there was a large city on the flat land below. There are consistent unattributable reports that at the bottom of some of the deep crevasses in the huge lava flow can be seen traces of homes and buildings, and there are some who believe that this was the site of the fabled Azatlán, the city from which the Aztecs originally came.

In 1882, when the Santa Fe Railroad was being constructed west of Albuquerque, workers digging through the lava flow unearthed three large pottery ollas around which the lava had flowed. In each olla was a human skeleton. The discovery was printed in an Albuquerque newspaper of July 27 of that year, but no mention was made as to the disposition of either the ollas or the skeletons. A few days later, the workers came across another olla. A supervisor noticed the men gathered around the discovery and confiscated the olla. Inside he found three Spanish coins, all dated 1543. Whether or not there were more that were divided up among the workers before his arrival has never been determined. In 1950, highway workers cutting an improved road through the lava flow came across a small iron chest which contained about $10,000 in Confederate paper money. The iron chest was rather badly rusted, but the paper was in excellent condition, despite the fact that its purchasing power was nil. Most think it was thrown away by fleeing Confederate soldiers as worthless baggage at the conclusion of the Civil War.

The lava flow stretches for many miles in all directions south of Mount Taylor. The crevasses are deep, sometimes wide and twisting. During World War II, the pilot of a medium-range bomber, who was on a training mission, radioed Kirtland Field in Albuquerque that he was having engine trouble. He gave his location as approximately one mile south of Mount Taylor. The plane was never seen or heard from again.

In 1947 one of these writers, while piloting a small plane over the area, spotted the olive drab empennage of a bomber lying on top of the lava about four miles south of Grants. The color blended so closely with the black lava that it was visible only from an altitude of about one hundred feet. Somewhere nearby in one of the lava canyons lies the rest of the missing plane.

The writer who found the tail of the missing bomber was looking for a different aircraft, a single-engine Lockheed Vega that is believed to have gone down in the treacherous lava beds in 1936. This latest legend of Mount Taylor and its lava flow is tied into the election contest of that year between Franklin D. Roosevelt and Kansas Governor Alf Landon.

Shortly before the election, there were several rumors that Mexico was planning to expropriate the United States oil companies operating in that nation and that Roosevelt, in the interests of his "Good Neighbor" policy, was not going to protest the action so long as the oil companies received a reasonable payment for their investment. The oil companies felt that Landon would take a stronger position against the pending expropriation if he was elected and Landon, whose chances for winning were not rated very high, desperately needed campaign funds. The oil industry in California raised $100,000 from among its members for a Landon donation.

As is the custom in many political donations, the money was raised in cash. It was urgently needed by the appropriate Republican campaign officials in New York and thus, a pilot by the name of Touchmann was hired in Los Angeles as a courier to fly the money to New York. He took off from Burbank, California, in a red Lockheed Vega, after telephoning ahead to a privately operated airport in Albuquerque to request that it remain open until his arrival so he might refuel. He was assured that it would.

Shortly before dusk of the same day, an insurance man and pilot from Albuquerque, named Homer Bray, who was flying to Gallup, noticed a red Lockheed Vega far below him. Bray had just passed over the western edge of the lava flow, a few miles below San Fidel, and was approaching the Cíbola National Forest. From where he was, it appeared that the Vega was skimming the ground. A few seconds later it occurred to Bray that the pilot of the Vega might be in trouble. Bray's first thought was that the strange pilot was going to be in a hell of a lot more trouble if he were heading for a forced landing in the lava beds. Bray made a 180-degree turn and dropped down for a second look. He could see no sign of the Vega.

Bray was flying a Bellanca, a much slower plane than a Vega, and after he had flown back about twenty or thirty miles without seeing the other aircraft, he decided that the plane was probably in no trouble and that its low altitude had merely been an optical illusion. It was not until he returned to Albuquerque the following day that he learned a red Lockheed Vega had disappeared on a flight between Phoenix and Albuquerque.

Bray reported what he had seen and led an aerial search party to the area later that afternoon. There was no sign of the aircraft. If it had crashed in the lava beds, it was unlikely that there ever would be, as both Bray and the other local pilots well knew.

Nevertheless, the search was carried on for two more days before it was abandoned. About three days after this, a well-dressed young man who was highly articulate and said he was a private detective from Los Angeles came into Bray's office. His name, the detective said, was Roger Smith, and he was most interested in locating the wreckage of the missing Vega. He said he represented a group of California businessmen who would pay all expenses for another air search of the area, and a $5,000 bonus if the plane was located. He advanced Bray $1,000, a considerable sum in mid-Depression days, to meet his immediate costs and said he would be available for any reports at the Alvarado Hotel.

Bray told his visitor that if the plane was down in the lava beds, the odds were a thousand to one that it would be found, but Smith was prepared to accept the risk.

Once again an aerial search was launched, this time with more than a dozen planes taking part. The search went on for a week. Every night, Bray met Smith in the bar of the old Alvarado Hotel. He soon learned that the visitor was not a professional private detective and that his name was not really Smith. He discovered also that Smith could not hold his liquor very well.

On the night the second search was called off, Bray and his companion had three or four martinis at the Alvarado. "This plane seems to have some extraordinary importance," Bray said.

Smith nodded, then looking around him, he lowered his voice and told Bray the story. When he was finished, he sat back and ordered another round of drinks.

"Thank you for trusting me with your confidence," Bray said, wondering whether or not the stranger was telling him the truth.

The man shrugged. "It is really nothing," he replied. "It would be denied by everyone, even if you told it."

"If I tell everyone, then everyone will be out looking for the plane."

The pseudo-Smith laughed. "Wait until I get back to Los Angeles," he replied.

Bray, who was a strong Democrat, told New Mexico's Senator Dennis Chavez. The Senator thought the story probably was true, but agreed with the mysterious Smith that if it was told, it would be denied. In addition, if it was made public, it might backfire because the Democrats would be accused of resorting to "smear politics." He asked Bray to keep it quiet.

Two years later, the Mexican government did expropriate the United States-owned oil companies in Mexico and, as Smith had predicted, Roosevelt made no protest. Bray spent some time cruising over the lava beds and the adjacent Ácoma Reservation and the Cíbola National Forest, but he could find no sign of the missing aircraft.

The war kept him busy for the next few years and the mystery "was stored in the back of his mind. Shortly after the end of the war, however, he was reminded of it forcibly. General Patrick J. Hurley was running for a New Mexico senate seat against Clinton Anderson. One evening, during the campaign, Bray was in the lobby of the Hilton Hotel when Hurley entered the building. With Hurley was the mysterious pseudo-Smith. When Smith saw Bray, he stared at him for a moment, then smiled slightly, nodded, and turned his attention back to the general. It was most obvious that he did not wish to renew the acquaintanceship any further. The insurance executive asked several people around the lobby if they knew who the man was, but none of the local politicians ever had seen him before. All that Bray could learn was that the man had accompanied Hurley on a flight from Los Angeles earlier in the day.

Bray no longer kept the story quiet. He was a colonel in the Civil Air Patrol and on several occasions he led members on a search expedition of the lava flow, but with no success. For several years, amateur pilots have been making passes over the lava beds looking for the lost Lockheed Vega, which surely is buried in one of the steep twisting fissures of the black rock. If anyone has found it, he has kept the discovery quiet.

Some day, the wreckage of the plane surely will turn up, like the tail from the lost bomber, like the iron chest full of Confederate money, like the ancient coins of Coronado's era and the three skeletons in the large ollas.

A TRIO
OF LOST
MONSTERS

Apparently the first genuine sea serpent ever sighted by a man not in his cups was seen by an aging cleric named Bishop Pontoppidan off the shores of Bergen, Norway, back in 1734. The good bishop was a teetotaler, was well respected in his parish, and when he told of seeing a sea serpent more than one hundred feet long less than fifty yards from the shore, where he was meditating, enough of his flock believed in him to mount a long watch in hopes of glimpsing it. The bishop's sea serpent apparently was a transient because it was never seen around Bergen again. When the insistent bishop referred to the serpent as a heavenly manifestation in one of his sermons, some of his more stolid parishioners reached the conclusion that the cleric was well past the retirement age and suggested that he go back to his meditation along the seashore on a more permanent basis. Thus, the Reverend Pontoppidan occupies the unique position of not only being the first person to see a sea serpent, but the only person ever to be damaged in any manner by these monsters of the deep.

Shortly after the good bishop reluctantly acceded to the wishes of his parishioners, however, sightings of the elusive sea serpents became more common. One of the best chronicled sightings was that of a monstrous sea reptile that cavorted for two weeks in Gloucester Harbor, Massachusetts, in 1817 before hundreds of skeptical New Englanders. Scientists even came from distant Boston to view the antics of the strange beast, but if their conclusions were ever published, they have long since been lost.

It was off the coast of the Western United States, however, that the aging Bishop Pontoppidan finally was cleared of senility charges almost two hundred years later. Not only were a mother and child sea serpent sighted, but the baby was captured and photographed.

It started in February of 1901 when a fisherman named Al Dixon was setting his lines at the 100-fathom curve of Newport Beach, California. Dixon first became aware that something unusual was happening when he heard "the goddamdest loudest whistle that was ever made" from behind his back, over the bow of his boat. He dropped the line he was holding and spun around. A huge animal "with a face somewhat like a bulldog" was slowly sinking back into the sea about fifty feet away from his skiff. In the back of the slowly submerging face was a body built "like a straight roller coaster," which was a least two hundred feet long.

Dixon, open-mouthed, watched it disappear beneath the water and then, as he stared, a much smaller version of the same animal raised its head out of the water and portions of its body also broke the surface of the calm sea. Two wicked canine teeth projected from the lower jaw. The smaller version of the monster moved slowly toward the skiff. Its mouth closed slightly and Dixon once again heard the peculiar high-pitched whistle, although somewhat softer than the first cry. As it drew almost abreast of the boat, it too sank below the surface of the water. A second later, one of Dixon's lines began to scream on its reel. Dixon didn't hesitate a second. He picked up the pole and reel and threw it as far from the skiff as he could. He then quickly cut his other lines and "started rowing like hell for shore." The larger monster surfaced, screamed toward him with its shrill whistle, "as if telling me to hurry up." Dixon needed no encouragement. He was exhausted by the time he reached the dock in Newport Bay.

"There's a big eel out there," he replied. "A couple of 'em. One's about two hundred feet long. The other's about twenty-five feet," he told a man on the pier. "They got away with all my gear."

His friend started to laugh, then stopped and turned his head away when he saw that Dixon was serious. By evening the story was all over town, and Al Dixon was being looked upon in about the same manner as the Norwegians had looked upon the good Bishop Pontoppidan.

About two weeks later, a young man named Joe Baracca decided to take a swim from the beach in an area that now has become the end of Thirty-sixth Street. Just beyond the surfing line, he noticed a fish pole lying in the water. Taking hold of it, he started back to shore. When he reached knee-deep water, he noticed for the first time that the other end of the fishing line was snagged on something in the water. He pulled on it tentatively, felt something give, then started to reel it in. A moment later, a huge body rose in the curl of a wave and raced toward him. Baracca dropped the pole and ran.

When the wave receded, the monster was lying on the sand. For a long while, Baracca watched it cautiously from a distance, then, satisfied that it was dead, he went back to it. Never had he seen anything like it. Two large canine teeth protruded from the lower jaw and there were smaller teeth in both the upper and lower jaws, with small spaces between. Through one of these ran the fishing line which continued on into the animal's stomach. The body was thick near the head, then gradually tapered down into a reptilian tail. Baracca pulled it farther up on the beach, then ran into the town to report its discovery.

Within the hour, half the town was out on the beach to look at the strange serpent with the head of a dog. The tailor in the town had his tape measure with him. The creature was thirty-one feet, six inches long. While he was measuring it, Al Dixon appeared, looked at it for a moment, then, taking a jack-knife from his pocket, he cut the line and departed with his fishing pole. Several other men hauled the serpent further up on the beach. A photographer from Los Angeles, who was visiting Newport Beach, took a picture of the sea serpent with twenty-six of the town's residents posed behind it.

The local correspondent for the Los Angeles *Times* dutifully reported the discovery, but the editors apparently thought the tale of the find too unlikely to warrant printing it. The photographer, George Peabody, gave the photograph to the local Newport-Balboa *Press*, but this newspaper apparently also was short of space and did not bother using it.

Several years later, the photograph was given to Harry Welch, secretary of the Newport Beach Chamber of Commerce, who had copies made and sent one to the Los Angeles County Museum. A probable identification, that of an oarfish, was made by the museum; a fish that sometimes does grow to the length of thirty feet. Dixon knew better, however. "That one was the baby. The other was at least two hundred feet long."

No one can remember what happened to the baby sea serpent that swallowed Dixon's bait. It probably started to smell and was buried.

There is no mystery, however, as to what happened to one of the gigantic sixty-pound minnows that was caught in Lake Mojave, California. The first of these big minnows was caught by an Indian in November of 1952 and was rather well devoured by the fisherman and several of his friends before it came to the attention of the United States Fish and Wildlife Service. By the time a ranger reached the village, some cats had pretty well worked over the head of the strange fish, but there was enough left for the ranger to determine that the fish was of a species thought to have become extinct hundreds of thousands of years ago.

In November of 1962, a sports fisherman from Las Vegas, Nevada, caught another prehistoric sixty-two-pound minnow while fishing in Lake Mojave. This fisherman had never seen anything like it before and he took it to the Fish and Wildlife station for identification.

The Fish and Wildlife Department was ecstatic. It was in perfect condition. "You have caught a most rare, prehistoric fish," a ranger told the Las Vegan.

"No kidding," the fisherman replied.

"We'll preserve it and send it on to Washington," the ranger said excitedly.

The fisherman shook his head. "Like hell you will," he replied. "That's going over the mantel of my den."

The ranger shook his head and refused to give it back. While the ichthyologists gently prepared it for its long trip back to Washington, the Las Vegas sports fisherman went to court and demanded that his fish be returned to him. The judge thought his argument was a reasonable one. If a man who is properly licensed catches a fish, he is entitled to keep the fish.

The government fought back. The sixty-two-pound minnow lay in a carefully prepared preservative solution while the case was appealed and appealed once again. The government lost.

The giant prehistoric minnow now is mounted and hangs over a fireplace in a Las Vegas den.

A few miles to the southeast of Newport Beach, over the mountains and into the desert country, there is the legend of the abominable sandman. In January of 1964, a Marine major was exploring some of the more remote canyons in the lower Borrego Valley when he came across some incongruous tracks. Excitedly, he recalled the abominable snowman legend. The tracks were splay-toed and immense, staggered in some areas, parallel in others, with clearly definable digits which terminated in tiny depressions, as if made by claws. The prints pointed downhill, each pair falling at an interval of approximately forty inches from the preceding set. Upon reaching the desert floor, the tracks continued into the bed of a wash, then disappeared in the wind-blown sand of an arroyo. The major continued his search and found identical prints on a nearby hill, where there was some scrub grass and softer ground. These tracks were about seven feet apart and slightly larger than the others. From this, the major deduced that the monster which had made them was capable of prodigious leaps.

Upon his return to San Diego, the major went through the files of the San Diego *Union* and, although he found little on an abominable sandman, he did learn that some years earlier a monster had been killed by a Frank Cox at Deadman's Hole near Warner Hot Springs. This monster was described as having feet twenty-four inches long, weighing about four hundred pounds and with a small head and buck teeth. It appeared to be a cross between a man and a bear.

The following weekend, the major returned to the Borrego Valley and made several plaster casts of the tracks he had discovered. He then took pictures of the casts and wrote a story about his discovery, which he sold to *Desert Magazine*. Within a few days after the story was published, the Borrego Valley was swarming with explorers seeking the abominable sandman, a foray which caused considerable frustration to rangers in the Anza-Borrego State Park, who for months worked around the clock pulling the vehicles of abominable sandman hunters out of the deep sand.

One of the editors of *Desert Magazine* went to Borrego for a personal inspection of the phenomenon. She noticed a steer grazing on a scrub a short distance away. A few moments later, she noticed some dried dung lying on the ground. She kicked it aside and took a plaster cast of the impression left by the dung in the sand. The cast was virtually identical to the casts made by the curious major.

Not so easily explained is the mysterious Big Foot of the Pacific Northwest, sometimes known as the Sasquatch, which has been sighted in wilderness areas on many occasions, has been tracked for miles, and photographed by both motion picture and still camera.

According to many tribes of Indians, the Sasquatch has been around for centuries. The first known chronicled sighting of the eight-foot Big Foot appeared in the *Daily British Colonist* of Victoria, B.C., on June 30, 1884. The newspaper reported that the crew of a freight train which ran between Yale and Lytton in British Columbia had captured, alive, a Big Foot which had been sleeping near the railroad tracks. The monster was described as "half man and half beast" and was shaped like a human being. Except for its hands and feet, the body was covered with shiny black hair approximately an inch long. The creature was reported as being "extraordinarily strong, with forearms much longer than a man's. It had the ability to break a three-inch-thick stick by merely twisting it in its hands." The animal was in the possession of a George Tibury of Yale. There appears to be no further record as to what Tibury did with his monstrous pet. About two weeks after the monster was captured, the train running between Lytton and Yale was wrecked and the more avid of the Big Foot fans contend that the wrecking of the train was an act of vengeance carried out by Big Foots because of the earlier capture.

Other sightings of Sasquatch have been compiled by writer James B. Shuman for the Los Angeles *Times*. Mike King, a timber cruiser, spotted one at a waterhole on Vancouver Island. Charles Flood of New Westminster saw another eating berries in 1915.

In 1924, a Big Foot scared the daylights out of some prospectors in two widely separated parts of the Pacific Northwest. The first incident occurred in July of that year at an isolated canyon near Mount St. Helens in Washington when a band of the giant Big Foots attacked a cabin where five prospectors were sleeping. Earlier in the day, one of the prospectors had shot at what he thought was a large bear. He thought he had killed it, but he could find no sign of the animal when he went into the trees to skin it. The Big Foots who assaulted the cabin threw huge boulders onto the roof and charged the door consistently, in an attempt to get past the barricade. They were driven off only after a number had been wounded by the guns of the prospectors.

The following morning, the prospectors went for help and a posse of deputy sheriffs, citizens, and reporters returned with them to the cabin. The building was badly damaged and, surrounding the cabin, were hundreds of giant footprints. The posse made a thorough search of the area, but the Big Foots had vanished.

A little more than a month later, a seventy-five-year-old prospector named Al Ostman drifted into Vancouver with an incredible story. He had been sleeping in his bag a couple of weeks earlier in a remote area about one hundred miles north of the city when he awoke to find himself being picked up off of the ground. He was slung "like a sack of flour" over the shoulder of a huge gorilla, who set off at a trot across country. Shortly after the break of dawn, he was dropped on the ground and knocked out. When he regained consciousness, he found that he had been removed from his sleeping bag and that he was surrounded by a family of Sasquatch. The females were around seven feet tall and the males at least a foot taller. Ostman said he was held captive by the Big Foots for six days, confined in a small bowl-shaped valley which had only one narrow exit. He escaped, he said, when he fed the Big Foot guarding the exit a tin of snuff, fleeing when the Big Foot rolled on the ground in a paroxysm of sneezing. Understandably, the adventure of Mr. Al Ostman attracted little attention.

According to Shuman, the next sighting that can be taken seriously occurred in September, 1941, when a Big Foot strolled into the isolated home of Mrs. George Chapman at Ruby Creek about thirty miles up the Fraser River from Agassiz, British Columbia. She and her three children fled out of the back door.

When she returned with her husband, the Big Foot had departed, taking along some salted fish. Donald Hunter, of the University of Oregon, saw a Big Foot in the Oregon Cascades near Todd Lake in 1942. His wife was a witness to the sighting of a Sasquatch, this one about nine feet tall. In 1955, William Roe of Edmonton, Canada, spotted another Big Foot on Mica Mountain, near the Indian village of Tête Jaune Cache in British Columbia.

In the summer of 1964, Scott Claghorn, an Arlington, Washington, newspaper publisher, went for a Sunday afternoon drive with his wife. Early in the evening, well before dusk, they were heading back toward Arlington on a little-used road about thirty miles east of the community, when he noticed two giants running across an open field. They were so tall that Claghorn instinctively jammed on his brakes for a better look. The squealing of the tires apparently caught their attention, as the two "giants" stopped, straightened up, and stared toward the car.

"Two Big Foots," Caghorn said in amazement. Slowly, he reached for his camera lying on the back seat of the car. The Sasquatch apparently noticed the movement, for suddenly they ran at an incredible speed toward a clump of trees, where they disappeared.

"I always thought they were a myth," Claghorn said a few moments later. "It's a hell of a story."

"You've been on the wagon for twenty years," his wife said. "Everyone will think you have fallen off."

"I won't say they were Big Foots. I'll just say they were two ten-foot giants wearing fur fatigue suits."

"Not even that," his wife said firmly. "It will ruin our circulation."

Claghorn sadly agreed. Only a few close friends know of his experience.

Roger Patterson, a thirty-five-year-old rancher from Yakima, Washington, was luckier with his camera. His avocation has been running down the legend of the Big Foot. He probably has the most complete collection of sightings in existence and he is the author of a book entitled *Do Abominable Snowmen of America Really Exist?* which is a rhetorical title, as he is convinced that they do. He even has a sixteen-millimeter motion picture film of a Sasquatch in action to prove it.

The film was shot in October of 1967. Shortly before it was taken, a Big Foot-phile telephoned Patterson to report that Big Foot tracks of recent origin had been found near Bluff Creek in northern California. Patterson, accompanied by an expert tracker named Robert Gimlin, departed immediately for California where, for the next week and a half they scouted the area searching for some signs of the elusive hominid. On the afternoon of October 20, as they rounded a bend in a canyon, Patterson's horse suddenly reared and, as the rancher brought the animal under control, he saw the Big Foot.

"He was about one hundred and twenty-five feet across a creek," he says. "Its head was human, although more slanted and with a large forehead and wide, broad nostrils. Its arms hung almost to its knees when it walked. Its hair was two to four inches long, brown underneath, lighter at the top and covering the entire body, except for the face around the nose, mouth and cheek. And it was a female. It had big, pendulous breasts."

This Big Foot was more cooperative than the ones seen by the Claghorns. It moved slowly across a sandbar, but Patterson had time to get out his motion picture camera and start shooting. He had time to use up a full roll before the Sasquatch ambled into some nearby woods and disappeared.

The rancher next made plaster casts of some of the footprints and covered the others with bark, in order that they could be studied by experts. One of the experts was Robert Titmus, of Kitimat, British Columbia, who measured the tracks. After a close study, he pronounced that they were undoubtedly not a hoax and were made by a creature he had never seen. Each track was fourteen and one half inches long and from the deepness of the impression, Titmus estimated they were made by an animal weighing between six and seven hundred pounds.

There were some who branded the film a hoax. Others, equally expert, claimed it was not. The great Pacific Northwest is still a wilderness area of more than 150,000 square miles, so it is entirely possible that there could be an unknown species of animal living somewhere within its confines.

The Norwegians did not believe the story of Bishop Pontoppidan and his sea serpent, yet a fisherman named Al Dixon caught one off Newport Beach. Few people believed that gigantic prehistoric minnows still cavorted in Lake Mojave until two of them were caught.

Someday, someone may catch a Sasquatch, if he is man enough.

A LOST SHIP OF THE DESERT

There are many who swear that camels still roam the deserts of the United States Southwest. Prospectors often come back into town with a story that while they were sitting alone near some saguaro cactus, or some greasewood, or some cholla, they saw anywhere from one to fifty camels silently moving past, silhouetted in the light of a full moon. One of these tales was proved beyond all doubt when, shortly after it was reported, some drivers recaptured a trio of camels who had escaped the annual Date Festival celebration in Indio, California. A number of years ago, however, there were many camels roaming the American deserts. They were brought to this country by the United States Army and large numbers of them were turned loose when the experiment in camels was brought to an end.

Most credit the idea of importing camels to Edward F. Beale, who was undoubtedly the greatest military publicity hound of the mid-nineteenth century. The idea for the drafting of camels into the United States Army first was suggested by a Major George H. Grossman, who thought they would do well as beasts of burden in Florida. Crossman's idea was pigeonholed until 1848, when Major Henry C. Wayne suggested to the War Department that a camel purchasing expedition be sent to the Middle East and that the ungainly beasts be used for transporting military supplies in the American Southwest. When the War Department failed to act, Wayne took his idea to Jefferson Davis, who was a senator at the time.

In 1853, after President Franklin Pierce had appointed Davis as Secretary of War, Davis once again resurrected the plan. If the camel was a "ship of the desert" in the Sahara and the Sind, Davis reasoned, then there was no reason why he could not fulfill the same function in the Mojave and Death Valley. Accordingly, the United States Camel Corps was established and Wayne, accompanied by Navy Lieutenant David Porter, set sail for the Middle East two years later on board the Navy ship *Supply*. Their assignment was to buy camels.

Their first port of call was Tunis, North Africa, where they soon found that dealers in the used-camel market were about as ethical as a Los Angeles used-car dealer today. They discovered, also, that there were many different kinds of camels. There was a dromedary who came with one hump and a Bactrian who came with two. Some camels were slow and could carry heavy loads. Others were fast, but with a much lighter capacity for carrying weight.

Wayne spent a few hundred dollars of the War Department's funds on some camels here, loaded them on the *Supply*, and continued on to Smyrna, Turkey, which, he had been told, was the Detroit of the camel market.

Before the *Supply* cleared the harbor, one of his camels died and was given a quick burial at sea. Another developed a camel's itch, which Wayne soon learned was an itch to end all itches. While Wayne was being treated for this ailment, the beast from which he had caught it broke loose, jumped into the Mediterranean and started swimming back toward North Africa. There apparently is no record as to whether or not the camel made it.

When the Navy ship put in at Smyrna, customs officials came aboard. Five of the camels on board the *Supply* would have to be kept on board in their pens. A camel's hump that sagged over onto its side did not mean that the camel was young and approaching adult life, the officials explained to Wayne. It meant that the beast was either very old or very sick and camels this sick were not going to be allowed in Turkey.

The *Supply* put out to sea, where mass services were held for the dying camels before they also were pitched over the side. By the time the *Supply* returned to Smyrna, Wayne had decided that he needed a professional consultant. After a considerable search, he found one man who appeared to be reasonably honest, was an expert on camels, and was willing to join the United States Camel Corps as a paid consultant and to recruit other camel drivers, who would return to the United States and train enlisted men in the art of camel driving. This man was Hadji Ali, which was pronounced Hi Jolly forevermore by all the Americans with whom he came in contact.

Hi Jolly took over the War Department's mission. He saw that proper camel pens were built on board the *Supply* and he bought 28 camels. The price was high, but the beasts all appeared reasonably healthy. Hi Jolly also rounded up a half-dozen other camel drivers who had no objections to coming to the United States.

Four of the camels died en route to the New World, but six baby camels were born on shipboard, so when the *Supply* docked at Indianola, Texas, on May 14, 1856, there was a total of thirty camels on board. There was a large crowd present to watch the unloading.

The camels were very docile while they were led down the gangplank, but as soon as they hit solid earth, their attitude changed. "They reared and kicked and cried, broke their halters, tore up picket lines and pawed and bit each other. The Indianola mothers who had come to the docks to see the strange beasts, gathered up their children and fled."

"Those are just the pehlevans, or wrestling camels," Hi Jolly explained. "They are very fast and good for chasing Indians."

"What about those who are spitting on everyone?" Wayne asked.

Hi Jolly shrugged. "Maybe it's because they have never seen anyone wearing such funny clothes," he said.

Among those on hand to greet the camels was the ubiquitous Edward Beale with orders in his possession to take charge of the camels and relieve Wayne.

Beale first led the camel caravan to Camp Verde, Texas, some sixty miles northwest of San Antonio, and it was on this trek the United States Army first learned that the Americanization of the camel was not going to be as easy as it had appeared on paper. Whenever Hi Jolly or one of the six other camel drivers brought from the mid-East spoke to one of the "ships of the desert," the beast would respond immediately. The only language the camels seemed to understand was Arabic. Not one camel in the lot would learn English and not one American soldier in the caravan would learn Arabic. Beale tried to overcome this language barrier while the camels were penned in Camp Verde, but to no avail.

Beale accused Hi Jolly of not cooperating sufficiently. Hi Jolly protested vehemently. The next day he went to see Beale once again. The gist of the conversation was that all of the Arabs were homesick, an illness that possibly could be cured quickly if their salaries were doubled. Beale followed Hi Jolly's advice. For more than a year, the camels were kept at Camp Verde. During this time, an additional forty-one were brought across the Atlantic. The second shipment was made under the tutelage of a good friend of Hi Jolly's, a George Xaralampo who, forever-more, was to be known as George the Greek.

On June 25, 1857, the United States Camel Corps, under Beale's command and Hi Jolly's authority, departed Texas for an overland trek across the deserts to Camp Drumm, which is now within the city of Los Angeles. According to Beale, the trip was an outstanding success. Beale explained it in a long letter to Jefferson Davis. "When there is plenty of water, the mule has no desire to drink. There is no way to explain to the mule that for the next ten days water is going to be scarce. When there is no water, the mule wants a drink. The camels, on the contrary, drink gallons of water at one time and never suffer from thirst, no mat-ter what the nature of the country, for another ten days or more."

It was an interesting observation, coming, as it did, more than a year and a half after the camels had been purchased.

The cross-country trip took five months. Shortly after ar-riving at Camp Drumm, Beale moved on to better things. The camels chewed their cuds when they were not breeding, which was rarely. By the end of 1859, the camel count was in excess of two hundred. The soldiers of the Camel Corps had little to do. George the Greek bought a ranch in El Monte.

When the Civil War broke out a short time later, the Camel Corps was brought to the attention of the new Secretary of War, Edwin M. Stanton, and he immediately ordered the government to sever all connections with the project that had been the idea of his Confederate predecessor. Several of the camels were driven over the mountains to the desert and turned loose.

The officers in charge at Camp Drumm then decided that this might not be a practical manner for getting rid of them. They met regularly to debate an alternative method which could evoke no criticism from Washington.

In 1864, Stanton found out that the Army still had a camel corps in California. Angrily, he ordered that all of the camels be driven from Camp Drumm to Benecia, California, many hundreds of miles to the north, and sold at public auction. George the Greek was too busy at his ranch to make the trip. When Hi Jolly insisted that he could not move all of them north by himself, George the Greek compromised. He took half of the herd, drove it over the desert, and turned it loose. As nearly as can be determined, about four hundred camels were given their freedom in this manner.

Hi Jolly took about one hundred up to the Benecia Arsenal north of San Francisco, where they were put up for public auction on February 28, 1864. There was only one bidder, a Samuel McCleneghan, who had an idea that he could use them for transportation between Sacramento and the silver boom town of Austin, Nevada.

Hi Jolly and the five camel drivers from the mid-East agreed to work for McCleneghan. When the caravan reached Sacramento, however, Hi Jolly and his friends suddenly were seized by another attack of homesickness. McCleneghan explained that he did not have the unlimited resources of the United States War Department and a compromise was reached. McCleneghan and Hi Jolly would put on a camel race at the annual state fair, which was just opening in Sacramento.

The race was well-publicized and more than two-thousand

Californians paid a dollar admission to witness the Great Dromedary Race "brought directly to this fair from Smyrna, Turkey." Whether or not McCleneghan made any money on the betting that accompanied the race is unknown. Hi Jolly cleared two thousand dollars in gate receipts.

When the fair ended, the remnants of the United States Camel Corps were moved to Austin. The welcome McCleneghan and Hi Jolly received there was less than welcome. It started when a horse shied as the caravan entered the town, which in turn caused one of the camels to break loose. Before the incident had ended, every "horse and mule within the town limits had disappeared."

A contract was arranged, however, with the owner of an ore reduction plant to haul in supplies and other material from both Virginia City and Carson City, but it did not last long. Oddly, although the camels had traversed from Texas to California without causing any trouble, they were a source of constant friction to the native Nevadans. Horses and mules inevitably panicked every time a camel caravan entered a town. Virginia City passed an ordinance prohibiting the use of camels within the town limits. A short time later, the Nevada legislature passed a law outlawing the use of camels on a public thoroughfare, thus making that usually tolerant state the only state in the union that has an anti-camel ordinance on its books.

The day the law became effective, Hi Jolly once again became sick. This time it was not a longing for his native Turkey that troubled him. It was a more serious disease: gold fever, an ailment for which there is no cure. Hi Jolly did one more favor for McCleneghan before he took off. He drove the camel herd a few miles outside of Austin and turned every one of them loose on the desert. The next morning, Hi Jolly left for Arizona on a mule with a burro in tow and a complete prospecting outfit. McCleneghan went back to San Francisco. Hi Jolly eventually married a Gertrude Serna in Tucson. He died in the small town of Quartzite, Arizona, in 1902. His gravestone is a pyramid with a camel effigy at its apex.

Most of the camels that were turned loose in Nevada moved south to the warmer deserts of California and Arizona. Many were killed by Apaches, who discovered camel meat was a tasty dish. In 1913, a herd of camels was pursued by a posse near Ajo, but easily outdistanced the horses in the soft sand. There are many who still claim to sight camels in the more remote sections of the Southwest, but, unlike the Big Foot, no one ever has come close enough to take pictures of them.

One of the camels that roams the area is a ghostly beast known as the Flying Dutchman of the Desert. According to the legend, one of the officers of the Camel Corps decided upon a unique punishment for an unruly enlisted man. One evening, as the original caravan was making camp near the Gila River, the officer decided that he would force the soldier to learn to ride a camel. He chose the biggest beast in the herd, a Bactrian, and had the soldier's legs tied to the saddle of the animal.

When the camel rocked to its feet, it suddenly broke away and raced off in the general direction of Death Valley. (The soldier quickly died in the intense heat.) Despite a three-day search, no trace of the soldier or the camel could be found. Soon the soldier's body became a skeleton that fell apart, all except for the legs that still were tied to the huge camel, which roams Death Valley to this day.

The Flying Dutchman of the Desert is easily recognized by the slash of white on his saddle, the skeletal legs of the unruly soldier in the United States Camel Corps.

EPILOGUE

THE LOST GOLD BARS OF JUAN BLANCO

In the mid-sixties, a new tale of buried gold began to circulate among the fraternity of treasure seekers in the Southwest. The details were vague. The only information that was consistent was that a part of a large hoard of Dominican gold bars had been found somewhere near Tecate, Mexico, a small border town a few miles east of Tijuana. Soon it became a legend.

The source of the story was discovered in late 1966 by a young engineer from Los Angeles named Paul Devlin.

After spending a weekend in Enseñada, Devlin started out on his return drive to Los Angeles. As he neared Tijuana, the traffic became heavier and he remembered the early Sunday

185

evening jam at the border as thousands of United States citizens returned home from the bullfights, the races at Agua Caliente, and shopping sprees into Tijuana. About the time this thought occurred to him, he noticed a square pink building on top of a small hill some distance from the highway. A narrow, rutted road led up to it and at the junction was a Coca-Cola and a Dos Equis beer sign with an arrow pointing toward the building. It was the beer sign that sent Devlin up the rough road.

Originally, the building had been constructed as a private home. A partition between two small rooms had been knocked out to make room for a very small bar and restaurant. There was only one patron, a man who appeared to be in his late sixties with snow-white hair and nut-brown skin drawn tightly over the high cheekbones of his face. When Devlin sat down, the old man looked at him incuriously for a moment, then turned away and stared at the bottle of tequila in front of him. Near his right hand was a dish with quartered limes, a shot glass, and a salt cellar.

"Good evening," Devlin said politely, but the man did not answer. His voice, however, caused a reaction in the room in back of the bar, for he heard a chair being pushed back. Presently an enormously fat woman appeared. She looked at him in surprise, then after he placed his order, giggled delightedly and opened a bottle of Dos Equis for him.

"Not many tourists come here," the woman said, with another giggle.

"I do not think of myself as a tourist, señora," he replied in Spanish. "I think of myself as a guest in your country."

The old man turned on his chair, stared at Devlin for a moment, then with a steady hand, poured the shot glass full of tequila. "You speak our language well, señor," he said.

"You are very kind, señor."

The old man wiped his mouth with the back of his hand, then turned toward Devlin. His eyes were a deep black that contrasted sharply with his thick, white eyebrows. "I do not like gringos," he said.

"That is a pity," Devlin replied.

"Calm yourself, Don Juan," the fat woman said.

"You calm yourself," the old man retorted. "The gentleman is not a gringo. He is a *Norteamericano*." He stood up and held out his hand. "Allow me the honor of presenting myself. I am called Juan Blanco."

Devlin stood up, shook the proffered hand and introduced himself, then slid back on his stool.

"I will tell you why I do not like gringos," Senor Blanco said presently. He poured another shot of tequila in his glass. "Would you like to hear why I myself do not like the gringos?"

"Why not?"

The fat woman sighed and went back to the other room.

Devlin sipped his beer and listened to the old man recount his tale of woe. Two days after Easter, in 1960, two men had arrived at his farm in Tecate. They arrived in a brand-new Lincoln and they wore very expensive suits that seemed to change color as they moved in the sunlight. One of the men tried to speak in Spanish, but he spoke the language so badly that Juan Blanco was forced to send for his young grandson to act as an interpreter. The two men wanted to buy his farm, they told Juan Blanco, and the price they offered for the land was more than twice its value. They were very disappointed when Juan Blanco explained the law. No foreigner could buy land in Mexico within thirty miles of a border. Then the two men withdrew a short distance and talked to each other in English, apparently forgetting that Juan Blanco's grandson, who was squatting on the ground, could understand them and was translating their conversation to his grandfather.

It developed that the two men had discovered a bar of gold buried in the ground in the United States just across the border from Tecate and they also had found a map buried in a tube of lead which told of the location of many similar bars of gold, a treasure hidden by the Dominicans after their missions had been abandoned. The larger of the two gringos became angry with his companion. He said repeatedly it would be easy to come back during the night and dig it up and that the old farmer, who was Juan Blanco, never would know. The smaller man would not agree to this. He argued that they should tell the old farmer of the discovery and, because the treasure was on his land, it was right that he should have half of it, and that also there was so much gold that even after it was divided, they all would be rich.

Eventually the bigger man threw up his hands and agreed to the plan of his friend. When they came back and told Juan Blanco of the treasure, he acted surprised and happy. They showed him the map found in the lead tube. The words upon it were written in a strange language which the smaller gringo identified as Latin, a language he knew well, he said, because he had studied for the priesthood as a boy.

The two gringos carried a metal detecting machine in the trunk of their expensive car and the smaller man showed Juan Blanco how it worked and let him operate it. The map was very accurate. Juan Blanco himself, with the aid of the machine, found the location of the treasure in little more than an hour. The cache was in an area just out of sight of the highway. Juan Blanco himself dug up the first bar, which was next to another tube of lead. The bar was very heavy. On one side was an etched cross and on the other, the word *ora*. The smaller gringo, the one who was honest, picked up the lead tube, scraped away the wax around one end with his penknife, then extracted a very old piece of parchment paper. He unrolled it carefully and after he had finished reading it, he crossed himself.

He showed the old paper to the big gringo and Juan Blanco. This, too, was written in Latin, he said, and it told that directly below them were buried two thousand golden bars identical to the one they had discovered. They could not, however, dig it up immediately. The smaller gringo read the contents of the old paper. If the gold, he translated, had not been recovered by a Dominican priest before it was found by another person, then this was God's will. If it were found by another, there were certain requirements that must be met before it was removed from the ground. The finder must journey to the City of Mexico and pay for 365 masses at the basilica. If, when he returned, the gold was still in its burial ground, then it was God's will that it become the property of the finder. The finder could pay for his trip and the masses with the golden bar that had been left by the tube. If these instructions were not followed, then the finder would be confined to hell forever.

The big gringo laughed, then picked up the shovel and started to dig. His friend became very angry and pulled the shovel away. If these instructions were not followed, he cried, they all three would be confined to hell for eternity. The big man sighed and became quiet.

Juan Blanco covered up the hole and they walked back to the house. The big gringo took some scales from his car, weighed the gold bar, then whistled. Its weight was worth two thousand American dollars, he said. They were millionaires, for there were two thousand more identical bars in the ground.

There was the question of the conditions, the smaller man reminded them. The answer was simple, the other gringo said. The old man, Juan Blanco, should go to Mexico City because he was the one who actually had found the treasure. Juan Blanco shook his head. He was needed on the farm, he told them through his grandson, but the real reason he would not go was because the big gringo was a thief who would return when no one was at the farm and steal all of the treasure. For a long time they discussed the problem and it became evident that the smaller gringo did not trust his companion, either.

The small gringo offered another solution. His friend

189

would make the trip to Mexico City by airplane from Tijuana and he would pay for the masses. He could easily be back within three days and then they could all recover the gold together.

His companion at first objected because he did not know how to ask a padre to say a mass. The big gringo thought for a moment, then said both of them would go to Mexico City and that Juan Blanco would do something to show his good faith, such as letting them hold five thousand United States dollars of his while they were gone. Again, the smaller man, the one who had studied for the priesthood, objected.

Juan Blanco became tired of the bickering. He offered an alternative. He would give them two thousand dollars and they would leave behind the gold bar that had been discovered next to the tube. The two gringos agreed to it, apparently not realizing that Juan Blanco had outwitted them because the bar they had discovered was worth the two thousand dollars. That very afternoon, they drove to the bank in Tijuana where Juan Blanco withdrew two thousand dollars, which was almost all of the money he had in the bank. He gave it to the smaller man, who was more honest, and the smaller man gave him a receipt for it as they drove back to Tecate in the shiny new Lincoln.

For a week, Juan Blanco remained on his farm checking constantly to see that no one disturbed the ground where the treasure was buried. On the eighth day, he became suspicious. He took his gold bar to Tijuana where an examination disclosed it to be a piece of bronze-plated lead.

Devlin rapped the bottom of his beer bottle on the counter and the fat woman came in and took another from the cooler, "Did you tell the police, Señor Blanco?"

"Of course. They laughed." He reached into his pocket and pulled out his wallet from which he extracted a small piece of ruled paper. He passed it to Devlin. It was a receipt for two thousand United States dollars signed by John Doe, at what undoubtedly was a fictitious address in Los Angeles. "You know why they laughed so hard, Señor Devlin?"

"Possibly because the name John Doe in English is used for someone whose real name is unknown."

The old man nodded. "This is partly the reason, my friend." He poured tequila into the shot glass. "Do you know the name that is used on such occasions in Mexico?"

Devlin shook his head.

"It is Juan Blanco . . . my very own name." The old man laughed, upended the shot glass and bit into the fresh lime. Then he pushed himself to his feet. "For the night, I think I shall take one of your rooms, Gordita," he said.

"At your orders, Don Juan."

Juan Blanco nodded toward the woman, then bowed gravely toward Devlin before he walked steadily out of the door.

"He should have taken his shotgun and told them to go back to the United States in their shiny new Lincoln." Devlin signaled Gordita to join him in a beer.

"Then he would have not learned about the gold on his farm," she answered.

Devlin laughed. "But there was no gold."

"At the time, he did not know this," she gestured with the beer bottle. "What if there had been many bars of gold? Surely he should find out first if the gold was there."

"That is the whole point. He did not find out. He should have dug the hole deeper."

"How could he do that? If the gold was there, then he would have been disobeying the orders of the padres and would be sent to hell for all eternity."

Devlin smiled. "You are a logical woman, Gordita," he replied. "It was a problem."

"No, señor, it was not a problem. It was a matter of faith."

Some three months later, Devlin was at a small party in

Los Angeles where someone told the story of a vast Dominican treasure that had been buried in Tecate. In turn, Devlin repeated the experience of Juan Blanco. The man who had told the story agreed that such a thing could have happened, but, he added, this did not necessarily mean that a Dominican treasure was not buried in Tecate.

Legends start from fact. They are kept alive through faith.

LOST TREASURES
OF THE WEST

CONTENTS

INTRODUCTION

There have been hundreds of books written about lost treasures and mines of the West. Most of these books derive from death-bed confessions or revelations by grizzled prospectors or remorseful murderers who invariably manage to gasp out the story of the treasure but expire in the arms of a friend or doctor before they can pass on anything but the most meager clues to its location.

In this book, as in our previous books, we have avoided this approach to the tales of treasure. Although we have not written this work with the attitude of dedicated historians, there is tangible evidence as to the existence of treasure in each of the following stories. Thus, if the reader wishes to pick up a metal detector or a scuba tank and go seeking, he may do so with the knowledge that what he seeks is not entirely based on fantasy. However, the writers admit candidly that in most of these tales there is the probability that somewhere in the story the facts have been augmented by legend. For example, at the time the *Brother Jonathan* sank at the entrance to Crescent City Harbor in California, it was reported to be carrying approximately $500,000 in gold dust and gold nuggets. Now, a little more than a century later, there are few people in Crescent City who do not know for a fact that the side-wheeler went down with more than $2 million in precious gems, currency, and gold bullion on board. The increased value of the treasure is not based upon the inflated value of gold. It stems from the expansion of a legend over the years.

Inflation does increase the value of a treasure, however. A diamond that sold for $1,000 in the late thirties might well bring ten times that amount today. With this in mind we shall make an exception immediately to our ban on deathbed confessions and tell a story about diamonds that came from the late Jake Ehrlich, the well-known San Francisco criminal attorney.

Shortly before the outbreak of World War I in Europe, a young Frenchman named Antoine Rosselet decided that the odds on his reaching middle age would be much better if he avoided military service by migrating to the United States. Arriving in San Francisco a few months later, he went to work as a waiter in one of the city's better restaurants. When he was twenty-eight, he met and married Helen Riley, a pretty young girl ten years his junior. A few months later the romance was over. Before Helen was twenty, she literally was not speaking to Antoine, nor was he speaking to her. They communicated with each other only by note, and although their mutual hatred intensified during the ensuing months and years neither husband nor wife, because of religious beliefs, sought a divorce as an answer to their problem.

They lived modestly. Rosselet saved his money, and shortly after the United States entered World War I he opened his own restaurant. Apparently it was a success, but the bonanza for Rosselet came with the passage of the Volstead Act. He opened one of the best speakeasies in the city where he served fine liquor and wines with good food. He also be-

194

came active in the illegal importation of liquor from both Canada and Mexico, and the profits from bootlegging and his restaurant made him rich.

With the repeal of Prohibition, Rosselet closed his restaurant. The Depression was at its lowest ebb, and there were few who could afford his cuisine. He bought a small bar on the North Beach, anglicized his name, apparently to avoid the stigma of his rum-running days, and moved with the bitter and noncommunicative Helen into an upper-middle-class section of the city. His bar prospered, not to the extent that his restaurant had during the Prohibition era, but enough so that he did not have to dip into his capital.

In 1948 Rosselet was informed by his doctor that he had a brain tumor and that his life expectancy was only a matter of a few months. Rosselet was approaching sixty. For thirty years, almost half of his entire life, he had been married to a woman to whom he had not spoken a word. He hated her. Yet, he believed that under the California community property laws, his wife would inherit everything he owned, no matter what kind of will he left. There was no way to prevent her from getting possession of their house. She was aware of a small insurance policy and, of course, she knew about the bar. Because of their peculiar relationship, however, she did not know that her husband was worth approximately three-quarters of a million dollars. This money, the dying Rosselet decided, would never cross the palms of Silent Helen.

He sold his bar, cashed in his stocks and bonds, and with the proceeds he quietly bought $750,000 worth of diamonds. Then he was faced with a dilemma. If he put his hoard in a safe-deposit box, Helen certainly would find it after his death. He had no relatives or friends close enough to trust with such a fortune. He had no plans for disposition of the money after his death other than a passionate desire that his wife not get it. As a temporary solution to his problem, he placed the precious stones in a large metal box, then buried them in the backyard of his home when Silent Helen was out of the house.

A few weeks later Rosselet collapsed and was taken to a hospital. Apparently he realized that his hold on life was tenuous, and so, rather than taking his secret to the grave with him, he told the doctor what he had done, adding that the doctor could have the treasure any time he could get it.

The doctor accepted the offer appreciatively and discreetly. A few days later, Rosselet died. The doctor went to the house to offer his condolences to the widow. Apparently he decided to wait until she too passed on, then return to pick up his inheritance without the bother of a probate.

In the fall of 1965, while Silent Helen was enjoying perfect health and still living in the same house, the doctor suffered a mild heart attack. He consulted with Jake Ehrlich, an excellent investigative attorney about his will, and during the conversation he mentioned the peculiar bequest from Rosselet. He identified the donor only by his French name, but he did describe part of his background.

A few weeks later, the doctor, his wife, and his son were killed in a freeway accident in Los Angeles.

The most difficult part of Jake Ehrlich's investigation was finding the court order through which Rosselet changed his name. When Ehrlich discovered the doctor's name on Rosselet's death certificate, he knew he had found the man. The lawyer went to Rosselet's house where his widow still lived.

She was a small woman, very spry and charming. Ehrlich

found it difficult to reconcile her with the Silent Helen described by the doctor, but she made it quite clear to the lawyer that she had found life much more enjoyable since her husband's death. She was not the least bit interested in selling her house.

"Every day I read the obituaries," Ehrlich told one of the authors of this book early in December 1971. "When I read that this very nice little old lady has passed on to her reward, I'm going to buy that house. Those diamonds are probably worth two million by now."

"What if someone else has the same idea?" he was asked.

"That could be," Ehrlich replied. "All the clues to this treasure are in the court records. You just have to know where to look."

A few days before Christmas in 1971, Jake Ehrlich suffered a fatal heart attack in his Nob Hill apartment. His death was front-page copy for the San Francisco newspapers. It is quite possible that Silent Helen may have been reminded of Ehrlich's offer to buy her home when she read of his death, but it is unlikely that she knew of the treasure in her backyard.

Maybe Silent Helen is still alive. Maybe her house has withstood the onslaught of the high-rise apartments in San Francisco. Maybe she will read this book and learn of the treasure her husband buried in her backyard. If this happens, all that will remain for her to do is to obtain a metal detector and run it over her property. Possibly it has already been found and quietly cashed, but if it has, the writers have been unable to find any record that this is the case.

Some of the lost treasures described in these tales may have been found. In other of the tales, such as the shipwreck on Nehalem Spit, a part of the treasure is known to have been recovered and is the best clue to the location of the rest of the fortune.

We have chosen little-known legends of lost treasure and we have told you where to look.

Los Angeles, California   *Brad Williams and Choral Pepper*
June 1973

BEESWAX AND BULLION

When Lewis and Clark reached the end of their long overland trek at the mouth of the Columbia River, they were given a large chunk of beeswax by a group of welcoming Clatsop Indians. History does not record what these two explorers did with their gift, but if they had realized its significance they probably would have made a beeline to its source.

The beeswax came from one of the most spectacular areas of the Oregon coast, some thirty miles south of where the Columbia River pours into the Pacific Ocean in what is known today as Nehalem Beach, Oregon. Immediately to the south of Neahkahnie Mountain, the beach is adjacent to the Nehalem River on a wild spit of land covered only by shifting sand dunes and large clumps of sea grass. There is nothing there that would appeal to a busy Oregon bee even if he had the strength to fight the steady prevailing offshore winds.

This beeswax, which still can be scavenged by beach-combers, was manufactured by bees in India almost three

centuries ago. Its presence on this remote Oregon beach probably solves the mystery of what happened to a huge Manila
galleon that vanished in 1705 with a cargo of millions of dollars worth of gold, silver bullion, and precious gems.

The name of the galleon was the *San Francisco Xavier*.
Built in 1691 in Cavite, in the Philippines, it was approximately
175 feet long, 50 feet wide, carried 80 guns and, when fully
loaded, about 1500 tons of cargo. If it was built like most of the
other Manila galleons, its frames were made of teak, and the
other parts of the ship were constructed of Philippine hard-
woods such as *lanang* and *molave*.

For more than two hundred and fifty years, the Manila
galleons operated a regular route between Manila and
Acapulco. Usually one ship traveled in each direction once a
year. The westbound ships headed south from Acapulco to pick
up the prevailing winds and current near the equator, then
north as they neared Guam, an island which the Spanish
named Los Ladrones (The Robbers) because of the light fin-
gered habits of the natives. The galleons usually paused here to
reprovision their stores before continuing on into Manila.

Eastbound ships headed north to catch the prevailing
winds and the Japanese current, usually turning east at the
northern end of Japan for the long voyage across the Pacific.
Landfall of the North American continent varied anywhere between the thirtieth and forty-fifth parallel or, roughly, between
the northern coast of Baja and the northern coast of Oregon.
More often than not, landfall was made far enough north so
that the galleons could put into either Monterey or San
Francisco for reprovisioning.

Westbound, the galleons carried unexciting cargos of
cocoa, chocolate, and similar products, plus cash. Diocesan
records indicate that the *San Francisco Xavier* carried 2,070,000

pesos in 1688. When voyaging back to Acapulco, however, the cargoes were much more exotic.

William Lytle Schurz, in his book *The Manila Galleon* reports that the ships carried silks, taffeta, and delicate Cantonese crepes from China, rich vestments for the churches in New Spain, and gauzes, napkins, and handkerchiefs from the Mogul Empire of India. Persian rugs imported into the Philippines from India and the Malabar and Coromandel coasts were very much in demand.

No galleon ever departed for New Spain from Manila without large shipments of gold and silver bullion and precious stones. One cargo manifest from a galleon that arrived in Acapulco in 1767 lists diamond earrings, necklaces, pendants, and bracelets by the hundreds, a large diamond-encrusted cross, sword hilts studded with jewels, and thousands of uncut or unset precious stones. No vessel ever made the trip without a large shipment of Ghedda beeswax, made in India, and much in demand in New Spain for use as votive candles and for lighting.

The galleons were known to have carried another cargo: slaves brought to the Philippines from the east coast of Africa. The traffic in slaves was small, but each passenger aboard ship was permitted to have two personal servants. Often these were blacks and were sold by the passenger when the galleon arrived in Acapulco.

From the first crossing in 1565 to the last in 1815, there was a record of thirty Manila galleons lost on the westbound trip. Most of these foundered in the turbulent straits of the Philippines. One went aground on the coast of Japan, another was captured by English freebooters, and still another broke up on the northern edge of San Miguel Island off the California coast. Of these lost galleons, only two vanished without a trace:

the *San Francisco Xavier* and the *San Antonio*. There are some reports, however, that the *San Antonio* was the galleon lost at San Miguel. If this is true, it leaves only the *San Francisco Xavier* unaccounted for, and there is considerably more evidence than several tons of beeswax to indicate that this long lost Manila galleon may be resting under one of the sand dunes on Nehalem Spit in Oregon.

It is not an improbable location for the *San Francisco Xavier* to have been battered ashore by an early fall storm. Nehalem is a very short distance above the forty-fifth parallel, which was the northernmost point of a Manila galleon's eastern route. The Nehalem River enters the ocean here, and the spit curves upward at the river mouth to form Nehalem Bay. It would have been possible for a galleon seeking sanctuary from a storm in this sheltered water to have been blown or pushed ashore on the Nehalem Beach by the river's currents.

The tons of wax that have been picked up on Nehalem Beach are the strongest clue that the *San Francisco Xavier* was wrecked there. Beeswax is virtually indestructible, except by heat, and the Oregon beaches are always cool. It is still used in the manufacture of votive candles because of its higher melting point and slow burning characteristics. The origin of beeswax can easily be determined through analysis. European, Japanese, and North American beeswax is manufactured by the common bee, *apis mellifica*. Beeswax from India, which is the slowest burning of all, is made by the bee known as *apis dorsata*. This Indian beeswax is commonly called Ghedda wax and it was used in the seventeenth century by the churches and the rich of Mexico City and Guadalajara. Analysis of the beeswax found on Nehalem Spit shows it to be Ghedda wax.

The wax also was "sized" to the proportions required by a Manila galleon, and vast numbers of the pieces bear numerals and letters which have been interpreted by some scholars to be the equivalent of a modern bill of lading.

The Clatsop Indians told Lewis and Clark that the beeswax came from a shipwreck, and, according to a legend that has been passed on for centuries, some of the men on board the doomed ship survived. Most of the survivors set off toward the south. Among those who made it to shore successfully was a giant black man.

The late Senator Richard L. Neuberger of Oregon, who was an avid historian of the Pacific Northwest, was fascinated by the beeswax and its possible origins. He told of one variation of a Clatsop Indian legend which goes back to the shipwreck and involves a gigantic Negro.

According to Neuberger, the black giant and a white man were the only survivors of the shipwreck on Nehalem Spit. The day after the storm subsided, the giant, who was apparently the white man's servant, went back out to the wave-pounded wreckage of the ship and presently returned carrying a large chest. The giant and his companion then proceeded to bury the chest well above the tide line and away from the spit, marking the site with a triangular placement of large rocks. Then the pair set off to the south. They had covered only a short distance when they ran into a group of hostile Indians and were murdered.

Early in the 1930s, a farmer named Edward G. Calkins turned up a skeleton while he was plowing a field near Three Rocks Beach, only a few miles south of Nehalem in Oregon. A short time later, after some careful digging, he discovered two skeletons, and one was that of a giant about 8 feet tall. A delayed autopsy showed that both men had been murdered by blows to the head more than two hundred years earlier. The skeleton of the giant was that of a Negro.

In her book, *Lost Mines and Treasures of the Pacific Northwest*, Ruby El Hult, tells of a discovery by Pat Smith, a beachcomber, at Nehalem in 1898. Combing the beach after a heavy storm, he came across the remains of an ancient ship, bared by the shifting sands on Nehalem Spit. The frames were made of teak, the same wood used in the construction of the Manila galleons. After he salvaged several pieces of the wood, which he fashioned into canes and sold as souvenirs, Smith was convinced the wreck was that of a Manila galleon and made several attempts to get into the hold areas. All proved futile because of the shifting sands. A short time later another storm buried the wreckage once again under the dunes.

The shipwreck surfaced once again after a heavy storm in 1929. This time the galleon remained in view a sufficient time to attract the attention of Phillip I. Cherry, the British vice-consul in Astoria, Oregon. Cherry knew of the incredible value of a Manila galleon's cargo, and, after a close inspection of the wreck, he attempted to interest a salvage company in raising the hull.

The year 1929, however, marked the start of the Great Depression. To raise the hull of the ancient ship would have required the construction of a $30,000 cofferdam. Cherry could induce no one to risk that much money in those parlous times.

The shipwreck still lies on Nehalem Spit. The ribs of the vessel are bared occasionally after a storm, sometimes for a few hours only, sometimes for months before they are again inundated by the sand.

The legend of the buried treasure chest has many variations and has attracted more treasure seekers than the lost galleon. More than one thousand holes have been dug around Neahkahnie Mountain in quest of a treasure chest, which contains only a tiny part of the treasure left on the galleon. However, if the wreck is the remains of the *San Francisco Xavier*, there's a fortune in gold bullion, silver, and precious gems in those sand dunes.

There is even a greater treasure in the wreckage of the other lost Manila galleon, the *San Antonio*, which is believed by many to be the one that foundered on the western side of San Miguel Island, a few miles off the California coast.

The island lies approximately thirty miles south of Point Concepcion. Shaped roughly like a triangle, it is about 9 miles long and 5 miles broad at its widest point. Technically, it does not belong to the United States despite its geographical position some two hundred miles north of the Mexican border. It is one of the so-called Channel Islands, none of which were mentioned in the treaty by which the United States acquired California from Mexico, a point brought up at regular intervals by Mexican politicians. The U.S. State Department never has debated the matter seriously with our southern neighbor because neither country really cares who has the title to the unpopulated and barren Channel Islands, except for Santa Catalina Island.

San Miguel is the most mysterious of the eight Channel Islands. It is a barren, windswept place, haunted by ghosts of prehistoric tribes. There is a legend that any man who attempts to make it his home is doomed to die violently. It is here that Juan Rodriguez Cabrillo, who many believed was the first conquistador to sail up the California coast, is reported to have been buried. It is a graveyard for many ships including the *San Sebastian*, which sank in 1754, the *J.F. West* which crashed into its hostile shores in 1889, the *Comet* in 1911, and the *Cuba* in 1923. It also is the probable site of the wreckage of the *San Antonio*.

In the year 1603, the Chinese and the Filipinos in Manila joined in a massive revolt against the Spaniards. At the start of the revolt, the *San Antonio* was in port and preparing for its return trip to Acapulco. In addition to the regular cargo, most of which had already been loaded, the captain suddenly found that his ship had become the sanctuary for the families, with their valuables, of the leading Spanish politicians. Millions of dollars in precious stones, jewelry, cash, and bullion were carried on board the galleon by refugees. More valuables were loaded to be shipped to the New World where the political climate was believed to be more stable.

When the *San Antonio* left Manila it carried more riches than any other galleon in the entire two hundred and fifty years of the run. It was never heard of or seen again. Spanish historians state flatly, however, that the *San Antonio* was wrecked upon the treacherous west shore of San Miguel Island, and there is strong evidence to support this contention. Visitors to the island have found lumps of Ghedda wax on the western side of the island. Like the *San Francisco Xavier*, the *San Antonio* carried a large shipment of this Eastern beeswax.

The area to search is small, but the breakers will thwart the efforts of any scuba diver.

THE NAIL ON THE HEAD

The wagon trains usually gathered in Fort Boise, Idaho, to reprovision and rest up for the final trek along the Oregon Trail into the lush valleys of western Oregon, but rarely were there so many wagons in the outpost as in the midsummer of 1845. In the early part of August, six wagon trains, comprising a total of three hundred wagons, about one thousand adults, twenty-three hundred cattle, eight hundred oxen, and one thousand goats were straining the hospitality of Fort Boise as preparations were made for the last segment of the long trip over the Blue Mountains and down the banks of the Columbia River.

Five of these wagon trains had been made up in Missouri; the sixth originated in Iowa. The land voyage across the plains and over the Continental Divide had been long and dull. Without exception, all of the travelers were eager to reach their destination, and, thus, most were easy marks for a persuasive promoter of indeterminate age named Stephen Meek when he offered to guide them over a 200-mile shortcut to Oregon's Willamette Valley for a five-dollar fee per wagon. If there had been no Meek, there would be no legend of the lost Blue Bucket gold. Today there is a plethora of versions about the lost Blue Bucket, all versions verifying that the whole affair started with Meek.

One of the wagon trains was commanded by William G. T'Vault from St. Joseph, Missouri, a man who, either by luck or cunning, proved to be the smartest wagon master in Fort Boise at this time. Of the six commanders, only T'Vault resisted the blandishments of the smooth-talking Meek. The other wagon masters collected the five-dollar fee from the members of their train, gave the money to Meek, then lined up to follow him into disaster.

The huge wagon train started west from Fort Boise as a unit. Then, on August 24, it split into two parts. T'Vault, with about one hundred wagons, continued along the well-established Oregon Trail; the other two hundred wagons followed Meek to the south.

For the first day or two the Meek contingent found the way passable. Then the trail gradually disappeared under a mass of boulders which shattered wheels and pounded the hooves of the cattle so severely that many could not stand. The heat grew intolerable and tempers strained to the breaking point. Meek said the boulders were the result of some unknown natural phenomenon that had occurred since he had last used the trail.

Two weeks later the battered wagon trains came down from the mountains into the smoother, but more deadly, parched alkali plains northeast of Malheur Lake in an area known today as Crane Prairie. The caravan paused beside a spring, but the water was too polluted to drink. Even the cattle refused to touch it, and some literally were dying of thirst.

The wagon train commanders called an emergency meeting with Stephen Meek, who finally admitted that he was indeed lost. Shortly after this meeting Meek disappeared. There are two versions of his disappearance. The more charitable states that Meek sought sanctuary in one of the wagons and that he escaped some weeks later. The other version reports that Meek was shot and quietly buried without the usual services, for there were no mourners. A week later, as the caravan struggled across the desert, it stumbled upon a series of small sloughs that contained stagnant but potable water. They named the area Stinking Hollows, a name it still bears, and here the immigrants made camp.

Mostly sick, more than one thousand men, women, and children, approximately two thousand cattle, five hundred oxen, and eight hundred goats crowded into the sloughs. It was here that the first victim of Meek's mistake, a woman named Mary Smith, was buried. The following day a young boy died.

Scouting parties were sent in search of water and, within a few days, one of the scouts returned with news of a spring some forty miles to the north. Camp was struck and the caravan moved on.

There is an interesting sidelight to the encampment at Stinking Hollows. The tale may be apocryphal, but many years later an Indian told a newspaper reporter in The Dalles, Oregon, that when he was a small boy he had, on several occasions, crept to within a few yards of the immigrants and watched them. He knew that several of the travelers were dying of thirst, and he also knew the location of a large spring within an hour's ride of the camp.

"Why didn't you tell them about it?" he was asked.

"I couldn't," the Indian replied. "I was an Indian and would have been shot before I could have told them."

The spring found by the scouts was in the foothills of the mountains, not far from the headwaters of Crooked River. The water in the small spring was crystal clear but was far from sufficient to slake the thirst of the wagon train that descended upon it. It was in an area covered by juniper trees and splattered streams of lava from some prehistoric volcanic eruption. Dry creek beds wandered throughout the lava pot-holes. Once again the wagon train came to a halt as the scouts explored for a way out of the dilemma. The water shortage began to take its toll. On September 23, four persons died. On the following day, six more died. Another half-dozen perished in the ensuing six days. The wagon masters broke camp and struggled on.

On the last day of the month a small girl died. Each wagon in the train was, of necessity, self-sufficient, and the mother of the small girl had no time to mourn. The wagons paused only long enough to dig a grave, then moved on. Late in the afternoon the train came across another lava flow. As the wagons struggled over this, there was a sudden desert cloud-burst. The dry wash became a flowing stream for only a short time, but even when the water seeped through the gravel, enough remained on the surface in the potholes of the lava to warrant making camp for the night.

The husband of the bereaved mother was a drunkard. He had been in varying degrees of intoxication ever since he left Fort Boise, and not a night went by in which he did not drink himself into a stupor. This night was to be no exception. While the wife prepared the evening meal, her husband opened a fresh bottle of whiskey. Their ten-year-old son picked up a small blue bucket, ran over to the bank of the creek bed, and presently began collecting small pebbles, tossing those that appealed to him into his bucket. The husband upended the whiskey bottle several times, belched, then sullenly told his wife to get out of his sight and into the back of the wagon, which she did. Her son then returned and climbed into the wagon. As the boy entered the wagon, the flap was pulled back and the woman saw her husband eating alone, swilling all of the food down with his whiskey. Later, as it grew dark, she watched her husband stretch out on the ground, a fist clenched around the neck of his nearly empty whiskey bottle. She crept down from the wagon, started the fire again, and prepared another meager meal for herself and her son.

Much later that night, while everyone in the caravan slept, the woman once again climbed down from the wagon. In her hands she carried a hammer and a long thin nail. She moved quietly toward her husband, knelt down beside him, placed the point of the nail against his skull, and drove it into his head with one powerful blow of the hammer. Then she covered up the head of the nail with his thick and matted hair and crawled back into the wagon.

There was no autopsy the following morning when his body was discovered. There had been too many deaths and if any thought at all was given to the cause, it probably was attributed to alcoholism. He was buried, and a pile of stones was left behind to mark his grave. No one knew how he died until some thirty years later when his widow made a deathbed confession to her son.

The day after his death an advance party returned to the caravan with news that the Deschutes River was only two days' journey away. A week later the wagon train arrived safely in The Dalles. The widow and her small son settled in an area of the Willamette Valley now known as Oregon City. Without a man, she was forced into servant status. One day Charles Dillingham, one of her employers, noticed her son playing with some yellow stones in a blue bucket. Astounded, Dillingham picked up a stone and discovered it was a nugget of pure gold. One of the "pebbles" was almost a pound of pure gold. All of the pebbles had been picked up by the boy on the banks of the dry creek bed where his mother had murdered his father.

The woman was understandably vague as to the location of the gold vein. Whoever found the gold would probably find her husband's body, and, although she undoubtedly looked upon the killing as justifiable homicide, she had no intention of standing trial for murder, no matter how much gold was involved. Her reticence probably also accounts for the many versions of the legend of the Blue Bucket gold or, as it more often is called erroneously, the Blue Bucket Mine. Only on her deathbed did the widow tell her son the location of the gold and her reason for keeping it secret. Thirty years, however, had dimmed her memory, and her son was more adept at practicing law than prospecting, so it is unknown whether or not he made even a cursory search for the treasure.

Another version of the lost Blue Bucket gold legend contends that T'Vault accompanied the Meek group. According to this account, all of the wagon masters lined up behind Meek in Fort Boise. Two of the trains pulled away from Meek, shortly after he embarked upon the "shortcut," returning to the Oregon Trail. Then, after the trail became nonexistent, the trains split into smaller units for more efficient movement. For a while Meek escorted a train commanded by a Captain Herren, but when this unit reached an area known as Wagontire Mountain, Meek went back to look for T'Vault, whose train was bringing up the rear. He found T'Vault, but was unable to find his way back to Wagontire. It was in T'Vault's wagon train, guided by Meek, that the murder of the alcoholic husband occurred and where the gold was scooped into a blue bucket by a small child.

This version is more explicit as to the probable location of the gold. It says that T'Vault threw Meek out of the train and sometime later brought his wagons to the fringe of a marshland now known as the Hart Mountain Antelope Range. Here they found a series of small holes containing stagnant but potable water. A camp was set up and scouts sent out to look for a way out of the mountains. Three days later one scout returned with a report of a better water hole some forty miles to the north. The train moved to the site. A new campground was established between two rises now known as Coyote Hills and Rabbit Hills. It was there that the blue bucket was filled with gold nuggets and the drunken husband was killed with a nail.

The motivation for the murder was stronger in this version. The little girl who died on the trail was the drunkard's daughter. He had beaten her so severely that she fell into a coma. She died about three days after the train moved on. She was buried on a hillside with an ox yoke and a toy cup to mark her grave. The drunkard's grave was marked by a wagon tailgate.

The search for the Blue Bucket gold has continued throughout the years. One of the more spectacular searches was organized in Portland in the summer of 1861. A man named Harold Adams spread the word around the Willamette Valley that he knew the location of the Blue Bucket gold. His boasts attracted the attention of a young man named Henry Griffin, an adventurer with a talent for organization.

Griffin made a deal with Adams that Adams would be paid $1,000 to lead a prospecting party to the site, and, if gold was discovered, he would be cut in for ten percent of the profits. Adams agreed.

Griffin made up a party of experienced prospectors, and in early August the well-equipped expedition set out from Portland under the guidance of Adams. The group wound a crooked trail through the Cascades, crossed the dry Oregon desert and, many days later, found itself in the area of the headwaters of the Burnt River. This was a spot considerably far from where Adams had indicated the Blue Bucket gold would be found.

That night, around the campfire, Griffin asked Adams for an explanation. "We're almost there," Adams replied.

"Will we be there tomorrow?" Griffin asked.

"Tomorrow or the next day."

"Will you stake your life on it?"

Adams did not answer. Later that night, however, after he thought all of his companions were asleep, he quietly saddled a horse. Before he could mount the animal, Griffin stopped him at gunpoint. The other prospectors were awakened. A unanimous vote approved the immediate "trial" of Adams, with Griffin acting as judge. It was probably one of the shortest trials in the history of the West. "You were running away because you have no idea where the Blue Bucket gold is," Griffin suggested.

Adams nodded his head.

The "jury," consisting of the other prospectors, then voted unanimously to strip Adams of all of his possessions except the clothes he wore and a canteen of water and to throw him out of the group.

Incredibly, the confidence man survived the long trek back across the desert. The following year, he was charged in Seattle with extortion for raising money to finance another expedition to find the Blue Bucket gold.

The prospecting party that had thrown him out in Oregon split into two segments the day after Adams's departure. The largest group turned toward the northwest and discovered what later became known as the rich John Day mines. The party, headed by Griffin, also is reported to have found gold in an area known as Elk Creek.

One of the most intensive expeditions in search of the lost Blue Bucket gold was a month-long foray financed by the late Erle Stanley Gardner shortly before his death. His search was based upon information furnished by Mrs. Lois Pierce of Hoodsport, Washington. She is descended from one of the families who took part in the historic Meek's Mistake.

According to journals in her possession, three persons in the wagon train died on consecutive days starting the day after a life-saving cloudburst. Her journals also indicate that the lost wagon train found water in what is now known as Lost Forest near Wagontire Mountain in central Oregon. Since a wagon train traveled about twelve miles a day, Gardner reasoned there should be three graves about twelve miles apart. He found a grave near a windmill on an abandoned ranch midway between Christmas Valley and Highway 395. About twelve miles away, another grave was discovered near Alkali Lake Station, and a third was located about another twelve miles south off Highway 395. Since the Gardner expedition worked backward, this placed the area of search between Rabbit Creek and Foley Creek, an area covered with potholed lava beds.

Gold often has been discovered under lava caps, most frequently in northern California, a short distance south of the

Gardner Expedition site. The gold originally was in streambeds that became conduits for lava spewed up by volcanic eruptions. Through continuing erosion over aeons, the streams once again wore away the lava, picked up the gold during cloudbursts, then deposited it in potholes as the stream again subsided.

Although Gardner failed to discover gold in the lava potholes between Rabbit and Foley creeks, there are many such lava beds in the area. If one finds the proper skeleton, he will have hit the nail on the head.

CACHIE'S CACHE

Cachie was an unfortunate Indian princess. She had the face of a burro, a deformed foot, and was as flat-chested as a table-top. Possibly to make up for these deficiencies, she was given more intelligence than many other Indians in her tribe. This only added to her difficulties, for if there was one thing an Indian warrior shunned more than a short, ugly woman, it was a squaw with brains. Not even the fact that she was the daughter of the Yavapai Indian Chief Quashackamo helped her lure a brave into her teepee. She was friendless and forlorn.

Whenever anyone did make a kind gesture in her direction, she became overwhelmed with gratitude. It is unknown what she did to repay kindly Indians. It is known, however, that on three separate occasions when she was befriended by a white person, she repaid the favor by divulging the location of a fortune. She was not believed on any of these three occasions. Two of the treasures later were found. The third is still undiscovered in Arizona.

Cachie was an only child, born in a teepee at some overnight camping site in the mid-1880s. Nothing is known of her mother, other than she died when Cachie was very young. If Cachie had not been an Indian princess, she probably would have been abandoned during her infancy because of her physical condition. By the time she reached puberty, she required a crude crutch to hobble around. She was an expert rider, however, and, because she was the daughter of a powerful Indian chief, she had her own pony, even though she was a girl.

When she was in her early teens, she was sent west by her father, Quashackamo. Apparently he was motivated by the dangerous political climate of Arizona in the late nineteenth century.

The commanding general of the army in the territory was the devious George Crook. Crook sought headlines in his war to exterminate the savages.

Massacres were not uncommon. After a group of whites raided an Indian concentration camp at Camp Grant and raped most of the women before slaughtering the entire community, Quashackamo decided that Arizona was, for the time being, no place for his crippled daughter. He sent her to live in a community of Chemehuevi Indians with whom the Yavapais had long enjoyed a friendly relationship.

The Chemehuevis, located near San Bernardino in California, accepted Cachie into their village, then ignored her. Cachie quickly learned to speak the dialect of the Chemehuevis, but even after she could communicate, she was ostracized. The Chemehuevis also had little use for an ugly squaw with brains, but Cachie did make friends with an elderly white couple who traded with the Indians. The two itinerant merchants operated out of San Bernardino, visiting several Indian villages in the area and trading knickknacks and baubles for moccasins and rugs, which they sold in their city store. Since there were no blood ties to hold the Indian princess to the Chemehuevis, one day she threw a blanket over her pony and followed the merchants to San Bernardino.

One of the other city merchants, an Englishman married to a Mexican woman, took Cachie into his home as a servant. Whether or not he realized that his guest was an Indian princess is unknown, but he certainly must have been impressed with the ease with which Cachie achieved fluency in English and Spanish. Within a few weeks, he had her working in his San Bernardino store as a clerk and interpreter. But it was a style of life that did not appeal to the princess.

It is unknown how long Cachie remained in San Bernardino or how she returned to Quashackamo, who then ruled his tribe from semipermanent headquarters on the banks of the Colorado River in Arizona. There are historical records, however, that refer to Quashackamo's daughter who sat at his side as an interpreter during meetings with Army men and merchants. Two of these accounts refer to Cachie's ugliness— one written by an emissary from General Crook who was trying to pressure Quashackamo into bringing his tribe into a reservation at Camp Date Creek, the other written in the diary of a miner named Charles Genung.

Genung was an enigma to his fellow white citizens in the territory. Both a prospector and a farmer, he was also a literate man in his early forties when he first met Cachie and her father. Although all the other white settlers were fighting the Indians, Genung preferred the company of Indians to whites. He lived by himself in a modest house in an area known as Peoples Valley, and apparently met Quashackamo during the time Cachie was in California. He met the Indian princess when she returned and became her father's interpreter. He described her as a "female of most ugly countenance to the point of fascination."

Genung's fascination with Cachie was not missed by the Indian princess. Anticipating that such interest probably would occur but once in her lifetime, she saddled her pony after one of Genung's visits and followed him back to Peoples Valley. Genung was not as forthright with his diary as could be desired. Although it is known that Cachie moved into Genung's modest home in Peoples Valley, there is some question as to whether she became his mistress or his housekeeper.

Cachie had been living with Genung for about a year when she decided to reward her benefactor. She told him the Yavapais knew of three locations where there was more gold than one man could spend in his lifetime. If Genung so wished, she would lead him to one of these locations. Genung smiled tolerantly and thanked her. Although he knew that Cachie was more intelligent than most Indian women, Genung had discovered that she also had a fertile imagination, and he did not want to embarrass her by accepting her offer.

Several months passed. Genung went on a prospecting foray and returned to Peoples Valley empty-handed. Again Cachie repeated her offer and when Genung again smiled, she drew him a map. "Go by yourself, then," she said quietly, passing him the paper.

Genung went to his small office, collected a gold nugget, a rock containing copper particles, and another filled with pyrites, sometimes known as fool's gold, then returned to Cachie. "One of these is gold," he said, placing the three specimens on the table. "Can you pick it out?"

Cachie instantly picked up the rock containing the shining copper particles. Genung patted her on the shoulder and carried his specimens back to his office. The next morning

Cachie was gone, and Genung heard a few days later that she was back with her father.

Five years later, gold was found in the Harquahalas Range in southwestern Arizona, resulting in the largest gold rush in Arizona's history. One mine alone in the area produced more than $15 million worth of gold before it was sold to an English syndicate for another $5 million. The Bonanza vein produced $4 million before it went dry, and the Golden Eagle vein adjacent to it was worth approximately $3 million.

When the gold rush was at its peak, Genung chanced across the map that Cachie had drawn for him earlier. The directions led him straight from Peoples Valley to the gold fields of the Harquahalas.

Cachie did not remain with her father very long. The U.S. Army was increasingly active in attempting to break up the Indian tribes. More white settlers were migrating into the fertile lands abutting the Colorado River. Quashackamo retreated deeper into the interior of the territory. Cachie, however, remained behind, moving in with a Mexican woman named Maria Valencia in the small mining town of La Paz.

Maria Valencia was an enormous woman with a husband who showed up about once a year. How Cachie and Maria became friendly is unknown, but it is known that Cachie also became friendly with the Ochoa family of La Paz through her relationship with Maria.

Long before the Harquahalas strike, Cachie attempted to give the Yavapais' secret away to Maria. Maria believed the story and she convinced her wandering husband upon one of his rare visits to La Paz to accompany Cachie to the site. Her husband, whose first name has long been forgotten, did accompany Cachie to the Harquahalas. Either Cachie did not show Valencia the gold fields, or Valencia could not recognize the gold ore. He returned to La Paz several hours ahead of Cachie, told his wife and the Ochoas that the squaw was crazy, and out-lined in detail the course and destination of his journey.

Maria died shortly after this foray, and Cachie disap-peared. Three years later, when the gold strike was made in the Harquahalas, Peter Ochoa, a son of the people Cachie be-friended, wryly recalled the scoffing comments made by Valencia about his trip into the mountains with the crazy Indian squaw.

When he was in his late teens, Peter Ochoa was given a job driving a freight wagon between Ehrenburg and Prescott, Arizona, along a route which took him through Peoples Valley. On one of these trips he met Genung and eventually discov-ered that they had a friend in common, Cachie. Ochoa learned also that Cachie, now forty years old and in poor health, had returned to Peoples Valley and was presently living in an aban-doned miner's shack.

Ochoa stopped to see her. Quashackamo was dead. Cachie had no money and little to eat, but she still was an Indian princess—too proud to live on a reservation. Ochoa gave her a small supply of food and on his next trip a larger amount and some medical herbs prepared by his mother. During the late spring and the entire summer, Peter Ochoa never went through Peoples Valley without stopping to see Cachie to give her supplies and medicine.

One day in the early fall, Cachie hobbled out to his wagon as he was preparing to leave. "If you can come with two ponies, I will take you to a place where there is so much gold that you will never be able to spend it in your lifetime," she said.

"In the Harquahalas?"

Cachie nodded.

222

Ochoa stifled a sigh. "It has already been found, Cachie," he replied. "I thought you knew."

"Only on the north side. No one has found the gold on the south slope."

"How do you know?"

"My father showed me when I was a child."

Ochoa was convinced. Genung had told him of his experience with Cachie, and Ochoa had heard the words of Valencia. He promised to return within two weeks with the ponies.

It was closer to three weeks, however, before Ochoa was able to get back to Peoples Valley. There was no one in the shack that Cachie called her home. Peter Ochoa found her body under a tree about three hundred yards from her cabin.

For several years after Cachie's death, Ochoa searched the south slopes of the Harquahalas for the Yavapais' gold. He found several specimens of "rusty gold in quartz" at the bottom of arroyos, but he was never able to trace them to their source.

A story in the Yuma *Sentinel* in 1892 tells of two Frenchmen who deposited $8,000 worth of rusty, rough gold in the safe of the Hooper Company General Store and never returned to collect it. The description of the gold matches that found by Ochoa.

Another report of rusty gold in quartz is attributed to George Sears who, for many years, operated a small mine near Ajo, Arizona. En route from Ajo to Phoenix, he decided to do some prospecting. He made a detour into what he thought was the Eagle Tail Mountains, which are adjacent to the southern slope of the Harquahalas. In the side of a canyon, he found some loose rock that he thought worth assaying. He had loaded about twenty-five pounds of the ore on his mule when the skies suddenly darkened, then were split by lightning. Sears knew a canyon or a wash was no place to be during a mountain storm. Flash floods usually follow the downpour and to be caught in an arroyo means certain death. Sears hurriedly gathered up his tools, jumped on his horse, and galloped (leading his mule) down the canyon until he found a spot where he could climb up to a higher and safer elevation.

The storm was extraordinarily heavy and continued for several hours, leaving Sears and his animals thoroughly soaked. Below him, and between him and Phoenix, water raced down the canyon as forcefully as if it had escaped from a ruptured dam. Prudently, he decided to go back to Ajo and dry out. A day or so later he again set out for Phoenix, this time going there directly. An assayer confirmed that the ore he had picked up in the Eagle Tail Mountains did contain gold, lots of it.

Sears spent years looking for the lode. He was convinced that he knew where the canyon was, but he never could find it again. His only explanation was that the flash flood which followed the heavy storm had altered the terrain sufficiently to thwart recognition.

Today the Harquahalas are completely unpopulated. The booming town that arose coincidentally with the development of the mines is a ghostly accumulation of old foundations, crumbling fireplaces, and fragments of broken glass turned purple by the sun. Its post office, established in 1891, was discontinued in 1918, then revived from 1927 to 1932 under the name of Harqua. It has since vanished.

On most maps of the area there is a reference to the unbelievable Indian princess. Someone has named a water hole after her. It is known as Cachie's Tank.

HONEST HARRY MEIGGS

The North Beach section of San Francisco is an extension of the city's once infamous Barbary Coast. It is packed with night clubs, bars featuring topless and bottomless entertainment, cocktail lounges, restaurants with flamenco dancers and bull-fight movies, and Irish pubs where the darts fly in all directions. Buried or cached somewhere in this part of the city that is awake around the clock is $1 million worth of gold bullion stolen from the Bank of California by an alderman named Harry Meiggs. In all fairness to Honest Harry, however, he apparently was more concerned with making a name for himself than hustling a fast buck. He succeeded in the former endeavor but he was also fast with a dollar.

Honest Harry was born in New York, had an average school education in New England, and then was apprenticed as a hand in a lumberyard in Williamsburg, New York. He did not remain a hand very long, however, and there are conflicting stories as to how he wound up as proprietor of his own lumber-yard within two years. The most unkind theory suggests that Honest Harry simply stole enough lumber from his employer during the two years he worked for him to stock a competitive yard.

The life of a successful lumber merchant in Williamsburg soon palled for ebullient Harry, and, when word reached him of the gold strike in California, he decided to go west. He chartered a small ship, loaded it with the inventory in his yard and every other piece of lumber he could purchase on credit, and then filed for bankruptcy. It seemed pointless for him to wait around to answer embarrassing questions so, a few days after the petition for bankruptcy was filed, Harry sailed on his lumber-laden bark for San Francisco.

He could not have picked a better time to arrive in the "City by the Golden Gate." Although rich in gold and silver, San Francisco had no lumber to meet the building boom. Estimates of Honest Harry's profit on his cargo range from $50,000 to $500,000. The latter figure probably is more accurate in view of the fact that his New York creditors had met most of the initial cost.

Harry quickly decided there was more gold in lumber than there was in the Mother Lode country. He built a mill on North Beach, hired five hundred destitute miners, trained them to swing an axe, and launched the first assault upon California's redwood trees in the nearby canyons. A little more than two years after his arrival in the mid-1850s, the Mendocino mills of his California Lumber Company were supplying San Francisco with almost three million feet of redwood monthly.

If Harry had been content to remain a lumber baron, his name would long since have been forgotten. "I'm a lot bigger than a few planks of wood," he told a newspaper reporter immodestly. Harry raised funds to build the city's first opera house and sold them the lumber used in the construction. When a competitor raised funds to build the Jenny Lind Theatre, Harry exposed him as a swindler.

Harry ran for the city council and was elected. A few months later the city awarded the California Lumber Company a contract to build Meiggs Wharf, a monstrous pier that stretched from North Beach halfway to Alcatraz Island. A few days later, Honest Harry's lumber company won the first of several lucrative contracts to construct a road from Clarke's Point, around the face of Telegraph Hill, to North Beach. (The streets and roads at this time were constructed of heavy planking.)

It was a bank failure in the Panic of 1854 that started Honest Harry on his downfall. No one knows how much he lost, but it was enough so that he could not withstand the rising financial pressures of the depression. He was overextended on credit, and some reports claim that he was paying almost $250,000 annually as interest on loans. Harry, however, showed no visible signs of his problems. He still was considered a financial genius by his colleagues on the city council, and his offer to serve as chairman of the finance committee was gratefully accepted.

In this capacity it was easy to steal about a ream of "street warrants"—authorizations for payment by the city for the construction of roads and sidewalks. He filled out the forms for some $2 million worth of contracts to the California Lumber Company, then pledged them as security for loans from other banks in the city that had not folded.

No questions were raised. Honest Harry was the largest builder of streets and sidewalks in San Francisco, so it was natural that he should have such warrants tendered to him by the city. That Honest Harry sought the loans in gold bullion also was considered normal after Harry dropped the hint that he was involved in a large international financial transaction.

227

But when an observant bank clerk noticed that one of the warrants was payment for a sidewalk construction project that had been completed more than five years earlier, the matter was brought to the attention of the president of the bank, William C. Ralston.

A few nights later Ralston ran into Meiggs at a social function in the Occidental Hotel and cautioned him against holding the warrants for such a long period of time before cashing them. Honest Harry laughed off the advice, commenting that he had not needed the money, but the conversation was overheard by another alderman who became curious. He discovered the next day that the warrant for this construction project had been cashed two days after it was issued, and he thought it indeed strange that the same warrant could be used five years later as security for a loan. He went to Ralston who, in turn, called upon Meiggs.

"I don't understand it either," Honest Harry replied with a laugh. "I'll go through my books and let you know tomorrow."

Two hours later Honest Harry chartered the bark *America*, telling the captain to provision himself for a very long cruise and to plan for a midnight departure from the Broadway Wharf. During the afternoon Ralston and the suspicious alderman pored over the warrants hypothecated by Meiggs. Ralston checked with other bankers. By ten that evening, the banking community of San Francisco began to accept the truth: Honest Harry Meiggs, a pillar of the city, had indeed taken the city's leading bankers for almost $2 million in gold by pledging forged street warrants as security for loans.

Stopping only to pick up a deputy sheriff, the bankers sped by buggy to Meiggs's palatial home. A manservant informed them that Meiggs had not yet returned from dinner. They waited.

The suspicious alderman, whose name has long been lost, meanwhile had driven to the offices of the California Lumber Company on North Beach. A heavy fog was rolling in from the Golden Gate and it put a chill in the air. The alderman said later that he did not know why he waited, but he did. Sometime around eleven, he spotted Honest Harry. Meiggs was coming out of the building carrying two canvas bank bags that appeared to be very heavy, a hammer, a saw, and a shovel. Honest Harry saw the alderman at the same time, shouted something unintelligible, then dove into a waiting cab. The driver whipped the horses and the hack disappeared in the fog, but not before the alderman got the cab number.

The cab driver returned to his base shortly after midnight to find the alderman and a policeman waiting. His story was short. Honest Harry had engaged him at the hack stand in front of the Occidental Hotel. They had gone directly to the California Lumber Company and upon leaving there had driven toward the Broadway Wharf. About halfway to their destination, Meiggs had told him to stop and again wait. He then disappeared in the fog, carrying both canvas bags and his tools. He returned in about twenty minutes carrying the tools and one canvas bag. They then went to the Broadway Wharf, where Honest Harry left him with the tools and a five-dollar tip.

About an hour after midnight, Ralston, other bilked bankers, the alderman, the deputy sheriff, the police officer, and a reporter from *The Alta*, were clustered on the Broadway Wharf. Despite the dense fog and the lack of a breeze, the bark *America* had cast off shortly after midnight. Although no one had seen Honest Harry board the vessel, it was the

229

only ship to have sailed since he had arrived at the wharf. Therefore, it was reasonable to presume, the pursuers decided, that Meiggs was on board the *America*.

The only wrath greater than that of a woman scorned is that of a mulcted banker. On the Broadway Wharf were five of the city's leading bankers and every one was in a fury. They knew Meiggs was escaping with $2 million worth of their gold, and they wanted him caught, no matter what the cost.

At the end of the wharf was the small coastal steamer *The Active*. The bankers, the police, and the reporter descended upon the boat en masse. The captain of *The Active* was reluctant to sail. It would take an hour to get up steam, and the fog was so dense that it would be impossible to find the bark. The bankers waved money, so the skipper decided to try the impossible. In little less than an hour, *The Active* cast off, headed full steam in the general direction of the Golden Gate, and promptly rammed into the side of a coal barge.

With the dawn coming, a slight breeze sprang up. It blew away the fog and the bankers found they had drifted to a point about a mile east of Alcatraz Island. Less than three hundred yards off their starboard bow, which still was impaled on the coal barge, was the bark *America*. The same breeze that blew away the fog puffed the sails of the bark. Leaning over the taffrail as the *America* swept toward the Golden Gate was Honest Harry Meiggs.

Ralston was convinced that Honest Harry had only taken half of his gold with him. The hack driver identified the canvas bags carried by Meiggs as similar to those the bank used for transporting coin and bullion. He repeated his story: that

230

Honest Harry had left his office with two heavy canvas bags, that he had stopped about midway between the office and the wharf where he had mysteriously disposed of one of the bags. A small clump of moist dirt remained on the shovel that was left in the hack. Weeks were spent searching for some signs of hasty digging in the area, but nothing was found.

Honest Harry did not disappear. From Hawaii he wrote letters to acquaintances, and this so infuriated Ralston that he prevailed upon Governor John Bigler to start extradition proceedings. By the time the papers arrived in Hawaii, however, Honest Harry had moved on.

He next appeared in Chile where he immediately began to operate in much the same manner as he had in San Francisco. Here, with the help of government officials as silent partners, he built railroads instead of planked streets. According to one published report he realized a $1,300,000 profit on a 33-mile stretch of track laid between Valparaiso and Santiago. He built a large castle, which he named La Quinta, for his home. On one occasion he put it up as the grand prize in a charitable lottery, but Honest Harry's "luck" still held for he had purchased the winning ticket.

The unforgiving Ralston continued to labor for Meiggs's extradition, as Honest Harry still made no secret of his whereabouts. Extradition papers sent to Chile disappeared. Ralston went to Governor Bigler and then wrote to Washington. A short time later, Bigler was appointed to the position of American Minister to Chile. He personally carried Honest Harry's extradition papers with him. A short time after his arrival in Chile, Bigler personally quashed the extradition. Meiggs wrote to friends in San Francisco that he still planned to return "to pick up some investments."

A change of administration in Chile sent Honest Harry

Meiggs north to Peru where he remained for the next decade and where he left a name that never will be forgotten in South America. It was Meiggs who promoted the construction of the Trans-Andean railroad, described as one of the awful tragedies of history. More than ten thousand lives were lost in its construction and its $200-million cost virtually bankrupted the Peruvian government. Much of this passed through Meiggs's wallet, but, like many confidence men, Honest Harry spent his money as soon as he touched it. At his hacienda near Callao, he hosted parties that cost more than $200,000. Usually, a few days after a party a contract for another segment of the useless railroad would be let to Meiggs and his silent partners in the government.

The end of the Peruvian venture came in the mid-1870s. The government could borrow no more capital to finance rail construction and soon could not raise enough money internally to meet the interest payments on money borrowed earlier. The railroad remained unfinished.

"I am planning to return to San Francisco," Honest Harry wrote to an acquaintance there. "I have a million-dollar investment in the city, and, if certain formalities are undertaken successfully, I plan to spend the waning years of my life there quietly."

The "formalities" soon became evident. A special bill was introduced in the California assembly which would grant amnesty to Meiggs should he return. It was passed and then referred to the California senate where it also was quietly passed, but not so quietly that word of the maneuvering did not reach Ralston.

The banker rushed to the state capital and prevailed upon the governor to veto it. Honest Harry's influence apparently was well financed, for both the assembly and the senate promptly overrode the veto. Ralston then reached the state attorney general who announced that the bill was unconstitutional and that he would carry the matter to the state supreme court. Once the issue had attracted the attention of the newspapers, the lawmakers promptly lost interest in the future plans of Honest Harry Meiggs.

Shortly after news of this defeat reached Meiggs in Peru, he was seized by apoplexy. He lived for only a short time afterward in a state of paralysis, and died on September 29, 1877, at the age of sixty-six in his Callao hacienda.

Soon after Meiggs died, Ralston committed suicide when his Bank of California collapsed.

Somewhere in the North Beach there surely is hidden $1 million worth of gold bullion, stolen by Honest Harry Meiggs from Ralston's Bank of California. It lies somewhere along the old road that led from the offices of the California Lumber Company to the Broadway Wharf. Perhaps it could be found with a metal detector, but the treasure seeker would have to put up with such distractions as nude or flamenco dancers, dart-throwing gamesters, bullfight *aficionados*, or someone simply enjoying a good steak. But it might be a good escape for the treasure seeker who is tired of the desert and the sea.

THE SINKING OF THE "ADA HANCOCK"

At approximately five o'clock on the afternoon of April 27, 1863, a small ferry steamer named the *Ada Hancock* blew up midway between the Banning Dock in Wilmington and Dead Man's Island in Los Angeles Harbor. Twenty-six of the fifty-six persons on board were known to have been killed.

Investigators, probing in the primitive manner of the times, were unable to reach a conclusion as to the cause of the explosion. The vessel was carrying several barrels of gun powder loaded from a coastal freighter earlier in the day, but not yet placed ashore. One employee of the company which owned the ship reported that the boiler was defective. Not much attention was paid to his testimony, however, because not only was he a Mexican, but he had been fired the morning of the accident because of a knee injury that slowed him down on the job.

There were a few potential murder victims aboard the *Ada Hancock* who were killed in the accident. One was a busi-

234

nessman whose life had been threatened by a competitor. Another was a Southern Californian who was trying to get rid of a clinging mistress. A third was a doctor who was running off with another man's wife. A small-time robber baron was blown from the deck of the steamer and, according to one report, "landed ashore on his feet escaping injury." This qualifies as a miraculous escape indeed as the *Ada Hancock* was about a mile from shore when it blew up. One of the most intriguing solutions to the sinking of the *Ada Hancock* did not appear until a half-century after the explosion, long after the tragedy was forgotten by most people. This solution, which is the most probable, not only accounts for the explosion, but also for the disappearance of more than $125,000 of Wells Fargo gold.

When it exploded, the *Ada Hancock* was ferrying passengers from the dock to the S.S. *Senator*, a coastal steamer anchored at Dead Man's Island, scheduled for an early evening departure to San Francisco. At this time there were but two piers in Los Angeles Harbor. One was the Banning Dock owned by Phineas Banning in the town of Wilmington, a community that Banning ran like a fiefdom. The other was owned by a man named Timms and was located in the adjacent and somewhat larger town of San Pedro. Neither the docks nor the harbor entrance were large enough to accommodate the deep draft of a coastal steamer the size of the *Senator*.

The only communication between these waterfront towns and Los Angeles, other than by messenger, was by telegraph wire with terminals in San Pedro and Camp Drumm. The latter was a small military outpost in Wilmington that had achieved fame of a sort for being the headquarters of the military's ill-fated camel corps.

Shortly before four o'clock, about one hour before the

235

Ada Hancock cast off, someone cut the telegraph wire at about the midway point between San Pedro and Los Angeles. As a result, more than five hours passed before news of the *Ada Hancock* tragedy reached Los Angeles, less than twenty miles away.

The seasonal high fog and clouds hung over the harbor, and there was a slight chill in the air. Most of the passengers already on board the *Senator* were either in their cabins or in the salon when the *Ada Hancock* left the Banning Dock for the last time. One of the exceptions was a Dr. Paul Henry who was on the deck of the coastal steamer.

"The ferry started to cast off, then was made fast again to allow a man to board," he reported. "Then it backed away from the dock, made its turn, and proceeded toward me. I watched it for a short period of time, then stepped back to make way for one of the crew. It was then that I heard the gunfire. I looked back just in time to see the explosion. The *Ada Hancock* simply disintegrated. Bodies and debris from the vessel rose into the air, appearing to move very slowly. After the explosion, the only sound I heard immediately was a long piercing shriek of a woman. The vessel had disappeared. Then the bodies and flotsam fell back into the water. A huge bubble of air escaped from the bottom of the harbor. A moment later a large wave, created by the explosion, rocked the *Senator*. It was after this that I became aware of the faint cries for help, and that I realized that incredibly there were some survivors of this disaster."

Dr. Henry reported at once to the captain of the *Senator*, and the main salon of the ship was prepared as an infirmary while the lifeboats were lowered to pick up the survivors. There is no record as to how many of the survivors were taken to the *Senator*. The coastal steamer sailed that night for

236

San Francisco carrying its injured with it. Dr. Henry's version of the explosion was given to San Francisco reporters upon the ship's arrival there. It is known only that there were fifty-six people on board the *Ada Hancock* when it exploded and that there were twenty-six known fatalities.

One of the survivors taken to San Francisco was Edgar Smith. He told reporters that there was a gun battle below deck immediately preceding the explosion.

Those survivors missed by the lifeboats of the *Senator* were not so fortunate. Because telegraphic communication with Los Angeles was severed, only the staff medical officer from nearby Camp Drumm was available to treat the injured. Most were transported by wagon for treatment at the military base.

All agreed that there had been gunfire immediately before the explosion, but those who had been on the top deck said the shots came from below. Conversely, those who were on the lower deck insisted the gunfire erupted on the top deck. Some contended that the vessel's boiler blew up. Others reported the heavy smell of gunpowder right after the blast.

Many bodies washed ashore during the evening. Most were promptly stripped and looted, then buried, either by soldiers from Camp Drumm or by waterfront derelicts.

The day after the explosion word of the disaster's extent reached Los Angeles. Among those seriously concerned were officials of the local branch of the Wells Fargo Bank, because one of the passengers scheduled to sail on the *Senator* had been a Wells Fargo messenger named William Ritchie. The messenger was carrying $25,000 in gold destined for the San Francisco Mint.

An official of the bank was dispatched to Wilmington where he learned that Ritchie had indeed been on the last voyage of the *Ada Hancock*. It was not known whether or not he was one of the survivors taken on board the *Senator*. More than a century ago, bank auditors were as suspicious of disappearing employees as they are today. An audit was taken of the bank's resources. The $25,000, as expected, had been picked up by Ritchie on the previous day. What was unexpected, however, was the disappearance of an additional $100,000 worth of gold bullion. In fact, the gold reserves of the Wells Fargo office in Los Angeles had been wiped out.

The investigation quickly disclosed that the authorized shipment of gold had been taken out of the bank by Ritchie a little past noon on the preceding day. Shortly before this he had been seen with Louis Scheslinger, another Wells Fargo messenger who, as a sideline, dabbled in usurious loans. Word was put out immediately for Scheslinger to come to the bank, but to no avail. He had disappeared as completely as Ritchie.

Louis Scheslinger had arrived in Los Angeles from his native New York when he was in his late teens. A big, powerful youth with a quick mind, he easily secured a job with Wells Fargo as a guard. Within a few months he was promoted to messenger and soon thereafter was entrusted with carrying large shipments of gold and currency between Los Angeles and San Francisco.

He also demonstrated a talent for making money. Within weeks after his arrival he was making loans to small Mexican landholders who did not qualify for a loan from the bank and who were sufficiently in need of funds to be willing to pay an exhorbitant interest. He usually foreclosed on the landowner the day after the note became due and sold the property quickly for a substantial profit. He was not the only loan shark operating in Southern California during this period, but most of the others were willing to wait until the crops were harvested before they collected their money. The idea of foreclosure was foreign to the Mexicans and to the community, so Scheslinger's habit did not make him a popular man in Los Angeles. It was unlikely that Scheslinger cared about his popularity for, by the summer of 1862, he had acquired sufficient capital to lend $30,000 to a Don Ricardo Vejar, who used his huge ranch east of Los Angeles as collateral. The interest charged on the loan is not known. It is known, however, that the loan was for one year's duration, and there was a clause in the loan agreement stating that the full amount would become due immediately in the event of Don Ricardo's death. On April 20, 1863, one week before the *Ada Hancock* blew up, Don Ricardo Vejar was injured fatally when he was thrown from a stallion on his ranch.

Scheslinger heard of the accident on the following day. He immediately had foreclosure papers drawn up and, accompanied by one Hyman Tishell and another unidentified man, arrived at the Vejar hacienda in late afternoon with his ultimatum: Pay me or I'll take the ranch.

Ramon Vejar, the eldest son of Don Ricardo, was not sympathetic to Scheslinger's claim. The body of Don Ricardo was not yet buried. There were members of the family who had not arrived for the funeral. At first he reacted as if Scheslinger were perpetrating a bad joke, but when he became convinced that the loan shark was indeed serious, he became very calm, picked up the papers Scheslinger had brought with him, asked the loan shark to wait for his return, then left the room.

Tishell described the scene later. "When we arrived there were all the usual sounds that one expects on a busy ranch. But shortly after Ramon Vejar left the room, it slowly became quiet outside. Soon, I could only hear the sound of the wind. I went to the window and looked out. The Mexicans and all of the animals had disappeared except for our horses. I told Louis we ought to get out of there."

Despite the pleas and suggestions from his companions, Scheslinger did not want to leave. Ramon Vejar had disappeared with the foreclosure papers and if Scheslinger left without them, he would be forced to make another trip from Los Angeles. Approximately three-quarters of an hour after Vejar left, Schlesinger went out of the room and searched for his inhospitable host through several other rooms on the ground floor of the hacienda. There was not a sign of a human being or animal. He called out Vejar's name. There was no answer. The building had been abandoned. He returned to the room where Tishell waited with his friend and now their uneasiness infected him. It took very little urging from Tishell to get him to agree to leave.

The trio waited by the open door a long time. The outside seemed emptier and more ominous than the deserted hacienda. Even the dogs and the chickens had disappeared. The corral was empty. The only signs of life were the three horses on which they had arrived. Still saddled, the horses remained tied to a hitching post near the main entrance to the building. Unsheathing their revolvers, the three men walked across the open patio to their mounts.

About a half-hour later, the three men breathed a collective sigh of relief as they slowed their horses from a gallop to a canter and replaced their guns in their holsters. Although they were still on the Vejar ranch, they were now out of sight of the silent hacienda.

"Louis was becoming very angry," Tishell reported. "He said he was going to come back with a posse and throw out the Vejars so hard they would bounce all the way back to Mexico."

A moment later the three men were ambushed. They had

just entered a small arroyo. The unidentified member of the trio was in front, with Tishell and Scheslinger following in that order. They never saw their attackers, who were lying on the ground concealed by rocks and boulders. Only one volley of shots was fired, but it instantly killed the unidentified man and his horse. Two bullets struck Tishell, but he managed to remain on his horse and race through the arroyo to safety. Scheslinger wheeled his horse around, fled out of the arroyo in the direction from which he had come, and escaped un-scathed. He took a circuitous route back to Los Angeles, catching up with the wounded Tishell near the San Gabriel Mission. Tishell was left at the mission for treatment of his wounds and returned to Los Angeles the following day.

It was a badly frightened loan shark who reported the ambush and killing to the Los Angeles sheriff later that evening. The sheriff's reaction to the incident is unknown, but apparently he was not very sympathetic to Scheslinger's cause as there is no record of his undertaking any punitive action against Ramon Vejar.

Investigators for the Wells Fargo Bank pieced together Scheslinger's movements. The day after the ambush Scheslinger began to sell off his mortgages, discounting some as much as fifty percent. He visited the wounded Tishell. "He was in mortal fear of the Mexican, Vejar," Tishell reported. "Vejar was half his size, but he [Scheslinger] was afraid of him. He offered to sell me the Vejar mortgage for five thousand dollars, but I refused. If Louis couldn't collect on it, how could I?"

Scheslinger did sell the Vejar mortgage, however, along with several others to a man named Clark who paid for them with cash drawn from a Wells Fargo account. On the morning of April 27, Scheslinger appeared at the bank shortly after it opened and withdrew his account in cash. The amount of money in his possession at this time is unknown, but the most conservative estimate would place it at several thousand dollars.

Late in the forenoon, Scheslinger was seen talking to William Ritchie in the lobby of the Bella Union Hotel. In the early afternoon he was again seen with Ritchie outside the Wells Fargo Bank just before Ritchie picked up the gold shipment that he was scheduled to take to San Francisco. Bank investigators in Los Angeles could not find anyone who had seen Scheslinger after this.

The bank detectives discovered that three metal boxes bearing Wells Fargo seals were carried by Ritchie on the stage to Wilmington. One of these boxes was more than sufficient to hold the legitimate shipment. The investigators went to Wilmington and learned that Ritchie had carried three bank boxes on board the *Ada Hancock*.

In the course of their investigation, the detectives ran across the Mexican deckhand who had been fired from his job on the *Ada Hancock* because of his knee injury. He told an intriguing story. He had been at the dock while the *Ada Hancock* was preparing for her final voyage. The stern lines had been cast off and the vessel was swinging away from the dock when Louis Scheslinger ran up demanding that he be taken on board. A crewman tossed the line back to a workman on the dock who fastened it around a bit. The crew then pulled the vessel back to the pier.

"He was very, very angry," the deckhand said, adding that he knew Scheslinger well because of his many trips to San Francisco.

There were several witnesses to confirm that there had been a late boarder, but other than the injured deckhand, none could identify him. Late boardings were not uncommon since tickets could be purchased on the vessel. The detectives learned that Scheslinger had not traveled to Wilmington by stage. He was known to the drivers, and none had seen him.

Three days after the explosion Ritchie's body washed ashore near Timms' Landing. It was so badly mangled that identification could be made only from clothes remnants and an ornate gun holster that Ritchie favored. The holster was empty.

Here is where the investigation conducted by the Wells Fargo detectives ended. In the final report on the case, it was deduced that Ritchie may have been trying to double-cross his partner, Scheslinger, in the bank theft and had been caught at the last minute. The gun battle on board the *Ada Hancock*, which immediately preceded the explosion, may well have been carried out by these two men. The report adds that the answer will probably never be known as there is nothing besides the statement of a disgruntled Mexican to indicate that Scheslinger was on board. The report did conclude, however, that the stolen gold was on board the *Ada Hancock* when she blew up.

By 1912 the activity around Los Angeles Harbor was much greater than in the days when Banning and Timms competed for the wharfage business. In the summer of that year, workmen excavating for footings for a new building unearthed a shallow grave. It contained the skeleton of a large young man in his late twenties. In the middle of his skull was a bullet hole. The only clue to his identity was a tarnished belt buckle lying near the bones. Inscribed upon the buckle were the initials L.S.

The location of the grave was not far from the old

Banning Dock. Detectives did not pursue their investigation of this apparent murder with vigor because the coroner's office placed the time of death about a half-century earlier.

It is not unreasonable to assume that in the remains of the *Ada Hancock* lies more than $125,000 in gold. Dead Man's Island has disappeared, long since dredged away, but its location still is known. Also long gone is Banning's Dock, but its former location also is known. In a straight line between the two points, about a mile off shore lies what is left of the *Ada Hancock*.

THE VASQUEZ INGOT

About an hour's drive north of Los Angeles is the Vasquez Rocks Recreation Area. These pockmarked rocks, thrust up to heights in excess of two hundred feet by temblors along the San Andreas Fault, sprawl over a large area near the southern end of the Mojave Desert. The Vasquez Rocks area is a familiar sight to countless Western Americana buffs, as they provide one of Hollywood's favorite location sites for motion picture and television Westerns. These rocks, clustered over more than a thousand acres, are as full of holes as a piece of wormwood. In all probability there is a 500-pound ingot of pure silver that was hidden in one of these holes by a rather prominent California bandit of a century ago named Tiburcio Vasquez.

The huge ingot was cast as a precaution against a planned hijack from a silver mine several miles from the town of Panamint. Panamint was one of the more violent mining camps of the era. The first man to discover silver in the area, William Alvord, was murdered by a berserk partner before an ounce of ore was processed. Mining started on a minor scale in 1861 and remained small for almost a decade because of the in-

245

accessibility of the community. The town was located at the head of a canyon more than a mile deep in the mountains adjacent to Death Valley. For more than a decade after the first silver strike, the only way into Panamint was over a steep trail not wide enough in some areas for two horses to pass.

Many of the mining claims were worked by outlaws. One story claims that since so much of Panamint's population was wanted by the law elsewhere, postmasters automatically forwarded mail addressed to known desperados there for delivery. Another tells of two highwaymen who sought refuge in Panamint after holding up a Wells Fargo stage. The pair struck a rich silver lode, sold out for $25,000 and went to San Francisco to collect their money. Here they were recognized. The loot from the stage robbery had been approximately $5,000, but the bank manager gave the two outlaws an out. If they paid the bank one hundred percent interest on the "loan," Wells Fargo would not prosecute them. The two former bandits sold their $25,000 check for $15,000 and departed.

Around 1869 Robert L. Stewart, with two partners, found an exceptionally rich lode in the mountains above Panamint. Unlike most of their fellow miners, these men were well financed. They brought in cheap Chinese labor from San Francisco, built a rough road down the side of the mountain and a small smelter. The smelter not only processed the ore of their own Wonder Mine, but that of some of the small mines in the area.

Early in the summer of 1872, Senator William M. Stewart of Nevada strayed from his constituency to visit his brother Robert in Panamint. Stewart had made a fortune in the famed Comstock Lode in Nevada. He was a miner and a gambler with a fondness for cards, and so, when he paused in Neagle's

Occidental Saloon and saw a game of faro in progress, he promptly invited himself to participate. Among the players were John Small and John McDonald, two men of dubious reputation, who operated a small mine near the Wonder Mine.

McDonald and Small were surly men, liked only by each other. They were poor card players, also, but were tolerated in the games because they consistently lost. Usually after they had lost all of the silver in their possession, they would skulk back to their mine, which they ran with cheap Chinese labor.

The witty and gregarious senator was the exact opposite of the poor miners and, possibly because of this, they made known their dislike for the politician immediately. Apparently Senator Stewart was thick-skinned, and he ignored the thinly disguised insults tossed in his direction by Small and McDonald. He finally reacted, however, by raising the stakes in the game. Either the senator was extraordinarily lucky or exceptionally skilled in the game because within a half-hour, Stewart had bankrupted the game.

The two miners were furious. They did not dare to accuse Stewart of cheating, but they did question the senator's lucky streak.

"It is bound to turn," Stewart replied amiably. "It is unfortunate that neither of you gentlemen any longer have the funds to take advantage of this turn."

McDonald reacted angrily. "I'll put up five percent of our mine against the five thousand you have won here tonight in one game of showdown."

"I know nothing about your mine," Stewart replied, "but I will accept your wager."

A patron of the saloon was pressed into service as a dealer. Showdown is a game in which five cards are dealt from a deck in turn, and the winner is the man with the best poker hand. Neither McDonald nor Stewart touched the cards. When the last card was dealt, McDonald was the winner with a pair of kings. He reached for the money, then paused as Stewart held up his hand. "Once again," the senator said. "Ten thousand cash against ten percent of your mine."

McDonald hesitated, then nodded. Again the cards were dealt and again he won. Stewart raised his bet again, this time to $15,000, and when this hand was lost, he doubled his bet again. McDonald was dealt a full house over Stewart's pair of kings. The senator now owed the miner $60,000. The drinking and the other games in the saloon had stopped; the players and the patrons crowded around the small, round table with the green-felt top. Stewart was calm. Both McDonald and Small were flushed with elation.

"You value your mine at one hundred thousand dollars," Stewart said. "I will double the bet once more for one hundred and twenty thousand against the entire mine."

This time McDonald nodded with no hesitation.

"I must remind you that I am due for a win," Stewart said calmly.

"Deal," McDonald replied.

The winning hand has never been forgotten in Panamint. The first two cards dealt to McDonald were queens. The last three cards dealt to the senator from Nevada were aces. For a long time the cards remained on the table where they had fallen. Then McDonald swept them to the floor with the back of his hand. "Show me the money you would have paid me if you had lost," he demanded.

The onlookers sighed collectively. Senator Stewart nodded, took out his wallet and extracted a blank check. He asked for a pen, and one was brought from the bar. He then proceeded to make out a check to cash in the amount of $120,000.

With a flourish, he showed it first to the dealer, then to McDonald and Small. Then he tore the check into pieces and dropped them on the table. "It's not safe to carry this much money around in cash," he said.

"How do we know it would have been good?" Small asked. This remark was nearly as dangerous as an accusation of cheating, but the senator brushed it off. "I didn't question your ownership of a mine," he replied, "and how many years will it take me to collect your debt from the ground?"

Small and McDonald remained in Panamint, angry and moody. Stewart was shown his newly acquired holdings on the following day by other residents of the town and he immediately ensured the loyalty of his Chinese employees by dividing $1,000 among them as a bonus.

For several weeks, Stewart remained in the area, commuting between a boardinghouse in Panamint and the mine. The two former owners ventured out of the community to prospect occasionally, but for most of the time they sulked in one of the saloons. At first they complained bitterly about their ill fortune. Then their complaints took another tack. They claimed they had been swindled out of their mine by a crooked politician. When this was followed by muttered threats of revenge, McDonald and Small were paid a visit by the sheriff.

"If anything happens to Senator Stewart, I won't have to go far to find a couple of men for the hanging tree," the lawman warned.

A short time later, a Mexican card dealer arrived at the mine to see Stewart. On the previous evening, he told the senator, he had been approached by McDonald and offered a share in the proceeds if he would participate in the robbery of Stewart's first shipment of silver to Los Angeles. A Mexican was needed as a front man, the dealer explained, so that the robbery would be attributed to the bandit Tiburcio Vasquez. The dealer added with remarkable candor that he had refused only because he distrusted both Small and McDonald. Both of the former owners had indicated they would go ahead with the robbery, with or without the Mexican's help.

Stewart had been planning to send out his first shipment on the following day on a couple of pack mules, but because of this warning he changed his mind.

Small and McDonald gave no indications of abandoning their plans as the days turned into weeks and the amount of silver increased with each day's production. After nearly two months had elapsed, Stewart received some more disquieting news from informers in Panamint. Small and McDonald were becoming impatient and were making plans to raid the mine.

Stewart was in a quandary. He and his brother had made arrangements to sell both mines to a conglomerate in Los Angeles. The prospective purchasers were somewhat worried over Panamint's reputation for violence. Both Stewarts had assured the purchaser that such reports were grossly exaggerated. A raid on the mine could defeat the sale. The posting of armed guards might have a similar effect.

No gangs or bands were involved. The senator had five Chinese workers on his payroll, none of whom would back him up in a gunfight. Small and McDonald were unpopular in Panamint and so were unlikely to attract a following in the raid. As soon as he had realized this, Senator Stewart came up with an idea.

His ore had been refined crudely at his brother's smelter, then returned daily to the senator's mine for storage. At that time, he had approximately one thousand pounds of silver in his possession. In a shed near the mine Stewart built a furnace. Then he had his employees build a large mold. The silver was remelted, poured inside the mold and allowed to harden. When the project was concluded, Stewart had two huge ingots, each weighing approximately five hundred pounds.

A few days after this, the Mexican card dealer visited Stewart in the Panamint boardinghouse. He told the senator that Small and McDonald were planning to raid the mine the following day, take all the silver they could carry on two pack mules, and carry it all the way to San Francisco. Stewart smiled quietly and asked his Mexican friend to join him in witnessing the raid. Before sunrise the two men, each carrying a pair of powerful binoculars, were ensconced on a steep hill overlooking the mine.

Small and McDonald arrived at the mine around 9:00 A.M. Each was on horseback and each was leading a pack mule. The Chinese, squatting silently near the mine shaft, offered no resistance to the armed men. The foreman cooperated by telling the miners that the senator had not arrived today and by showing them the shed where the huge ingots were stored. The instant Small and McDonald entered the shed, the Chinese workers disappeared, scrambling up the side of the hill to hide behind rocks. A moment later loud curses rang out from the shed. The foreman burst out of the door and also fled into the hills. He too was out of sight before the two miners came out into the open again. Still swearing loudly, they rigged a sling from some rope they had brought with them and used the mules to drag the heavy ingots out from the shed. Then both struggled to lift the ingot in its sling to the back of the mule, but they were small men and the weight was too much for them. For more than two hours they wrestled with the huge bars before they became convinced that they were too heavy for them to hoist. Then they spent another hour or so rigging up an A-frame with a pully. Stewart became slightly worried when the men raised one of the ingots to the apex of the frame, but as McDonald led a mule underneath it, one of the legs of the frame collapsed. The frame fell, striking the mule who bolted and followed the Chinese miners up the hill.

In mid-afternoon the two men gave up. They had twice rebuilt the A-frame. It had collapsed once. The second time, when they lowered the quarter-ton silver ingot to the back of the mule, the animal sank to the ground, unable to stand. Small and McDonald were too exhausted to swear anymore. They mounted their horses and departed. They were never seen in Panamint again.

"How are you going to get such a large piece of silver to Los Angeles, señor?" the card dealer asked Stewart after Small and McDonald had disappeared.

"I guess I'll have to use Remi Nadeau," Stewart replied.

Nadeau was known as the boss teamster of California. His twenty-mule freight teams with their blue wagons roamed all over the southern part of the state hauling everything from ore to borax. Unknown to Stewart was the fact that Nadeau, along with several of his muleskinners, maintained a very friendly relationship with the bandit Tiburcio Vasquez. Their friendship had started a few years earlier on a day when Nadeau was driving in his buggy to one of his desert way-stations. Earlier that day Vasquez had been shot during a stagecoach holdup attempt, was assumed dead, and was left on the desert trail. When Nadeau came upon Vasquez, the bandit was still alive. Nadeau carried him in the buggy to his nearest freight station where he told the keeper to hide Vasquez and nurse him back to health.

Vasquez repaid the kind deed by ordering that none of

his followers ever hold up a Nadeau freight team, a reaction the wily teamster boss might possibly have foreseen when he played the Good Samaritan role. The bandit kept his word. On several occasions his band of outlaws were seen swooping down on a Nadeau freight train, only to veer off when the distinctive blue wagons were recognized.

There was one exception however. This was on the day that Nadeau sent a buckboard to Stewart's mine to pick up the two 500-pound ingots.

The buckboard was driven by a man named James Funk. He loaded the ingots with no problem and hauled them into Panamint where, a short time later, they were transferred to one of Nadeau's freight wagons for the long haul into Los Angeles. For no apparent reason the buckboard was fastened to the rear of the freight wagon and was towed along when the train left Panamint. Also going along on the trip was teamster Funk.

Tiburcio Vasquez and his band struck the freight train near the rocks which bear his name and where he often sought refuge. With the band was a harnessed mule, which was quickly hitched to the buckboard. Other members of the band wrestled one of the ingots from the freighter to the buckboard. The other 500-pound bar of silver bullion was left on the train. Nothing else was taken. The buckboard and the band of outlaws headed for Vasquez Rocks; the freight wagon started once again for Los Angeles.

It was not until the following day that a posse reached Vasquez Rocks, and the buckboard was found abandoned. There was no sign of Vasquez or his band.

Funk and the mule skinners were shown pictures of Vasquez and all identified him as the leader of the gang which had held up the freighter.

Three weeks later Vasquez and three members of his gang appeared at the ranch of Alessandro Repetto, nine miles from Los Angeles in what is now Hollywood. Repetto was not happy to see the outlaws. On their last visit they had stolen a mule from him and had threatened to kill him if he reported it. This time Vasquez wanted eight hundred dollars.

"I don't have it," Repetto protested.

"Then write a check," Vasquez demanded.

Repetto did as he was asked, and a boy who worked for him was sent to the bank in Los Angeles to cash it. Some time after the youth had left the bank to return to the ranch, the banker became suspicious of the transaction and notified the sheriff. The sheriff sent a deputy to the ranch. Vasquez and his companions had left, but when Repetto identified the extortionist as the notorious bandit, the deputy quickly rounded up a posse to give chase.

Vasquez was trailed to an area known as Tujunga Pass and then back to Hollywood where, a few days later, he was wounded and captured in a vacant ranch house. When he recovered, he was taken to San Jose and charged with murder in connection with the death of two persons during a stage holdup. Shortly before he was hanged, he was visited in the San Jose jail by Stewart.

"What happened to my silver ingot?" the senator asked the outlaw.

Vasquez shrugged. "It's in a hole in the rocks," he replied. He would tell Stewart nothing more.

The bandit also had another visitor, Remi Nadeau, a few hours before his execution. "I thought we had an arrangement," Nadeau said.

Vasquez spread out his palms. "There was a problem," he said. "I have a cousin who is a card dealer in Panamint, and

254

it was he who told me of the shipment. I had an obligation to him. But I also am your friend, Remito. I owe you my life. This is why I only took one of the ingots. Do you understand?"

Nadeau was not sure that he did.

There are many holes in Vasquez Rocks. The huge silver ingot will be as tarnished as the rocks in which it lies hidden. The area is easy to get to—a paved road leads right into it. There are even facilities for overnight camping.

THE VEKOL INVESTMENT

John D. Walker had always been considered a little odd by those who knew him. He came to Arizona in the mid-1860s when the Indians were believed to be such a menace that they required extermination by the United States Army. Rather than join the hue and cry, he hired Indians to work his ranch north of Tucson. He was engaged to an attractive young lady in Chicago named Elinor Rice, but this did not deter him from marrying Consuela Arriega. Consuela was a Mexican girl who had been brought up by Pima Indians, and the wedding ceremony was performed according to Pima custom. Walker ignored the criticism of his neighbors, and at the same time still considered himself engaged to Elinor.

He ran his ranch profitably and with a firm hand. No liquor was allowed on the grounds. Those with the smell of alcohol on their breath were banned from his house. If anyone on his payroll visited a saloon while in Tucson he was immediately discharged. The one exception to this rule was a man named Juan José Gradello, a Papago Indian who apparently surfaced in Arizona coincidentally with Walker's arrival. Gradello could get drunk, disappear for days, or just

256

lie around in his cabin doing nothing and excite not the slightest reaction from Walker.

Often the two men would talk for hours. More often than not, the subject was silver. From the day of his arrival, Walker had heard the legend of the hidden silver mine of the Papagos and how prospectors from all over the territory had risked Indian attack for years in search of it. Walker also was searching for it, but doing it the easy way. Whether Gradello knew the location of the mine and withheld the information, or whether he was engaged in espionage among his fellow Papagos will never be known. What is known, however, is that thirteen years passed after Walker appeared in Arizona before Gradello took him to a site some miles south of the ancient ruins of Casa Grande and pointed out the source of the Papago silver.

Walker staked out a claim and named a town he planned on the site, Vekol. The name of the new community reportedly was a Papago word meaning "grandmother." The claim owners were listed as Walker, Gradello, and Colonel Peter R. Brady. Walker and Brady were listed as the founders of Vekol, and the date of the town's birth was set as February 5, 1880.

Gradello did not last as a claim holder. Approximately three months after the claim was filed, Gradello sold out to Brady and Walker for the proverbial undisclosed sum. A house was built for him in Vekol, adjacent to the more imposing structure erected by Walker, and once again Gradello became the only person exempt from the Vekol ordinances decreed by Walker. These were the same rules that applied on Walker's ranch: no liquor, not even the smell of it.

The Vekol was a profitable operation. Within a year the main shaft had been sunk to a depth of more than one hundred feet. The ore that the two partners were shipping to Kansas

City, Denver, and San Francisco was being assayed at about
$2,000 a month. A year later the main shaft struck an even
richer load, and Walker and Brady tripled their monthly net
income. Vekol had a population of more than four hundred,
and Walker, who owned the store and all of the buildings other
than Gradello's home, ruled it like a fiefdom.

Walker still corresponded with members of his family
and his patient fiancée in Chicago. Consuela bore him a daughter. Three years after Vekol was founded, Walker's brother
Lucien appeared. John Walker did not appear particularly
pleased, but thirty days after Lucien's arrival, the two brothers
paid Brady $65,000 for his third interest in the mine. What
convinced Brady to sell is a mystery for the *Weekly Arizona
Enterprise*, which reported the transaction, disclosed also that
the Vekol mine now was netting about $1,500 a day. A year
later, after the construction of a stamp mill, the same newspaper reported the production of $169,807 worth of silver bullion
within a three-month period. The town now had a hotel, but
no saloon, a public library, a school, two churches, a livery stable, a boardinghouse, and a total population of about eight
hundred.

In 1886, another brother, William Walker, arrived in
Vekol. John D. Walker appeared to be more upset by William's
appearance than he had been over his reunion with Lucien.
William, who apparently was the youngest and most energetic
of the three sons, immediately assumed a proprietary interest
in the operation of both the mine and the town.

For several days John sulked and remained in his house
talking only to Gradello.

"Why don't we throw them out?" Gradello asked.

John Walker shook his head. "There's more to it than
that," he replied ambiguously. He rose from his chair, started

to walk across the room, then suddenly staggered. He would have fallen had Gradello not caught him.

These seizures of dizziness occurred regularly throughout the afternoon and that evening, Consuela and Gradello took him by buggy to a hospital in Tucson. Here, after a few days of observation, doctors diagnosed his illness as a minor stroke. They suggested that during his recuperative period he take an extended vacation. Walker thought the suggestion a reasonable one. He decided to go to San Francisco, taking Consuela and his daughter, Juana, with him.

The day before his departure he returned to Vekol and withdrew $80,000 cash from his personal account in his own bank. Two days later, he paused in Los Angeles, long enough to deposit the money in a bank account he maintained in this Southern California city.

Lucien and William became furious over this apparent expression of distrust by their older brother. They retaliated by petitioning the federal court in Tucson to appoint them as conservators of John's estate. (Arizona was still a territory and so was under the jurisdiction of the federal government.) The court granted the petition on a temporary basis. At the same time, the court authorized the immediate incarceration of John D. Walker in an asylum where competent medical personnel could have the time and opportunity to determine the sanity of John D. Walker.

About two weeks after his arrival in San Francisco, John was picked up by United States marshals in the lobby of the Palace Hotel and was taken to the Hospital for the Insane in Napa, California. No one thought to notify his wife and daughter, who waited upstairs in a hotel suite. After her husband had been missing for two days, Consuela telegraphed his best friend for help. Shortly thereafter, Gradello arrived in San

Francisco. He immediately filed a missing-person report with the San Francisco Police Department. A short time later, detectives notified Consuela and Gradello of John's whereabouts and the reason for his incarceration.

The federal court in San Francisco did not move as precipitously as the one in Tucson had. It took the lawyers Gradello hired more than a month to get John D. Walker freed under a writ of habeas corpus.

The Walker family and Gradello returned immediately to Vekol where John faced his brothers for a showdown. The outlook was bleak. During the two months that John had been gone, title to the mine and everything he owned in the town had been transferred to Lucien and William as conservators. The only property left in John's name, and thus under his control, was his home in Vekol. Lucien and William were absentee operators. During John's incarceration, they had both moved to the less confining atmosphere of Tucson.

The hostility between the Walker brothers now became public knowledge. Lucien and William petitioned the court for another order to confine John. This request was rejected by the court on the grounds that if John were so incompetent as to be unable to care for himself, he would never have been released from the hospital in Napa. On the other hand, the federal district court refused to revoke the order of conservatorship, issuing an order instead for John to show cause why the order should not be made permanent. The conflict became a battle between lawyers flailing each other with depositions.

It was after one such deposition, taken several weeks after his return, that John returned to Vekol more angry than usual. It was cold. There had been several days of below freezing weather, which made the ground hard. After dinner John went to see Gradello, but his friend was not at home. John left a note asking Gradello to come and see him when he returned, no matter what time. It was shortly after midnight when Gradello arrived. Consuela was still up. John took Gradello into one of the bedrooms and opened a closet door. There, hidden under folded blankets, were some three hundred silver-bullion ingots, each weighing about twenty-five pounds.

"They say I am crazy because I have hoarded silver," he told Gradello. "They think I have it hidden in a vault in Tucson, and they are going to get a court order tomorrow to seize it. When they find nothing, they will search my house."

"You are crazy indeed if you keep it here, then," Gradello replied.

"Precisely," Walker said. "Now I want to borrow your wagon and your horse."

A half-hour later Gradello helped Walker load the ingots into the wagon. They worked quietly so as not to disturb the sleeping town.

"Where are you going to take them?" Gradello asked.

Walker shook his head. "If you don't know where they are you can say so truthfully if asked in court."

Gradello recalled something else that Walker said that night. "One of the grounds they are using to say I am incompetent is that I am living with a squaw. I have plans that will thwart this argument," he added, "but don't tell Consuela."

It was about two in the morning when John Walker drove off into the night with the wagon load of silver bullion. He turned north on the county road which led to Casa Grande. He had not asked Gradello to accompany him and help unload the silver, and Gradello did not volunteer such help. He waited at the house with Consuela and her small sleeping daughter, Juana.

261

A little after four in the morning, John Walker returned. He was in good spirits and the wagon was empty. "They are almost in plain sight," he said, "but they'll never find them."

The next afternoon, Gradello once again came over to the Walker home. John D. Walker had left. He told Consuela that the house was hers and that he would not be back. He also told her to write to him if she needed money. Gradello recalled that Consuela showed no emotion over the departure of her husband, a man to whom she had been married for more than a quarter of a century.

Walker moved to Tucson where the first steps of the court battle to win back his property were being taken. The reason that Consuela was left behind was disclosed a few weeks later when Elinor Rice arrived in the territory. After a thirty-year engagement, John D. Walker was ready to marry his fiancée. The wedding took place in Tucson on April 18, 1891. If John bothered to divorce Consuela, there is no record of it. The only record of the marriage was in the memories of a few Pima Indians who had witnessed the ceremony.

The newly married couple adjourned to a nearby health spa for their honeymoon. In no way was the honeymoon idyllic. A new federal judge had been appointed to the bench in Tucson, and the morning after the wedding John was taken into custody on another commitment order obtained by Lucien and William. Jailed in Tucson to await a competency hearing, he was rescued by his bride and his attorneys who explained to the new judge that this was the second time around on this hoked-up charge.

His freedom lasted less than twenty-four hours. This time he was arrested on a criminal complaint by Lucien and William over the embezzlement of more than three hundred silver-bullion ingots from the Vekol mine. After another night in prison, he was released on $50,000 bail. The case came to trial quickly and the charges were dismissed when the court ruled that it was a legal impossibility to embezzle one's own property.

John Walker again was summoned before Lucien's and William's lawyers for taking a deposition in reference to the pending litigation over the conservatorship. He was asked repeatedly what he had done with the silver ingots. He repeatedly refused to tell. His obstinate attitude was referred to a judge who ruled that John would be held in contempt of court unless he revealed his secret. Before the deposition could be resumed, however, John suffered another slight stroke. Lucien and William again sought a commitment order. It was granted, and this time, John was taken to Napa Hospital again for observation. On July 2, 1891, less than three months after his marriage to Elinor, John D. Walker died in the Napa Hospital for the Insane.

Thirty-one days later, Juan Gradello discovered the body of Consuela Walker lying on the floor of her home in Vekol. She had died of an apparent heart attack. Gradello took teenaged Juana home with him.

At the time of his death the estate of John D. Walker was estimated at $1.5 million, including the $80,000 in cash in a Los Angeles bank. Not included in the estimate was the three hundred silver ingots. Gradello immediately contacted lawyers to act on Juana's behalf. Apparently Elinor did not put in a claim for the estate and, according to some reports, quietly returned to Illinois. Lucien and William, however, bitterly fought Juana's claim.

The case dragged through the courts for seventeen years, with most of the estate winding up in the hands of the attorneys. In 1907 the United States Supreme court decided in favor of Lucien and William. The Supreme Court, which at that time had no interest in the rights of minorities, agreed that Juana Walker was indeed the daughter of John D. Walker and, under ordinary circumstances, should be entitled to the inheritance. What disqualified her, however, the court ruled, was the fact that she was half or one-quarter Indian. Because Arizona law decreed that marriage between Indians and whites was illegal, Juana Walker's claim was invalid.

With the death of John Walker, Vekol began to decline. The lode ran out. Its post office was shut down in 1909, and the last resident left in 1912. Today it is one of the barely discernible ghost towns that abound in Arizona.

One of the last persons to leave Vekol was Juan José Gradello. He spent years looking for the three hundred silver ingots that were hidden "almost in plain sight" somewhere near the old home of John D. Walker. The hiding place is near the old road because the ingots were taken there in a wagon. The silver had to be hidden near the house because Gradello said that John was only gone for two hours, and it would have taken him at least three-quarters of an hour to unload it.

One thousand and fifty pounds of pure silver should be worth a canvass of Vekol with a metal detector.

THE JARBIDGE INCIDENTS

There is nothing left of Jarbidge, Nevada, today. It is a ghost town located at the bottom of a canyon more than 2,000 feet deep in the northern part of the state near the Idaho border. Unlike many of its more lusty neighbors, Jarbidge never did boom.

It was founded as a gold mining camp. At its peak of prosperity, it contained only eight hundred inhabitants, six saloons, two brothels, a small hotel, and a few business shops along its main street. It served four mines of modest production and a fifth which was *almost* found in the area. The missing mine goes by the name of the Lost Sheepherder.

In the late fall of 1890, a prospector named John Ross was driven out of the Jarbidge Mountains by a snowstorm. He had been alone for weeks and hungered for human companionship. Thus, when he ran across a sheep camp run by Russ Ishman near Jarbidge, he paused to chat. Ishman was a hospitable man, and he offered Ross a shot of whiskey. This was followed by a few more, and, as Ross became more mellow, he took Ishman into his confidence.

Ross had discovered an extraordinarily rich float, he

265

confided, and had tracked the surface gold to a point high in the mountains before the snowfall had driven him out. (A float is made up of pieces of gold that have been washed out by natural causes from a gold vein.) Ross had left behind his pick and shovel to mark the start of the search in the spring.

Ross apparently gave some indications as to where he had left his pick and shovel because by the time the snows had melted the following spring Ishman had given up sheep-herding in favor of prospecting. He found Ross's pick and shovel with little difficulty. A more disconcerting discovery, however, was that of a human skeleton with a hole in the skull lying beside the miner's tools.

Understandably, Ishman was nervous as he began his search for the source of the float. There was a strong probability that Ross was a murderer and that he would be back in the mountains very soon. Nevertheless, Ishman continued to follow the float higher into the mountains. Two weeks later, he came to its source, a lode so rich that the rock was seamed with yellow. He pried a few samples of the rock loose from the outcropping before he made camp that night.

The next morning someone shot at him. The bullet was fired from an unseen rifle, and it hit the enameled coffee cup he was lifting to his lips, ripping it from his grasp. Ishman threw himself behind a nearby boulder. His finger bled copiously where it had been cut by the handle of the coffee cup. He thought he was going to be murdered and that there was no way he could fight back. His rifle and gun were inside his small tent. If he went to get them, he would be shot down.

There was no sequel to the rifle fire, however. Hours passed. Ishman could detect no signs of any other human within sight or sound. He spent most of the day hiding behind his boulder. In late afternoon, he realized that eventually he would have to move, so he gathered the courage to dash to his tent. The move attracted no attention, but Ishman found no relief from his fear. With the arrival of dusk, he picked up his weapons and the ore samples he had taken from the rock cropping and set off down the mountain. His route took him past the skeleton, and there he paused to pick up the skull.

When he arrived in Jarbidge he told his story to John Pence, a prominent sheep rancher and one of the town's leading citizens. When the ore samples were assayed and valued at a phenomenal $4,000 a ton, Pence decided to put aside his sheepherding in favor of gold mining. Because of the obvious danger, Ishman told four other men from the town, in addition to Pence, of the discovery. A six-man partnership was formed.

In late May, Ishman guided the heavily armed party into the Jarbidge Mountains. When they reached the spot where Ross had halted his exploration the preceding fall, both the headless skeleton and the miner's tools had disappeared. The expedition paused here to allow Ishman to get his bearings.

A moment later a rifle-shot once again echoed through the mountains. This time the bullet struck Ishman in the temple killing him before his body hit the ground. His companions took cover, but the mysterious killer fired no more bullets.

The surviving members of the expedition were prudent men. Logically, they decided that Ross was the killer, and that he could be apprehended much more efficiently when he came out of the mountains. This decision was reached quickly, and Pence led the group back to Jarbidge. Word was sent to Elko about the murderer loose in the Jarbidge Mountains along with the suspicions as to his identity. A week or so later Pence received a letter from the sheriff in Elko. The killer was not John Ross. Ross had died of pneumonia apparently contracted when he passed out from drunkenness outside a saloon the preceding February.

The year following Ishman's murder, Pence and his companions once again entered the Jarbidge Mountains cautiously. They had no difficulty in reaching what they thought was the site where Ishman was murdered. They were not attacked by an unseen rifleman, but they could find no trace of the surface float that led to the fabulously rich lode found by both Ross and Ishman. As nearly as can be determined, the lode still remains to be rediscovered.

Gold was discovered in other areas around Jarbidge, however. The richest strike occurred in 1908, but it caused no great boom in the fortunes of Jarbidge. Unlike many of the earlier mining towns, Jarbidge had no boosters. The railroad ignored it. Merchants had learned through previous experience that the life expectancy of a mining town in the West was short. If the mines continued to produce, they were purchased by conglomerates that operated them with cheap, imported Chinese labor. Jarbidge was born too late to boom, and, from its inception, it adopted a funereal habit.

Because it came into existence late, Jarbidge died at a later date than many of the other mining towns. But it was not for many years after it had begun to die that anyone realized Jarbidge, in one sense, was an epitaph for the entire Wild West.

To reach the remains of Jarbidge today requires considerable driving skill. The narrow road twists and sideslips down the side of a canyon almost 2,500 feet in a distance of less than 5 miles. In 1916, when the town was eight years old, the road and the grade leading to it was even more hazardous. One reporter, who made the trip by stagecoach, described the road as less than a foot wider than the conveyance.

At least two stage drivers lost their lives on the road. One was caught in an avalanche and the other plunged off the road during a blizzard. Shipping supplies into the community was a hazardous task, especially during the winter months. According to Nell Murbarger, a prominent Western historian, residents of Jarbidge paid one hundred dollars a ton for hay, and fresh eggs were more costly than watch charms.

The road linked Jarbidge to Rogerson, Idaho, approximately sixty-five miles to the north. The stagecoach, which ran about three trips a week, usually arrived in Jarbidge about three o'clock in the afternoon. On December 5, 1916, the stage was late, but this was not considered unusual because of the weather. Shortly before noon there had been a small avalanche near the Flaxie Mine, and there had been several snow flurries during the afternoon.

Some disagreement exists over the name of the stagecoach driver. One account identifies him as F. M. Searcy. Another reports his name as Frank Slattery.

When night came, and the stage still had not arrived, the Jarbidge postmaster sent out a couple of men on horseback to look for it. They returned several hours later to report that they had ridden to the top of the pass and had seen no signs of it, nor were there any visible signs that it had skidded off the road into the canyon. The postmaster, and almost everyone else in Jarbidge, assumed that the stage either had not left Rogerson or had broken down somewhere north of the pass. The delay would affect nearly everyone in the town because the stage carried the payroll (more than $30,000) for employees of the four mines, plus $10,000 in cash designated for the town's largest gambling casino and the general store.

About noon the following day, a freight wagon from Rogerson drove into Jarbidge. The two teamsters reported that the stage had left Rogerson on schedule the preceding day. The freight wagon had followed the same route that the stage took, but had seen no sign of it. Search parties were immediately sent up the grade to look for clues to where it might have gone off the road into the canyon. A detailed search failed to turn up any indications that the stage had tumbled into the canyon, but the consensus was that this was what had happened and that the skid marks had been erased by the snow flurries and winds of the previous day.

Shortly before dusk Mrs. Dexter, an elderly widow who lived about two miles north of the center of the town, appeared in the General Store and Post Office to pick up her mail. When told that the stagecoach apparently had gone off the grade, Mrs. Dexter shook her head. "Nonsense," she replied. "It passed my house, about five o'clock last night."

Mrs. Dexter was known to be a little confused at times, but she insisted that it was on the previous night that she had seen the stagecoach pass her house. "It was snowing and the driver was all slouched down into his greatcoat," she said. "If I could have caught him I would have asked him in for a cup of warm tea."

The postmaster still was skeptical, but he dispatched a couple of riders to look over the area between the town and Mrs. Dexter's outlying house. The searchers found the stagecoach in a small grove of trees about three hundred yards off the road and less than a mile from the center of town. The lead horse, nearly dead from the cold, was tethered to one of the trees. The brakes were frozen to the rim of the wheels. Frozen to the rear seat of the coach by his own blood was the driver, bullet holes in both his head and chest. The mail sacks which contained the money shipments were missing.

Investigation of the murder the following morning indicated two areas where the ambush could have taken place. One was about a mile north of the Dexter residence where tracks in the road indicated that the stagecoach had slithered from one side of the road to the other for approximately seventy-five yards. If the ambush had occurred here, it meant that the murderer had been driving the stage when it was seen by Mrs. Dexter. The other possible ambush site was at a point about fifty yards north of the small grove of trees where the stage had been hidden. Bloodstains were found there under some freshly fallen snow.

A small creek ran along the side of the grove farthest from the highway. A path had been trod into the ground by the side of the stream and a rickety footbridge had been built over it as a shortcut into town for pedestrians. Along this path and on the bridge, investigators made what they thought was a significant discovery: the footprints of both a man and a dog.

One of the miners who lived in Jarbidge was a young man named Benjamin Kuhl. He was a surly man whose only friend in the community was his dog, a large yellow mongrel. The dog was as friendly as his master was unfriendly, and it was no chore for one of the investigators to entice the animal away from his cabin and out to the grove. The paw prints in the snow matched those of the dog, according to testimony offered later.

The dog, however, pointed the finger of suspicion toward his master in a much more dramatic manner. After his paw-print had been compared, the animal bounded over to a fallen log and began barking and digging at its side. Upon raising the log, the investigators found underneath it a blood-stained shirt and coat. The shirt, a black-and-white woolen check, was similar to one often worn by Kuhl. One of the investigators also identified the coat as Kuhl's property.

The band of amateur sleuths then descended upon Kuhl's cabin. There, under the bed, they found a revolver with two shots fired from it. The records do not indicate whether or not the weapon was the same caliber as the gun used in the murder of the stagecoach driver.

When Kuhl returned to his cabin, he was arrested by his fellow townsmen and immediately taken to Elko to await trial. He denied any knowledge of the crime and claimed the gun was not his. He denied ever owning a gun. He produced witnesses at his trial who stated that Kuhl was in a Jarbidge saloon the evening of the murder. On cross-examination the witnesses were not sure which night they had seen Kuhl, even though the day-long trial was held only one week after the murder. His lawyer pointed out that Kuhl quite probably would have been stricken with pneumonia had he walked bare-chested from the spot where he allegedly buried his coat and shirt to his cabin. The jury did not accept this logic. It found Kuhl guilty of first-degree murder and, according to the custom of the day, recommended that he be hanged. The sentence was commuted by the judge, however, to one of life imprisonment. Kuhl served twenty-seven years in the Nevada State Prison in Carson City. He was released in 1944. Three days after his release, Kuhl was struck and killed by a hit-and-run driver as he was walking along the highway between Elko and Jarbidge.

The $40,000 taken in that stage robbery has never been recovered. Most of the money was in gold currency and would be worth considerably more than its face value today. If Kuhl was guilty of the robbery, then the treasure probably is hidden somewhere along the footpath (less than a mile long) that connected the town of Jarbidge to the grove of trees where the stage was hidden. It is not unlikely that Kuhl was on his way back to Jarbidge to pick up his treasure when he was killed.

If Kuhl was guilty of highway robbery and murder on the night of December 5, 1916, then history awards him a more unique distinction than that of an ordinary bandit and murderer. His act would signify the end of an era in the Wild West, for he would be the last man in its history to have held up a horse-drawn stagecoach.

THE MAN WITH HALF A NOSE

One of the most successful bandits of the Southwest was Pedro Nevarez, a cutthroat who, oddly, has attracted little attention from historians. He is better known as El Chato, which translates loosely as Pug Nose, because half of that appendage was lopped off during a cutlass fight with another desperado.

El Chato hid his band in the wilderness of the Los Organos Mountains, east of the Rio Grande in what now is southern New Mexico. For about a decade in the mid-1600s he preyed with impunity upon travelers along El Camino Real. Legend says that even the Apaches feared him. Other sources contend that half of his raiders were pure Apache and that the rest, including El Chato, were half-Apache. On several occasions Spanish troops were sent into the area to run him down, but the wily El Chato apparently received advance notice of such expeditions and retired to his mountain hideout until the danger was past.

His preferred victims were members of wagon trains

274

traveling between the garrison at El Paso and the more northern Spanish cities of Mesilla, Santa Fe, and Taos. These raids not only provided him with jewelry and money, but also with supplies that helped sustain his organization. He controlled a network of spies and informers in both El Paso and Santa Fe that, in addition to letting him know when a military expedition was being mounted against him, also told him whenever a loosely guarded convoy with valuable cargo was headed in either direction. El Chato also usually was aware of the route his victims intended to take; whether it was along the old El Camino Real or the more dangerous Jornada del Muerto, the Journey of Death.

The latter route won its gruesome reputation from the untold numbers of travelers who perished on it. It still was widely used, however, because it cut out approximately fifty miles from the journey between El Paso and Santa Fe. It went north in a straight line from what is now Las Cruces for a distance of approximately one hundred miles. The safer El Camino Real followed the Rio Grande, but bulged considerably to the west of the Jornada del Muerto.

El Chato canvassed both routes. On one occasion his band raided a northbound caravan in the morning on El Camino Real and another southbound in the afternoon on Jornada del Muerto. With two notable exceptions, the loot garnered from any individual raid was not much—precious stones taken from women, gold and personal valuables from men—but over a ten-year span the accumulation of such booty mounted into the hundreds of thousands of dollars. The exceptions were a shipment of gold reportedly worth a quarter-million dollars that was being sent from Santa Fe to Mexico City and another shipment of church valuables worth twice as much that was being taken to Santa Fe.

The gold bullion, also the property of the Catholic Church, was lightly guarded. The wagon carrying it, part of a six-wagon convoy, headed south at Fray Cristobal along the Jornada del Muerto. A few hours later, El Chato and his band nonchalantly galloped alongside the convoy, shot two guards, and pulled out the wagon with the bullion. El Chato also tore a diamond cross from the bosom of Señora Ortega before the gang departed with the wagon.

A detachment of soldiers was sent out from El Paso. The burned hulk of the wagon was found a few miles from the ambush site, but, as usual, no trace was found of El Chato or the gold.

The second exception to El Chato's small profits was a raid on a pack train accompanied by a group of Augustinian monks. The pack train had started out from Acolmán on the outskirts of Mexico City with an ultimate destination of Taos where the monks planned to open a mission. While the train paused in El Paso, El Chato's spies learned that the pack mules not only carried the usual church supplies but also an assortment of gold crosses, baptismal urns, chandeliers, chalices, an altar cloth woven with gold thread, and a large amount of gold coin.

El Chato struck the pack train a few miles north of Las Cruces. The raid was very brief. The bandits merely galloped into the train, cut the mules loose, then herded them back into the mountains. One of the enraged and frustrated monks said later that less than five minutes elapsed between the appearance and disappearance of the bandit with only half a nose.

The Church was furious. The military sent out a detachment four days later to search for the elusive bandit, but they did not find him. This time, however, the Church officials did not accept the Army's excuses for the failure of its search mission. Without the knowledge of the El Paso garrison, the Church put together an undercover operation in distant Durango. Here a large number of soldiers were dressed as monks. A pack train was assembled and accompanied by the pseudo-monks headed north. The caravan followed the identical route and pattern of the earlier one and, while the "monks" rested in El Paso, word was leaked that the pack mules were laden with gold and silver. El Chato's spies relayed the word of the bonanza headed his way.

The bandit attacked in almost the same spot as he had in the earlier raid, but the results were much different. From under the robes of the pseudo-monks came guns. Two of the soldiers were killed, and all of the bandits except El Chato were believed slaughtered. El Chato was taken prisoner. He remained in custody in El Paso for a couple of months, then was moved to Mexico City where, after a short and speedy trial, he was hanged.

Two centuries passed. Everyone had forgotten about El Chato and his raids from the Los Organos Mountains. Then, in 1877, a band of marauding Apaches attacked the mission in Doña Ana. They set fire to the church, then fled, taking with them some boxes that they apparently thought were of value. The boxes, however, contained nothing but papers, which the Indians threw to the winds on the mesa.

Among the papers that were salvaged was a copy of a letter written by a priest of the mission to the Acolmán monastery more than two hundred years earlier. The letter tells of the capture of El Chato and of the death of all but one of his followers. The survivor, according to the letter, had been left for dead, but had managed to make his way to Robledo, where he was nursed by friends. He recovered from his wounds, but on his first venture into the town was recognized

277

by one of El Chato's victims as a bandit and was arrested. He was tried in Robledo and he asked for absolution while waiting to be hanged.

Before the rites were administered, the bandit told the priest where El Chato kept his headquarters in the Los Organos Mountains near the cave where all of the booty other than currency had been stored. There are several translations of this letter, but the differences between them are minor.

The letter describes the cave as a natural one, facing south, near the top of a hill in Soledad Canyon. A cross cut into the rock crests the cave entrance which is partially hidden by a juniper tree. To the east of the cave are three medium-sized peaks, and within sight to the north is a dripping spring. It is two hundred and fifty paces from the cave entrance to the top of the hill. From the summit, one can look down on the Jornada del Muerto for as far as the eye can see. The interior of the cave is separated into two parts connected by a short tunnel. The cave contains more coins of silver than two mules could carry, as well as jewelry, gold bullion, and the relics of Acolmán.

The letter ends with an account of three trips the priest made into the area looking in vain for the cave. He abandoned his search when he was transferred to Doña Ana.

Many copies and many translations were made of the letter, and undoubtedly there were many searches for El Chato's treasure, all of them apparently unsuccessful.

One incident concerning the treasure is told by Dr. Arthur L. Campa in his book *Treasure of the Sangre de Cristos*. It occurred about a year after the priest's letter was discovered. In the early spring of 1878, a prominent rancher near Mesilla lost some of his prize cattle to rustlers. In the area was a man known as Don Demetrio, who had been trained by Indians as

278

a cattle tracker and had become more efficient in this skill than his teachers. The rancher hired Demetrio to track down his missing cattle.

According to Campa, Demetrio, accompanied by two ranch hands, set off early in the morning and by noon tracked the rustlers to a deep arroyo where they discovered the cattle had been slaughtered and the beef loaded onto several pack horses. Demetrio and his men continued to follow the trail that led toward St. Augustine Pass in the Los Organos Mountains. As they climbed higher the weather turned colder, and by late afternoon it started to snow. The snowfall soon turned into a blizzard that obliterated the rustlers' trail and forced the trackers to take shelter under a rocky ledge. The men built a fire. While searching for wood to keep the fire going, Demetrio stumbled across a cave with its opening partially blocked by debris. He crawled into the opening, stood up inside, lit a tallow candle, and found to his surprise that the cave was man-made. Timber supports still remained along the walls and signs of mining pick scars were still evident in the wall. A more sensational discovery, however, was a stack of rawhide sacks piled against one wall of the cave. Demetrio cut one of the sacks open and then another only to find that they contained solid-gold bars.

The tracker said nothing about his find to his companions, nor did he mention it to his wife when he returned to Mesilla. He was canny enough to realize that a secret once told no longer is a secret. The problem he faced was how to get the gold out of the cave and dispose of it successfully. The problem was still unsolved when he went to work on a mining claim in the Sierra Blanca in the early fall. He never was able to solve it because, during the second week of his work on the claim, an explosive charge he was lighting went off prematurely, driving shards of sharp shale into his body and eyes and blinding him permanently. His loss of eyesight loosened his tongue and, upon at least one occasion, he was led back into the mountains by eastern treasure seekers in search of the cave. His handicap, however, was too great, and the cave remained lost to him.

Campa also tells of the discovery by a prospector named Ben Brown in 1916 of a cave choked with debris, but for one reason and then another, Brown did not get around to excavating the opening to see if it covered the treasure.

The last time any public notice was given to the treasure of El Chato was in the fall of 1949. The Associated Press bureau in Albuquerque, New Mexico, reported that the body of an unidentified man had been found in Los Organos, apparently the victim of a hunting accident. The body had been found near a campsite. The dead man had been shot by a high-powered rifle fired from a considerable distance, presumably by another hunter.

Duke Reed, a curious newsman and newscaster from radio station KOB in Albuquerque, called law enforcement officials in El Paso, where the body had been taken, to ask why it was unidentified.

"Because there was no wallet, no keys, or anything else of an identifiable nature on the body," he was told.

"Does this mean you possibly suspect murder?" Reed asked.

"Not necessarily," the deputy replied cautiously. "But apparently someone rolled him after he was shot." The deputy paused, then continued. "Whoever rolled him missed the best part. He had two gold bars inside an old rawhide sack in his bedroll."

Reed remembered the legend of El Chato and included

it in his account of the affair during his evening broadcast. This, in turn, prompted a flurry of treasure seekers to descend on the area, but if anyone found El Chato's loot, he did not announce it.

The victim never was identified. What happened to the two gold bars is also a mystery. But there are probably many more in rawhide sacks in a cave near the summit of Mt. Soledad, where the Jornada del Muerto is visible for as far as the eye can see.

MISTAKES IN MOKELUMNE

It was never very peaceful on the Barbary Coast in San Francisco. Bordellos, gambling halls, saloons, and taverns clustered around this section of the waterfront. Murders were common. Fights were frequent. It was a recruiting ground for able-bodied men who often were drugged in bars and "shanghaied" aboard a vessel as part of a crew. It also was an excellent training ground for young physicians who could pass with impunity throughout the area, because every thug on the Barbary Coast assumed that the day would come when he too would require the services of a doctor on an emergency basis.

One of these doctors was Michael Berlin. He graduated from Harvard Medical School in 1900 and came west for some excitement and adventure before settling down to a practice in Boston. He opened a small office on Lower Montgomery Street and acquired a plethora of experience in the adjacent Barbary Coast. It was early in the evening in the fall of 1902 when he once again heard the running steps followed by the pounding on his door, which always preceded an emergency call into the Barbary Coast.

This time there had been a murder in one of the saloons. The victim was a bartender named Charlie Mason who had been shot three times in the head and was quite dead by the time Dr. Berlin arrived. Mason's murderer had been stabbed twice by Mason, and was lying in a pool of blood on the floor of the saloon. He was a man in his early sixties, in excellent physical condition, and his wounds were to prove not fatal. As was the custom on the Barbary Coast, the police were not called. The witnesses to the affray had quickly disappeared. What happened to the body of the dead bartender is unknown, but the man who killed him was taken on three planks fashioned into a litter to Dr. Berlin's office where he was sewn up and bandaged.

The bartender's killer apparently thought he was much more seriously wounded than he really was, or else he was a garrulous man. He spoke English with a foreign accent and identified himself as a Russian named Slava Tyroff. He said that the dispute with the bartender arose when he saw Mason drop some knockout drops into a drink ordered by a young man. Tyroff explained that he had become furious because, some thirty years earlier, he also had been shanghaied from the Barbary Coast. According to Tyroff, he had knocked the drink from the bartender's grasp and called out a warning to the unidentified young man for whom it was intended. Mason had then picked up a knife and stabbed Tyroff, whereupon, Tyroff had pulled out a gun and shot Mason. Tyroff continued talking as Dr. Berlin worked on the wounds.

"Most men can go through their lives without killing anything more than a fish or a chicken," Tyroff said. "Now, I have killed two men."

"You don't have to tell me about it," the doctor replied.

"A doctor at the deathbed is like a priest."

"You are not going to die. You are good for another twenty years."

Tyroff was not convinced. He continued talking. He had been born in Russia and came to this country by way of Europe when he was a young man. He had arrived in San Francisco about thirty years before, long after the initial gold rush, while the Mother Lode country of California was still attracting gold prospectors. It was the lure of gold that had brought Tyroff to California, but on his arrival in San Francisco, he was penniless and knew nothing about prospecting. He got a job as a cleanup man in a gambling spot on the Barbary Coast for a dollar a day and room and board. He worked there for about two years, becoming more fluent in English, but still learning nothing about prospecting. He did save money, augmenting his salary with tips from prostitutes who worked the casino and occasionally from the gamblers themselves. Near the end of the second year he met a prospector named Harry Oversem, an older man who had come to the gambling hall with gold he had taken out of the Mother Lode country. Oversem quickly lost his newfound money at the gambling tables.

When Oversem went broke, he became friendly with Tyroff. He told Tyroff that he still knew where gold could be found in the Mother Lode country, and when he learned that Tyroff had a three-hundred-dollar grubstake, Oversem was eager to cut him in as a partner. Tyroff quit his job, and a couple of weeks later the two men struck out into the mountains from Mokelumne Hill, the infamous town where, at the height of the gold rush, men were hanged on the average of one a day. Oversem knew precisely where he was going.

He and Tyroff headed straight east from town for three miles and crossed a large mesa toward a range of sharp hills divided by three canyons. About three hundred yards from the summit of the middle canyon, they made camp next to a spring. Before the day was out, the men dug away the camouflage that covered the entrance to Harry Oversem's mine.

The mine was still productive. After the first week of work Tyroff and Oversem had unearthed about two burro loads of ore which Oversem took into Mokelumne Hill. It was Tyroff's job to stay behind and guard the mine. When he returned, Oversem gave Tyroff a twenty-dollar gold piece as his half. Tyroff was content. Twenty dollars a week was a lot more than a dollar a day, and the work was a lot healthier than what he had done in the past.

A pattern was established that continued for about six months. Oversem would leave on a Saturday, return the following day, and pay Tyroff his twenty dollars. It took six months before Tyroff attached any significance to the fact that Oversem invariably left the camp for about a half-hour every Sunday after his return. On one Sunday Tyroff suggested that he accompany his partner on his weekly stroll. Oversem decided not to take his walk.

That night Tyroff feigned sleep as Oversem stealthily left the camp. Tyroff followed him a short distance down the canyon, saw Oversem upend a heavy granite boulder, and heard the heavy clinking of coins as they were dropped into some type of metal container. They were dropped in one at a time, and Tyroff counted twenty-one coins before the shadowy Oversem struggled to replace the rock that covered his cache. Tyroff quickly returned to camp and again pretended to sleep, as his partner silently slid into bed.

As he lay awake, Tyroff's temper began to build. If each

285

one of the coins he had heard was a $20 gold piece, this meant that Oversem was selling the ore for about $250 a week instead of $40. If this were true, Oversem was cheating his partner at the rate of $125 a week, and there was more than $5,000 worth of gold currency in Oversem's cache. In the early morning hours, while Oversem snored softly in his bedroll, Tyroff quietly arose, picked up a sledgehammer and swung it with all his might at the skull of the sleeping Oversem. No sooner was the deed done, then Tyroff was seized by fear and contrition. The fear stemmed from the hanging he would surely face when word of the murder reached Mokelumne Hill. The contrition came from the fact that he had killed a man. The fear was responsible for his actions, however. Without waiting to pack his bedroll, he saddled the mule he and Oversem had purchased and departed. He skirted around Mokelumne Hill without even arousing a dog and by dawn was well beyond Sutter Creek. A week later he was shanghaied as an able-bodied seaman on a schooner.

He had returned to San Francisco about three weeks before the altercation with the bartender, thinking it probably would now be safe to look for the gold cache hidden by his crooked partner. But now it was too late.

Dr. Berlin helped his patient to his feet and walked him to another room where he kept a cot for such emergencies. "You can rest here for the night," he told Tyroff, "then I'll get someone to help you to your hotel tomorrow."

For the first time, Tyroff looked at him with hope.

"They are only superficial wounds," the doctor said. "One went a little deep, but it missed everything important."

Tyroff nodded and slowly lay down on the cot. "That story I just told you," he said, "I made it up. It isn't true."

For the first time, Dr. Berlin believed the tale.

Tyroff went by hack to his hotel the following morning. A week later his body was found in a Barbary Coast alley, a bullet in his head. Rumor around the Barbary Coast was that the killing had been done by a brother of the dead bartender.

The cache of $5,000 worth of gold currency intrigued Dr. Michael Berlin. In 1904 he closed down his San Francisco practice, which had been more rewarding in experience than in money, and made plans to return to Boston. Before he left, however, he decided to take a trip to Mokelumne Hill and to see if, by any wild chance, he could find Harry Oversem's cache. He took a steamer to Stockton where he rented a horse for the long trek to Mokelumne Hill.

Dr. Berlin checked into the Hotel Leger, Mokelumne Hill's only hostelry, then strolled down the street and entered a bar. The bartender was young, but there was an elderly man among the patrons. Before the doctor went searching through the mountains, he wanted to make sure that there really had been a Harry Oversem.

With some prodding the old-timer remembered. "Sure, he was one of those miners who got murdered back up yonder," he said. "I think he was the one whose body was found. Had a foreigner for a partner. Never did find his body."

"Then how do you know he was murdered?"

"Caught the fella that done it. Had Oversem's gold watch on him. A bad Mexican, he was, named Guillermo Cabrera. We hanged him right outside here. Murdered them both, he did."

Dr. Michael Berlin spent a week in the mountains east of Mokelumne Hill. He found the large mesa, the range of sharp hills divided by three canyons and the spring near the summit of the center canyon that had been described to him by Tyroff. He also found what appeared to be an old mine shaft.

He did not find the cache of gold coins hidden by a cheating partner.

Mokelumne Hill looks today much as it did a century past. The Leger Hotel still stands. The main street of the town has been paved, but the stores still have their false fronts. To enter a bar is to walk into the past. It was only recently that the town council passed an ordinance prohibiting the discharge of firearms within the town limits. Somewhere outside of town there is 136 pounds of gold buried in two covered iron skillets. It belonged to an old prospector named Buster.

According to legend, the gold hoard represented Buster's life savings, accumulated at numerous washes around the Mother Lode country. Buster decided to retire on his gold in Mokelumne Hill. A few days after he built a small cabin on the outskirts of town, he decided to have his gold weighed at the general store in Mokelumne Hill. Buster was getting old and was a bit eccentric. He came into town leading his burro by a halter. Over the animal's haunches were two iron Dutch ovens and in these ovens was Buster's gold, weighing one hundred and forty pounds. Buster left four pounds on deposit at the store for credit against future purchases and returned to his cabin.

Unfortunately for Buster, the storekeeper was a talkative man. Word quickly spread around town of the peculiar containers in which the old-timer carried his gold. This information presently reached the attention of a transient badman named Smokey Hall who rushed on horseback out to Buster's cabin. Unfortunately for Smokey his interest in Buster had not been unnoticed; three vigilant citizens had followed him.

They arrived too late to save Buster, but they caught Smokey in the act of rummaging through the cabin. The body of his victim lay across the cabin threshold. Smokey was tried instantly, found guilty of murder, and was hanged from a tree in front of the cabin. The trio of vigilant citizens buried Buster in the front yard, they conducted an exhaustive search for the victim's gold in order that it might be safeguarded. There was no trace of the gold nor of the two Dutch ovens. There are no indications that it ever was found. It could not have been buried too far from Buster's cabin, for he had returned from the store with his treasure less than two hours before he was murdered.

There is still another legend of buried gold around Mokelumne Hill, and although the gold was found before it was buried, the story is worth telling as an example of the tales that circulated throughout the Mother Lode country of California.

About a century ago, the owner of the Leger Hotel left Mokelumne Hill for a month-long visit to San Francisco. He entrusted the operation of the hotel to the day clerk, a diffident young gentleman named Ely Smith, who had a penchant for gambling. One night, shortly after he had taken charge of the hostelry, Smith became heavily involved in a game of faro in one of the saloons. Three times that night, after his stake was gone, Smith returned to the hotel and replenished his bank roll with hotel funds.

He gambled nightly for several weeks, and his luck showed no sign of turning better. Eventually he reached a point where not only the hotel's cash was gone, but so was the gold stored in the hotel's safe by prospectors and semi-permanent guests. As crimes far less serious than this were hanging offenses in Mokelumne Hill, Ely Smith awoke one morning feeling very depressed as well as being very broke.

After weighing the matter most of the morning, he decided to beat the hangman to the drop. Taking a lariat from the livery stable, he walked off into the hills behind the town. Eventually he came to a large fresno tree that he climbed to fasten the rope for his suicidal hanging. After the line was fastened and the noose was made, Smith paused in the branches for some last reflections.

While he was so engaged, he heard hoofbeats and presently saw an elderly man on horseback heading in his direction. Smith drew himself back against the trunk. The stranger reined in his horse directly below Smith, looked around him, but not up, then dismounted. He proceeded to take a miner's shovel from the horse's pack and to dig a hole under the tree. Into the hole went a large leather sack. The stranger then quickly filled in the hole and carefully covered all signs of the excavation with leaves and twigs. He then rode off in the direction of Mokelumne Hill.

Smith waited for a long time after the stranger had disappeared before he climbed down from the tree. The dirt was soft and easy to loosen with his hands. Within a few moments, Smith had pulled out the sack and tumbled its contents onto the ground. The sack contained almost $3,000 worth of gold coins. Smith's depression gave way to instant euphoria, and he abandoned his planned suicide.

He raced back to the hotel, replaced the embezzled funds with the partial contents of the sack, and set the rest aside for his evening at the faro table.

Later that afternoon, he had a sudden start. The stranger who had buried the sack came into the hotel and registered as a guest. His name was Seth Powers, and he came from San Francisco. Smith quickly regained his composure. He had not been seen. There was no way Powers could ever find out who had dug up his gold.

That evening Smith's luck turned. He won back all that he had lost and more. The next day, as Powers was checking out, Smith briefly entertained the idea of returning his gold. He decided against it. It would require too complicated an explanation.

On the following day, the town marshal came into the Leger Hotel and asked if Seth Powers had been a guest there.

Smith paled. "For one night," he replied nervously. "Why?"

"Need his home address," the marshal replied. "The old man went and hanged himself from a fresno tree just outside of town. Dug a hole in the ground then hanged himself."

DIAZ'S LOST GRAVE

Not all treasures are of gold or silver, money or diamonds. Some of the most interesting are of an historical or archeological nature, such as the grave of Melchior Diaz.

The ubiquitous Jesuit priest, Father Eusebio Kino, is generally accorded the credit of being the first European to travel west of the Colorado River and the first to explore what is now Baja, California. There is, however, strong evidence that suggests that Father Kino was preceded by a detachment of Spanish soldiers led by Captain Melchior Diaz. The story starts with the Seven Cities of Cíbola—the lucky seven towns purportedly built of gold—which gullible Spaniards searched for over a huge portion of North America.

One of the most ambitious expeditions in search of Cíbola was launched by Vasques de Coronado, who marched overland from Mexico City to what is now Santa Fe, New Mexico. As a part of the logistics of this operation, supplies were sent north from Acapulco to the head of the Gulf of California. The small fleet carrying these supplies was com-

292

manded by one Fernando de Alarcón. The original plan called for Coronado to rendezvous with Alarcón near the mouth of the Colorado River. Coronado, however, followed the Rio Grande north from El Paso, a route that would miss the meeting point by several hundred miles.

According to the *Narratives of Casteñada*, an account of the Coronado expedition by his scribe, Pedro de Castenada, Coronado dispatched Diaz with a forty-man team to make the rendezvous with Alarcón and bring back the needed supplies. Accompanied by impressed Indian interpreters, Diaz headed west and reached the Colorado River about one hundred miles north of the Gulf.

Here he headed south and, after a three-day journey, encountered some Indians who told him that Alarcón had sailed up the river to the present location and, after a long wait, had departed. One Indian took Diaz to a tree, dug out a clay pot from the ground beneath it, and from it drew out a letter that Alarcón had left for Coronado which said, in effect, that he was tired of waiting and was going back home.

Diaz retraced his steps, following the Colorado north to what now is Yuma, Arizona. There he forded the river and once again turned south, hoping, perhaps, to find traveling quicker on the western than on the eastern side of the river. He also hoped that he might be able to catch up with Alarcón's supply ships before they were out of sight in the Gulf.

The detachment moved south and, after a few days march, skirted an Indian village. The group had with them a small flock of sheep for food, and it was these animals, more than the soldiers, which attracted the attention of a large dog from the village.

The dog raced into the flock, scattering it in all directions. While the men went after the sheep, Captain Melchior

Diaz furiously raced on horseback after the dog. At one point he hurled a lance at the animal. The weapon struck the dog a glancing blow that upended the weapon at the precise instant Diaz galloped past. The pointed end of the lance ripped open Diaz's thigh from knee to groin.

Historians disagree on how long Diaz lived. Casteñada says the quick-tempered captain lived only for a few days. Baltasar de Obregon contends that Diaz lived for approximately one month. All historians agree that the injuries were fatal and that Diaz was buried where he died.

In the early 1930s Walter Henderson of Riverside, California, and some friends, set off on an exploratory trip of northern Baja. He eased his Model A Ford roadster carefully over the unpaved highway and rocky gullies that led toward San Felipe, a small fishing village about 125 kilometers south of Mexicali. A few miles south of a window-shaped rock formation known as La Ventana, he pulled the car off the road. Henderson and his companions unloaded their camping gear, filled their canteens with water from a tank in the car, and set out on foot.

Henderson had made several similar trips into this wilderness section of Mexico with no definite goal in mind other than the hope of coming across some old Spanish mine. He never found a mine. He did find countless Indian arrowheads, occasionally the powerful horns of a bighorn sheep arched over its bleached and sand-pitted skull. Sometimes he was serenaded by the screeching wail of a lynx, or he caught a fleeting glimpse of a mule deer. If a covey of quail were flushed from a sparse cluster of desert greasewood, he knew that water was close by. Occasionally he found the spring, but more often he did not.

On this present trip, however, Henderson had a definite objective. He had heard that there was an oasis not too far distant from La Ventana where native blue palms rose above huge granite basins of water stored from mountain runoffs after storms. On this search he failed because the map he had was crudely drawn. Later he was to learn that he had been several miles south of the oasis he sought.

The country he was in was deserted and parched. Mexican woodcutters who gather the ironwood used to fire the tortilla ovens of Mexicali and Tijuana had not yet been forced this far south. The explorers came across no signs of man after they left their vehicles, only twisted cacti writhing along the sandy ground, an occasional stubby tarote tree, or a lizard basking in the sun.

After a while the group entered an arroyo. On both sides, boulders protruded from the canyon walls like huge cancerous knobs. In some areas the distant mountains were the dark red of an ancient lava flow, while in other areas the mountains were bleached as white as the sand in the gully. By the time dusk arrived, Henderson knew he had missed the oasis he sought and picked a level spot to make camp. At night the dry clear air of Baja brought millions of stars so low to the ground that they mingled with the campfire.

The following morning the group started back on a different course to the spot where they had parked the car. They left the arroyo and hiked over a range of hills. In mid-afternoon they came across a curious pile of rocks, obviously stacked by man, set back a short distance from a steep ravine. Yet for miles in all directions there had been no other sign of humanity.

This pile of rocks was as tall as a short man, and twice as long. Its top was smoothly flat and the sides spread out toward the bottom at about a thirty-degree angle. The stones were rounded, and a cursory examination of the surrounding terrain disclosed that they had been gathered from a considerable distance.

Henderson picked up one of the rocks and turned it over. It was dark on the top; light-colored underneath. He knew a lot about rocks. The dark coating acquired by rocks in the desert is called "desert varnish." It is caused by heat from the sun, which draws the moisture out of the rocks in a capillary action. The dark deposit is left from the minerals in this water. In an arid region, such as this section of Baja where there is practically no rainfall, Henderson knew it would take hundreds of years for such a coating of desert varnish to form. The fact that all of the rocks in this cubed formation were so coated indicated that they had remained in their position undisturbed for a very long time.

Henderson knew something else about this pile of rocks: it was an ideal hibernation spot for the deadly red rattlesnakes of Baja. It was the latter part of April when these dangerous reptiles came out of hibernation. He tossed the rock back on the mound and backed away from it. For a while he studied the terrain, seeking some logical answer.

The mound had been built close to the side of the ravine through which they were descending from the hills. Unless a person came directly upon it, as they had, it would not be noticed. Thus, obviously it had not been built as a landmark. Henderson walked around it. It was then that he noticed the thick piece of ironwood leaning crookedly against one of the short sides of the pile. Lying on the ground was a smaller piece of ironwood. If the small piece ever had been lashed to the larger one, it would have formed a crude cross. Henderson and his companions decided the mound was a grave, but a remarkably elaborate one for its isolated position. Even today the Indians of Baja will immediately bury a corpse if they chance across one, but usually the burial site is marked at most by a small outline of rocks. Never had Henderson seen or heard of one built to monumental height. He studied the mysterious mound until, reluctantly, he was forced to depart to find his car before dark.

He puzzled over the origin of the mound for several years until one day, while reading Casteñada's narrative, he came across a passage that read ". . . on a height of land overlooking a narrow valley, under a pile of rocks, Melchior Diaz lies buried."

Henderson spent years searching for the grave, retracing his route from La Ventana back through this remote and desolate section of Baja, but he never was able to find the proper ravine.

It would be easier to get into the area today with a car with four-wheel drive, but permits are necessary from the Mexican authorities even to search for historical treasures.

THE WATERMAN AFFAIR

The feud between George C. Lee and Robert W. Waterman started in 1875. It was inevitable that Lee would wind up the loser because he was only a successful prospector, whereas Waterman was a crooked politician.

Lee was a big man, a caricature of a prospector. His beard was scraggly and streaked with white. He always wore dirty clothes over an unbathed body. His manners were crude and he was a loud braggart. He was suspicious of just about every person he met, an attitude that did nothing to enhance his popularity.

He came to California in the early 1850s, while still in his teens, from some city in the Northeast, obviously lured by the gold rush, which had started a few years earlier. He searched for gold in the Mother Lode country of north-central California, and it is known that he found a small vein near Volcano that he worked for about a year before he sold it.

He next turned up in Nevada where he reportedly found silver near Austin. The lode proved more profitable than the gold vein he had found in California, and Lee managed to do a considerable amount of high living in Austin before this section of the country palled. Again he sold out and this time drifted into the eastern part of Southern California. In Barstow he met an attractive Indian lass who apparently was more impressed by his size than she was repelled by his smell. They married and moved to San Bernardino, where Lee bought a house to live in when he was not prospecting. It was in San Bernardino that he met Waterman.

Waterman was the exact opposite of Lee. Dapper, well groomed, and highly articulate, it is unlikely that the two men would have nodded toward each other, had not Waterman been a politician. They met in a saloon where Lee was spending heavily and, as usual, talking loudly. The subject of Lee's discourse was a silver lode he had discovered earlier in the week. To most of the saloon patrons, Lee was a bore. He talked too loudly to be believed, and he had exhausted his subject matter.

In Waterman, however, Lee found an attentive and sympathetic listener. In the haze of good whiskey, Lee's suspicious nature was dulled. As the evening progressed, he decided that he had at long last found a true friend. Before Lee stumbled home to his patient wife, he had agreed to sell Waterman a half-interest in his newly discovered mine, and told him it was located about two miles north of present-day Barstow in the Red Mountains. The two men also agreed upon a name for their property. They would call it the Pencil Lead Mine.

The air of camaraderie between the two continued into the following week. When Waterman suggested that he be taken out to the lode before he paid the money for the half-interest, Lee agreed. A couple of days later, the two men rode out to the find. Waterman left Lee at the site and returned to San Bernardino with some ore samples. An assay disclosed that the ore tested even higher than Lee had indicated.

What happened next is something of a mystery. Some sources contend that Lee had never filed his claim—that he had gotten drunk, forgotten to do it, and after he became sober, thought that he had. Other sources say that Waterman arranged to have Lee's claim disappear from the records. In either event, the Pencil Lead Mine was registered as the sole claim of Robert W. Waterman.

When Lee returned to San Bernardino about two weeks later, he brought with him four pack mules laden with silver ore. He could find no trace of his new friend, but it is unlikely that he conducted much of a search for him. The ore was assayed at almost twice the value of the first samples he had brought back, and he gloated in one saloon that it was lucky he had not signed an agreement to sell a half-interest in his mine to Waterman. The mine was twice as valuable as he had first thought, Lee bragged, and so, friend or no friend, Waterman would just have to come up with twice as much cash for his half-interest.

Two weeks later, Lee departed once again for his mine. He was prepared for a long stay, for this time he brought with him twelve pack mules and provisions sufficient to last six weeks. His stay, however, was exceedingly brief. As he pulled up to his claim he was met by three men carrying rifles. One of them pointed with the muzzle of his gun toward a sign which warned against trespassing.

"It's my claim," Lee said carefully. "I've got it registered all proper."

"Not this one, you don't," one of the armed men replied. "You'd better go back and look."

"If it ain't mine, then whose is it?"

"Bob Waterman's," the gunman said.

Lee, understandably, was furious, but there was nothing he could do with three armed men facing him. He found out a short time later that there was nothing he could do in San Bernardino either. The claim was legally registered in Waterman's name. Waterman could not be found. Lee went to the sheriff to report the claim jumping. The law enforcement official was sympathetic, but pointed out that the claim legally was Waterman's. He said also that Waterman had complained to him about the theft of silver ore from the Pencil Lead Mine and identified Lee as the principal suspect.

The prospector next went to an attorney who told him also that he had no recourse legally. He recommended that Lee abandon his announced plans of hiring some gunslingers to re-take the claim by force.

The irascible prospector told his story loudly and often around the San Bernardino taverns, but because of his manner and his general unpopularity, he found few sympathizers. Word of Lee's constant complaint, however, did come to Waterman's attention, irritating him to the point where he re-acted by filing a suit for slander against Lee.

Instead of shutting up, Lee was delighted. "When we get to court, I'll prove he is a crook," he boasted happily.

A few weeks later, Waterman dropped the suit. The feud, however, continued. Lee made his accusations against Waterman repeatedly and monotonously to anyone who would listen. Apparently the only person who paid any attention to him was Waterman, who was becoming increasingly angry. "Lee will have to be taught a lesson," he told a friend. "I have just about reached the end of my patience."

Lee, meanwhile, had just about reached the end of his

bankroll. He resumed his prospecting, but was never gone for more than a couple of weeks. When he was in San Bernardino he did not let up in his harangue against Waterman.

About a year after his claim at the Pencil Lead Mine had been jumped, Lee found another lode. The ore that he brought back to the assayer had an even higher silver content than that of his previous discovery. Word of his strike spread quickly around the city. "I ain't goin' to register it here," Lee announced in one of the taverns. "Bob Waterman's just waiting to steal another one like he stole the Pencil Lead Mine."

A short time later, Lee rode into Los Angeles where the only man whom Lee considered trustworthy lived. Lee's friend was a crippled assayer named Sam Stewart, a man confined to a wheelchair as the result of a gun duel a few years earlier. Ever since the accident Stewart had kept a finely detailed diary of each day's activities.

"George Lee came into the office after the noon meal," Stewart wrote. "He has made a very good strike near Old Woman Springs and he wanted to register his claim here. He doesn't have any faith in San Berdoo [sic] officials because they erased his claim on the Pencil Lead. I told him that he would have to register his new claim in San Berdoo because that is where Old Woman Springs is. I told him to bring along a witness and demand a certified copy of the filing, but he thinks he can still be swindled. He smelt bad."

Lee decided not to register his new claim, preferring to protect his find by keeping its location secret. The prospector could not refrain from boasting about his strike, however.

For the next several months he would bring in his mules laden with silver ore, then in the bars he would boast that his new strike was so rich that soon he would have silver doorknobs and silver stairs in his home. He also stated loudly to all

302

within hearing distance that his mine's location was a secret because otherwise it would be stolen by Bob Waterman. On one occasion, when told he was wrong about Waterman, Lee replied that at least twice he had been followed as far as Old Woman Springs by Hans Hoffman, one of the gunman who had driven Lee away from the Pencil Lead Mine. This charge was remembered by many in the ensuing weeks.

On a Monday morning, Lee once again left San Bernardino en route to his secret mine. The following morning, two horsemen, whose names have been lost in history, approached Old Woman Springs. Before they entered the grove of eucalyptus and willows that surrounded the spring, a horse and rider raced out of the grove and headed north toward Barstow.

Near the spring, the travelers found a man lying on the ground, a large bloodstained rock in his hand. At first, they thought the man was dead, but when they dismounted they could see no signs of injury other than blood on his shirt. He was breathing, and as one of the travelers bent over him, he smelled fumes of whiskey, and realized the man was dead drunk. A few minutes later, they discovered another body. It had been dragged under a willow tree. This man was quite dead. The back of his skull had been battered to a pulp. The two travelers proceeded to tie up the unconscious drunk, then one galloped to San Bernardino to notify the sheriff while the other remained behind to guard the murder suspect.

It was a long day for the unidentified traveler. About noon the drunk sobered up enough to ask for another drink and then fell asleep again before the request could be granted. The traveler looked around for horses on which the murderer and his victim could have arrived. At the eastern end of the large grove he found three hobbled mules under some cottonwood trees.

303

Shortly before dusk Sheriff John Buckhart and three deputies arrived at Old Woman Springs. The suspect was awake and begging for a drink.

"What's your name?" Buckhart asked.

"Hoffman. Hans Hoffman."

The sheriff pointed with his thumb toward the body. "Why did you kill him?"

Hoffman shook his head and swallowed rapidly.

"You want a drink?"

Hoffman nodded and a tear rolled out of an eye. "It's a mistake," he said. "Waterman just wanted him beat up until he told us where his lode was."

"Who is he?"

"George Lee."

Hoffman's horse had run away, so Hoffman was tied on one of Lee's mules and Lee's body was slung over another mule.

As the sheriff and his deputies were preparing to leave, they heard the sound of galloping horses approaching the springs. It was dark and cloudy and the new arrivals were well into the grove before they were aware that anyone was there. Then someone cried out. The group turned their mounts, ignoring Buckhart's shout to halt. One shot was fired. One of the newcomers screamed and fell from his saddle. Still holding his gun, the sheriff walked over to his victim. He had been shot in the leg. Buckhart struck a match. He did not have to ask who this man was. He was Regis Brown, a sometimes bodyguard for Robert Waterman and foreman of his ranch in Barstow.

Hoffman was charged with murder. Some of the best legal talent in the state appeared in San Bernardino as Hoffman's defense attorneys, and it was acknowledged that the fees were being paid by Waterman. Hoffman changed his story. His defense was that Lee attacked him when they happened to run into each other at Old Woman Springs. The sheriff testified about the admission Hoffman had made while he was first interrogated at the grove. The first trial set a record for longevity in San Bernardino, lasting for more than six months. It finally was declared a mistrial when the jury hung eleven to one for conviction. A second trial followed. This was of a much shorter duration, but the results were the same as the first one; a hung jury voting eleven to one for conviction.

After this, Hoffman was released under $15,000 bail while awaiting his third trial. Two days after he was released, he vanished permanently.

Lee's wife then sued Waterman for damages resulting from her husband's death and won a judgment for $300,000, an incredibly large sum a century ago. As soon as this case was concluded, Waterman was sued again, this time by his own brother. This suit contended that Waterman had cheated the brother out of his third-interest in the Pencil Lead Mine. The brother died before the case was brought to trial, but the suit was continued successfully by his heirs who were awarded a third of the mine's profits by a sympathetic jury.

Waterman continued on with a successful political career despite his adversities in the San Bernardino courts. In 1886 he ran for lieutenant governor of California and was elected. The following year he became governor when the incumbent, Washington Bartlett, died.

George Lee's lost silver lode near Old Woman Springs has never been found. Searchers quite possibly have been confused over a switch in names. Several years ago someone decided that the name Old Woman Springs was too parochial for such a beautiful spot and the name was changed to Cottonwood Springs. Another few years passed. A rancher decided it was a pity that the colorful names of the Old West were disappearing. He named some springs on his property Old Woman Springs.

The Old Woman Springs on a present-day map are not the Old Woman Springs where the irascible George Lee was slain a hundred years ago. He died in Cottonwood Springs, and it is near there that the rich silver lode might be found.

LOST GOLD
IN UTAH

When Brigham Young led his flock of persecuted Mormons from Nauvoo, Illinois, to the West, and came to the shores of the Great Salt Lake, historians assert that he exclaimed: "This is the place." The temporary site of the Mormon Church became the site of present-day Salt Lake City.

It is unlikely that the Mormon pioneer knew at the time that Spanish explorers had said a similar thing a couple of centuries earlier when they arrived in the area and found one of the more productive gold mines in the North American hemisphere. When Brigham Young did find the gold mine, however, he quickly spread the word among the faithful to warn prospectors in the area to keep away.

"We cannot eat silver and gold. Neither do we want to bring into our peaceful settlements a rough frontier population to violate the morals of our youth, overwhelm us by numbers, and drive us again from our hard-earned homes," he announced.

The fabulous missing mine has had a variety of names: the Indian, the Ute, the Walker, the Spanish, the Mormon, the Rhodes, and the Brigham Young. The last name is the most common, probably because he was the last man to work the mine.

The Spanish were the first, and once the gold was discovered, they worked the mines in the customary Spanish -manner. Soldiers rounded up hundreds of Ute Indians and forced them to work in the mine as slaves. Unlike some Indian tribes farther to the south, the Utes were not docile, and they did not succumb to the blandishments or threats from the priests brought in to rule them. A state of continual warfare existed between the Utes and the Spaniards for almost two decades in the mid-seventeenth century, when the mine was first operative. For every Spanish soldier killed, however, a dozen Utes died, primarily from overwork and malnutrition.

The ore was packed out only twice a year because of the severe winter weather at high altitudes and the extreme heat at the lower levels. During the late spring and early fall an extraordinarily large mule train, heavily guarded by Spanish soldiers, would take the long trek to Sonora where the ore was smelted.

In the spring of 1680, about two days after the ore train had set out on its semiannual southern journey, it was attacked by a large band of Utes, and every soldier and Spaniard in the convoy was slain. The ore was spilled along the trail and approximately one hundred mules were herded into Ute corrals. A couple of days later the same band of Utes successfully raided the mining camp, killing all the Spaniards. Their bodies were thrown into the mine shafts and the openings were blocked with debris. There remained only a mopping-up operation. In the early fall the northbound mule train was ambushed about a day's journey from the mine, and the Utes left no survivors. Legend tells that the Spanish twice tried to reopen the mine, but on both occasions met the same fate as the other Spaniards. The Utes had no use for the gold, but from one generation to

308

the next they told each other of the location of the mine and of the white man's greed for the precious metal.

The Mormons' attitude toward the Indians was much different from that of the Spanish. They called the Indians "Larnanites," believing them all to have had common ancestors originating in Jerusalem in 600 B.C., and the Book of Mormon teaches that American Indians are descended from the lost tribes of Israel. The Utes did not subscribe particularly to this concept of their origin, but they approved of the Mormons' belief in it because it resulted in the most harmonious relation they ever had experienced with white men. Instead of being attacked, they were fed. Rather than being forced into slave labor, they were paid in goods such as clothing and livestock. The Mormons were not prospectors. Their collective efforts were directed toward colonizing, cultivating, and proselytizing. But eventually Brigham Young discovered that he needed gold.

Within a few years of the founding of Salt Lake City, the migration to the West prompted by the California Gold Rush was gathering momentum. Many of the wagon trains came through the Mormon State of Deseret and stopped to rest in Salt Lake City.

The wagon trains often carried manufactured goods and supplies needed by the Mormon community. Some pioneers would trade for foodstuffs. Others, of a more commercial mind, would insist upon gold or cash in payment. On one occasion, a Ute Indian overheard a traveler demanding only gold in payment for some shovels. A short time later, a Ute chief named Walkero visited Brigham Young. He carried with him several "chunks" of the almost pure gold. Because of the Mormons' demonstrated friendship with the Utes, Walkero said that he would disclose to Young the location of a gold mine in the nearby mountains. This mine had been operated by other white men many years ago, but they had been driven away by the Utes.

There was a conditional clause to Walkero's offer. Brigham Young would have to arrange for the mining to be done only by Mormons, and the mine's location would be kept a secret from all but those actually engaged in the mining operation. The Mormons could be trusted, the Ute chieftain said, but other white men could not. The miners would be under the constant surveillance and protection of the Utes while they worked. In return for this the Mormons would agree to continue feeding any Ute Indian who was in need and came to Salt Lake City for help. Brigham Young thought the agreement a good one, and both he and Walkero sealed the oral contract with one hand upon the Book of Mormon.

Young was not greedy for gold. He wanted only enough to trade for supplies and he decided that it would require only the efforts of two men to gather this amount. Consequently, he summoned a man named Thomas Rhodes and his son, Caleb Baldwin Rhodes, to his home. Here he swore them to secrecy, told them of the mine, then sent them off with Indian guides. When they returned several days later, their pack mule carried ore so pure that it almost could be used in its natural state. Caleb described it as "gold bearing rock rather than rock bearing gold." He mentioned also that the ore was taken from an existing mine.

Brigham Young wanted no gold rush to his State of Deseret, an occurrence that surely would have come to pass had he used gold ore and nuggets to purchase his supplies. He, therefore, built a small smelter and stamping press with which he issued gold currency from Deseret. Apparently, no one ever questioned him about the origin of the gold.

For approximately three years the arrangement with the

Utes worked smoothly. Then, two Utes stole a couple of horses from the Mormon settlement of Nephi. The Mormons took the incident much more seriously than did the Indians, and after catching one of the thieves, they tied him to a post and flogged him. The Utes took this as a collective insult and, in retaliation, they raided the communities of Springville, Pleasant Creek, Monti, and Nephi, stealing a large number of horses and cattle. The Mormon militia raced after the Utes, caught up with one band, and in the ensuing fight both sides suffered casualties.

Eventually Brigham Young and Chief Walkero met in Salt Lake City and made peace, but the relationship between the Mormons and the Utes was never again the same. Walkero rescinded his agreement to allow the Mormons access to the mine.

Some sources say that Caleb Rhodes occasionally slipped into the area and picked up a few nuggets, but he kept the secret of its location until shortly before his death. When he realized he was dying, he drew a crude map on a piece of buckskin. The map is so vague, it is almost worthless. A small lake is shown in the lower right-hand corner. Two lines labeled "trails" veer upward toward the right, then one makes a sharp angle to the left ending at a spot marked "gold." Three crosses in the center of the map are believed to designate a mountain range. On the left side of the buckskin is a curving line which is identified as "Rock Creek."

This map is still in existence, and there is strong evidence that it was drawn by Caleb Baldwin Rhodes. It was last known to be in the possession of a Utah mining prospector named Benjamin H. Bullock. A copy of the map appeared in the *Uintah Basin Standard* in its issue of July 10, 1958, along with a story of the mine and the following affidavits:

311

TO WHOM IT MAY CONCERN:

To the best of my knowledge, the following is a true history of the Rhodes Mine Map, a copy of which I have in my possession.

The original map from which I made this copy on paper was made on a small piece of buckskin about as large as one's hand and was owned by Ortiza Rhodes who was slain by Indians and robbed of his map. The Indians then brought it to Price, Utah, and traded it back to the Rhodes family.

Living with the Rhodes family at that time was a young man named Jake Colbert who got it from a member of the family. My husband, Warren Sulser, quite some time later, secured it from Mr. Colbert and I became its owner when Mr. Sulser passed away.

> (ss) Mrs. Mary Sulser Steele
> I am in my 85th year
> Witnesses:
> (ss) Ray D.Steele
> Ben H. Bullock

TO WHOM IT MAY CONCERN:

My stepfather, Frank Horsley, told me that he had personally seen Caleb Rhodes come into Price from his mine in the Uintah Mountains with a pack donkey loaded with a bag of rich gold ore on each side; and that he had personally taken some of the ore from the bags and examined it with his hands.

> Signed and witnessed at Goshen,
> Utah, this 18th day of June, 1958
> Mrs. Mary Sulser Steele
> I am in my 85th year
> Witness:
> Ray D. Steele

If Bullock ever found the lost mine, he has kept its discovery a secret. Shortly before Bullock collected his affidavits, however, there is a possibility that a Salt Lake City hunter named Clark M. Rhoades may have stumbled on it accidentally. His discovery was kept secret for more than a decade until it was revealed by his son, Gale, writing in the July/August 1967 edition of *Desert* magazine.

In the late fall of 1956, Rhoades was deer hunting in an area east of Heber City in the Uintahs. When he came across some fresh bobcat tracks in the snow, he followed them to the animal's den. The wildcat's lair was one of two very old mine shafts. At this time, Rhoades did not enter either shaft because the snow inside was deep; he had no flashlight and no desire to tangle with bobcats in the dark.

During the following summer, however, he returned to the area. The bobcats were gone, so he was able to study the mine shafts more carefully. He decided they had been deliberately filled-in years earlier or had collapsed during the passage of time. Outside the shaft he found three or four old Spanish shoulder yokes that had been used to haul ore up from the shafts. He also gathered up several ore samples from the ground which, when assayed, disclosed a heavy gold and silver content. He made no attempt to dig in the shafts for fear the blockage covered a much larger shaft into which he could easily fall.

Gale Rhoades visited the area again in 1964. He describes it as being located only a mile and a half up a mountain. He discovered that the shafts were connected about twenty feet from the entrances and, like many other Spanish mines, the shafts had been constructed in such a manner that steps had been formed near the top. The blockage in one shaft was about ninety feet down, and about an additional thirty feet in the

313

other shaft. Cautiously, he started to dig in the deepest shaft. About three feet down he uncovered a hoisting brace, grooved from the burn of ropes. He also discovered that the dirt was becoming softer, indicating that the mine had been deliberately plugged, and posing the threat of collapse. Rather than risk a possible fall of hundreds of feet, Rhoades reluctantly abandoned his excavations.

If someone finds the time and a way to safely dig through the plugs, it should be easy to determine whether or not this is the lost Brigham Young—Rhodes, Walker, Spanish, Mormon, Ute—mine. If there are a large number of skeletons in the bottom of the shafts, then it is the lost mine where the Spaniards were buried.

There is an interesting companion story to this legend of the lost Spanish mine in Utah. The United States Army spent more than three years looking for it, not because it wanted the money, but because it wanted to destroy the Mormon hierarchy. In 1862 an egotistical U.S. Army general named Patrick E. Conner arrived in Utah with a detachment of California volunteers, and established Fort Douglas, east of Salt Lake City. Conner was unable to find any signs of plural marriage. This, plus the lack of proper deference shown him by Mormon leaders, quickly engendered a hatred on his part for all Mormons.

He knew that Brigham Young had knowledge of and access to an abundant gold mine, but no matter how much he threatened and blustered, he could not get a clue from the wily religious leader as to its location. The general then tried to break the Mormon control of the territory by spreading word that the area was indeed rich in silver and gold. He detailed his troops to prospecting duty and organized mining districts in the Jordan and Tooele valleys. He hoped to trigger a gold rush that would fill the area with prostitutes, miners, and gamblers, thus forcing the Mormons into a minority status. He circulated tracts, at government expense, pointing to the evidence of mineral resources in the territory and the great opportunities for those "opening up the country to a new, hardy, industrious population." There were few takers because none of his soldiers found any gold or silver or the fabulous lost Spanish Mine.

The failure of his first tract prompted the circularization of a more inflammatory one, again printed and distributed with the use of military funds.

> My policy is to invite hither a large Gentile population sufficient by peaceful means and through the ballot box to overwhelm the Mormons by force of numbers and thus wrest from the church, disloyal and traitorous to the core, the absolute control of temporal and civic affairs. With this in view, I have bent every energy, both personal and official, toward the discovery and development of the mining resources of the Territory using without stint the resources of every soldier of my command.

Conner also posted a reward of $5,000 for information resulting in the discovery of the lost Spanish Mine. There are unconfirmed reports that on two occasions, a Ute Indian actually collected the reward, then slipped away from Conner and his troops while "leading" them to the location.

The general finally was recalled to Washington and promoted to some obscure post. The transcontinental railroad, when it was joined at Promontory Point north of Salt Lake City in 1869, did open up Utah's ranges to mining. Gold, silver, copper, lead, and later uranium were found in the mountains, but the old Spanish Mine still is missing.

MASSACRE IN SAN MIGUEL

The Mission of San Miguel, the Archangel, located about nine miles above Paso Robles on the central California coast, is the site of one of the most grisly mass murders in the state's history. The murderers were looking for gold. They did not find it at the mission, and neither has anyone else.

San Miguel Mission was founded by Father Fermin Lasuen on July 25, 1797, the sixteenth in the series of missions built a day's journey apart in California. The small mud-roofed church, which was replaced by a larger building the following summer filled in the gap between the missions at San Antonio and San Luis Obispo. In the ensuing nine years the mission grew into a complex of several buildings including granaries and workshops, which were the center of a village of more than one thousand inhabitants.

In 1806 a disastrous fire raged through the mission, razing all of the buildings except for a part of the original church. More than six thousand bushels of grain and almost a decade's

317

accumulation of hides, wool, and cloth were destroyed. Help was sent to San Miguel from other missions, and within a year the mission, except for the church, was again operating normally. When the time came to rebuild the mission, the padres wanted a structure that would be permanent, one with a tiled roof and thick, fireproof adobe walls. It took eight years to gather the tile and make the adobe bricks and another two years to build the church. It was during this period that New Spain broke away from Spain and proclaimed itself the Republic of Mexico.

Independence had a far-reaching effect upon all of the California missions. Funds and supplies for the missions no longer came from Mexico City. The missions not only had to support themselves, but also the colonists and soldiers within their territories. Eventually, the Mexican government initiated long-delayed orders to secularize the missions.

The theory behind secularization was that the missions had completed their assignment to civilize the Indians and now could be replaced by a more politically manageable system of pueblos.

San Miguel was the last of the California missions to be secularized. The order for confiscation was signed by Governor Pio Pico in the capital at Monterey in August 1834. For the next decade, San Miguel was operated by a succession of bureaucrats. The livestock disappeared. The Indians drifted away. Eventually there was no one to grow the corn for the granaries. The mission was abandoned, except for a couple of priests. Three days before California was surrendered to the United States in 1846 at Monterey, Governor Pico sold the entire mission, except for the priests' quarters and the church, to an English adventurer named William Reed. The total price for the property was 300 pesos, or less than $250.

Bill Reed was a tall and handsome man who had arrived in California as a seaman some two years earlier and had jumped ship in Monterey. There he married Maria Antonia Vallejo. When his wife's uncle, Petronillo Rios, suggested to Reed that they go into partnership, buy the mission, and use it as a headquarters for a hacienda and also as a commercial center, Reed thought the idea an excellent one. The ranching part of the operation complemented the general store. Indians returned to work, and Reed and Rios prospered, then grew rich as gold miners swept into California.

The former mission was approximately halfway between Los Angeles and San Francisco, and it was a perfect stopping place for travelers journeying between the two cities. Reed sold them lodging, board, and provisions and would take only gold in payment. He called the money that the miners paid him his very own "lode." The usual reticence attached to the English was not a part of the cocky Reed's character. He overstated rather than understated. On one occasion he announced that he had paid 300,000 pesos for the mission and that he had recouped his investment within the first year. Understandably, Reed was a strong Anglophile, and on those occasions when an Englishman would chance through San Miguel, he usually was given the hospitality of the house on a complimentary basis.

There were no banks in San Miguel and Reed often commented that he did not need one; that he had found a hiding place for his mounting hoard of gold that defied detection. The size of his "lode" varied in his stories and, because of this, there were many who discounted the existence of any hoard at all. There were others who knew better. They knew the prices Reed charged could not bring anything other than huge profits. These were the people who noticed the bulging chamois bag of twenty-dollar gold pieces that Reed carried with him. Often, near the end of a week, when the bag became too full to hold another coin, Reed would leave the mission and return ten minutes later. The bag would be empty save for a few small coins needed for change. Reed would make no secret of where he had been. "Had to go out to my safe and add a little more to the lode," he said more than once. "I'm different from most of the miners. I put my gold back into the ground instead of taking it out."

On occasion, he would be followed when he left the saloon, but always sensing when this was happening he would turn back.

For five years Reed and Rios prospered. By that time Reed had a four-year-old son named Petronillo, a daughter named Concepción, and another baby on the way. Reed and his family lived with six servants in a large building adjacent to the mission, a former warehouse that he had remodeled into a comparatively luxurious home.

One cool winter afternoon five men rode into San Miguel from the north. They were not used to horses, and if the animals had been anything other than broken-down nags, the strangers would obviously have been unable to remain mounted. Reed watched them bounce up to the mission. His first impulse was to refuse them entrance. He quickly changed his mind, however, when one spoke to him. His accent was British, a lower-class cockney but, nevertheless, British. The other strangers spoke with the same accent as they slid down from their horses. Reed immediately welcomed his fellow countrymen and escorted them inside.

He fed them and gave them drinks, and as the liquor mellowed the strangers' tongues, Reed discovered that they were all British seamen who had deserted their ship in Monterey. They had "found" the horses all saddled outside a saloon and did not appear concerned when Reed told them that this might be considered a hanging offense if they were caught. One of the sailors, however, as a precaution, went outside and turned the animals loose, but the tired horses remained at the hitching post.

As the evening wore on, Reed confided to his newly found friends that he also had jumped ship in Monterey. He told them also of the fortune he had made in only five years. He showed them his chamois bag, heavy with gold, and repeated his tired joke of putting the gold back into the ground rather than taking it out.

"Where?" asked one of the sailors.

Reed smiled and shook his head. Another of the sailors stood up and walked behind Reed. The tavern was now deserted but for the English.

"Where?" asked the sailor again.

"That's a family secret," replied Reed, still apparently unaware of his danger. His choice of words was tragic.

"Then we'll ask your family," the sailor replied. The man standing in back of Reed pulled a dirk from its scabbard and plunged it into Reed's neck killing him instantly.

Reed's murder was the start of an insane, drunken slaughter. The quintet raced to Reed's bedroom where they woke the pregnant Maria. They demanded to know the hiding place of the gold, and when Maria screamed that she did not know, she was stripped, raped, and then stabbed to death.

The other victims of the gang murderers were killed because they might identify the killers. They included everyone staying in the mission and the Reed house. The next two to die were Concepción and the young Petronillo, followed in rapid succession by a midwife, her married daughter and grandchild, a servant and her son, a sheepherder, his wife and child, and another servant. The death toll was thirteen.

In a smaller house, a few hundred yards from the mission and the Reed house, lived Ramón Rodriguez with his wife and two sons, aged eight and four. When the screams of the killings awakened him, he immediately sent his family to hide in a growth of tall mustard weed that covered several acres nearby. He then crept up to the mission, keeping out of sight in the shadows. He saw one of the sailors carrying the nude body of Maria into the tavern. Rodriguez then took off at a dead run for the ranch of James M. Price, some three miles away. One of the sailors heard his running steps and started in pursuit, but could not match the fleet Rodriguez.

The sailor returned to the tavern, gathered together his companions, and within a few minutes they were on the trail headed south. Rodriguez heard them as they passed him in the dark.

Price and a friend, F.Z. Branch, returned to the mission with Rodriguez about an hour later. Twelve of the bodies were lying on the floor of the tavern. The body of the sheepherder had been dropped just outside the door. Oil-soaked straw and rags had been set afire inside the tavern, but had burned out too quickly to set fire to the structure.

The three men rounded up a posse and took off in the morning. Rodriguez accompanied the posse despite the fact that his four-year-old son had become lost during the night. The search for the killers went on for days. The posse was made up of experienced horsemen who either did not know or did not take into account the fact that the men they sought could only cover a few miles before being forced to rest.

The posse had almost reached Santa Barbara when they decided that the murderers had escaped. On their way back to

322

San Miguel, however, they ran headlong into the killers near what is now Guadalupe. Somehow the posse had passed its quarry during the chase.

During their flight the sailors had picked up sidearms, but they were slow in drawing them. They apparently had not anticipated a posse coming from the south. The gunfight was brief. When it was over, three men were dead. One sailor was fatally shot, another drowned when his horse bolted into the sea. The third victim was a member of the posse, Ramón Rodriguez. The body of his four-year-old son was found a few months later in the mustard weed near the mission, raising the total death toll to seventeen, including the two sailors.

The three surviving sailors did not live long. They were taken to Santa Barbara where they confessed, were tried, and hanged.

After the Reed massacre, San Miguel Mission slowly deteriorated. Finally, on the verge of collapse, the mission was returned to the church by court order in 1859, but it was not for another nineteen years, in 1878, that the church was reactivated. Some of the buildings were restored at this time, and a few more were rebuilt in 1901. The Franciscans assumed control in 1928 and used it for a parish church and monastery. Today it is open to the public.

The bodies of eleven of the victims of the Reed massacre are buried in one grave near the rear door of the mission sacristy. What happened to the other two bodies is a mystery. Also a mystery is the location of Reed's "lode," where he put his gold back into the earth.

THE LOST EVANGELISTS

There are many tales of lost missions, and in many cases there are records to substantiate them. One of them, possibly the Santa Isabel, was found, photographed, and then lost again. Another, the San Dionysius, appears on several old maps, but although its location is known exactly, no trace of it exists today.

One of the more intriguing of the lost-mission legends involves the Mission of the Four Evangelists. If there is written record of this mission, it has been lost in the files of the diocese in Guadalajara. Perhaps the mission was officially given a name other than the one it is called today by the Papago Indians. What makes the Mission of the Four Evangelists so intriguing is that periodically over the centuries it reappears briefly and that less than half a day's journey from it lies a fortune of gold buried beneath the skeletons of two Papago Indians.

The Mission of the Four Evangelists probably was located on the shores of the Laguna Prieta somewhere between Tinajas Altas on the Arizona-Mexican border and the tiny town of El Doctor on the southern fringe of the Gran Desierto in Mexico. A railroad line cuts through this vast North American Sahara from Caborca on the southeast to Mexicali on the northwest. The only other thoroughfare through this devastating wasteland is the old Camino del Diablo that stretches from Sonoyta to San Luis, a small border town a short distance south of Yuma, Arizona.

Two small bodies of water interrupt the endless miles of desert sand. One is a series of three pools, known colloquially as tanks, located in a jumble of large boulders high above the highway on the northern flank of the desert. This place is named Tinajas Altas. Its cavities, eroded in granite strata one above the other, catch the runoff from rare rains and a spring that functions sporadically. The other body of water is the Laguna Prieta, a brackish lake surrounded by fresh water seeps lying in the middle of naked sand dunes. Various maps show different locations for Laguna Prieta, but most cartographers place it about fifteen miles east and eight miles south of San Luis. Explorers have gone here, however, and found not a trace of Laguna Prieta or the lost mission.

One explanation for its elusiveness is the phenomenon of the "walking hills" that surround it. Rising as high as three hundred feet above the desert floor, the sand dunes change their shape and size with each passing gust of wind. Within each of these hills there is a "heart." It may be a root or a rock, or a lost mission, but there is always a barrier to collect the windblown grains of sand. These particles of sand accumulate in hills that grow larger and larger. Then a fierce desert windstorm will lift the sand from one side of the dune and sweep it over the top to the other. When the storm subsides, the dune has taken on another shape. Often the "heart" of the dune is exposed briefly. This is why the Mission of the Four Evangelists and Laguna Prieta suddenly reappear. They disappear again as the winds slowly cover them up with sand.

The most recent sighting was made from the air in 1970 by a student pilot, Masa Nakagawa, of Los Angeles, while on a cross-country solo flight. He became lost, veered to the south, and inadvertently flew into Mexico. He descended to a low altitude to get his bearings and soon, after deciding that he was too far to the south, noticed a belfry tower jutting out of the sand. He circled it a couple of times before heading north. When he landed at Tucson later, he reported the sighting, but no one had heard of a lost church.

"It was one of the times I have regretted being one of those rare Japanese who is not permanently attached to a camera," Nakagawa said.

The only known sighting of the Mission preceding Nakagawa's experience occurred in 1915 when it was rediscovered by a band of Papago Indians. The story was told by the late Juan Orosco of Quitobaquito who, at the time, was a youth of fifteen living with his family on the banks of the Colorado River. Late one afternoon a white man stumbled into the Papago village. He said he had been prospecting in an area about thirty miles away and, after deciding to move on, had packed his gear on his mule. The mule had bolted and disappeared. The Orosco family took the prospector into their home, fed him, and let him rest for a couple of days.

When they awoke on the third morning their guest was gone. A short time later the Oroscos discovered that one of their best horses, a saddle, and a rifle were also missing. In something of a switch on the usual chase in the Old West, a posse of Indians was rounded up, including fifteen-year-old Juan, and the band set off in pursuit of the felonious prospector.

In the early stage of the pursuit they followed his tracks easily. He had headed in a straight line into El Gran Desierto.

326

In the forenoon, however, the wind came up, blowing sand into the fugitive's tracks and obliterating them. By noon the winds had reached gale proportions, whipping up a stinging sand blizzard.

The Papagos, who knew the desert well, decided to abandon the chase. Putting the storm at their backs they headed north toward Quitobaquito. A short time later, as the posse struggled over a particularly large dune, the wind suddenly died. Then, as they crossed over the dune, they saw through the haze the belfry of the Mission of the Four Evangelists. It jutted up from the desert floor near the bottom of the next dune. The Indians did not pause. They all knew the story of the lost mission, but they also knew that the lull in the wind could be temporary, and their primary concern was to get out of the desert.

Upon their return to the Colorado River camp, however, they told of their discovery, and word eventually reached a priest named Father Paul Kelley in Yuma. The priest went to their camp and attempted to enlist an expedition to take him to the site. He abandoned the project, however, after the Indians convinced him that the mission would have once again sunk beneath the desert sands.

The story of the lost mission is best told by the Papagos:

Many years ago there had been a large oasis at the site. It had been protected for centuries by small mountains that rose to a low elevation on three sides of it. There was a spring in the center of this oasis which the Papagos called Open Jaw, and the area was extensive enough to support a village of more than five hundred Papagos.

Then the Spanish arrived, including a detachment of soldiers and about a dozen priests. The strangers were made welcome. The soldiers dug in the earth of the mountain and found traces of gold, enough so that when the detachment moved on, they left behind two priests and a half-dozen soldiers. The priests taught the Papagos a new religion, how to make adobe bricks from the earth of the mountain, and how to dig out the gold. The soldiers devoted their time to making sure that the Indians were attentive pupils.

From the moment of the strangers' arrival, however, trouble seemed to appear in the village. The level of the spring became lower, and three years passed without a drop of rain. Some of the Indians attempted to explain to the priests that they were using too much water in their placer mining (a process by which water is used to separate the heavier particles of gold from the lighter gravel), but the padres would not listen or did not understand. The mining continued and a church was built. Two more priests arrived on the day the church was completed, and they brought with them a small bell that was hung in the belfry of the new building. At first the new church was called the Mission of the Four Padres, but a short time later was changed to the Mission of the Four Evangelists.

As the drought continued, the mountains, which were nothing more than huge piles of gold-bearing dirt, began to erode. At the same time the spring became so low that there was not enough water to support the village and the mining. Gradually the Papagos began to slip away, heading for other villages. Then the sand from the desert began to blow in on the oasis. The mining stopped. Two of the priests left, leaving behind only six soldiers to guard the other two.

One morning the remaining Papagos awoke to find the priests, the soldiers, and two more members of their village gone. Also missing was a large amount of gold that had been stored in the church. The Indians gathered together and

328

worked themselves into a collective rage. The Spaniards had been welcomed upon their arrival. The Papagos had accepted their religion, their authority, and had worked as slaves in their mines. In return their village had been destroyed, and they had been deserted. The Spaniards even had taken gold, which rightfully belonged to the Papagos.

Before the day was warm, the men of the village were on the warpath and in full pursuit of the Spaniards. They were more fortunate than their descendants who chased a prospector over the same route a few centuries later. The war party caught up with the fleeing Spaniards before noon. In the first skirmish the two Papagos, who had been impressed as porters to carry the gold, were killed. The Spanish paused long enough to bury the two Indians, then resumed their flight. About an hour later the Papagos attacked again. The two priests and one of the soldiers were killed in this attack. Before nightfall the Indians had killed all of the Spaniards.

When no trace of the gold could be found, the Papagos understood why the Spaniards had paused long enough to bury two Indians while the other bodies were abandoned where they fell. They knew the Spaniards were well aware of the Papago superstition that to disturb an Indian's grave is to bring down a curse of death. The perfect way to cache the gold until it could be recovered would be to leave it guarded by two Indian spirits. The gold surely had been placed in the grave before the corpses of the dead Indians.

The most recent known search for the Mission of the Four Evangelists was undertaken in 1964 by the Arizona adventurer John Powell. Alone and on foot, he traveled the desolate route from El Doctor to Camino del Diablo.

He estimated that his trip would take two days. On the evening of the first day he made camp at the base of one of the

329

sand mountains that hide the mission and Laguna Prieta. Writing of his experiences later in *Desert* magazine, Powell described his surroundings as "a silent, yellow sea of sand, billowing endlessly, and void of all life and movement." In the morning he found a fragment of a pottery olla, a clay water vessel, but the heat was too intense for him to linger in the area. He was virtually exhausted by the time he stumbled onto the paved highway after dark on the second evening where he was picked up by a friend. Later, he guessed that he had missed his projected route through the Gran Desierto by approximately twenty miles.

There is another version of the legend of the lost Mission of the Four Evangelists, an account that is accepted more easily on the northern than on the southern side of the United States-Mexico border. This tells the story of Don Padriac Odonoju, which is a loose Spanish interpretation of the name Patrick O'Donahue.

O'Donahue joined the Spanish in fighting the British in various naval encounters during the late seventeenth century. He was rewarded for his endeavors by the King of Spain with a Spanish name and a land grant in Papagueria, an area now known as the Altar Valley in southern Arizona. Although the grant of more than twelve leagues was in one of the most desolate areas of the Spanish New World, Don Padriac liked his new title and his surroundings.

He called his vast hacienda "The Garden of Solitude," and the mission he built near his ornate living quarters was called the "Mission of the Four Evangelists." Both the mission and Don Padriac's house were covered with gold mined by the Papagos in the nearby Baboquivari Range. Additionally, a fortune in gold bars was stored in the hacienda.

The end of Don Padriac's prosperous existence came suddenly one morning shortly before dawn. A band of Apaches descended upon the hacienda, killing everyone from the lowest Papago servant to Don Padriac. They left, taking only the horses, other livestock, and brightly colored cloths. They had no use for the gold.

Because of their superstition of the dead, other Papagos shunned the Garden of Solitude and over the years it gradually became engulfed by the "walking" sands.

The Mission of the Four Evangelists will be bared again briefly, be it on the shores of Laguna Prieta or in the Altar Valley. In either case, somewhere nearby will be the spirits of dead Papagos guarding a fortune in gold.

THE MURDER OF LEVI MACGRUDER

Hill Beachy was something of an enigma to his many friends in Lewiston, Idaho. To begin with, his name was considered strange. There were some who thought it was an assumed name, for Hill Beachy, like many other residents of the West in the mid-nineteenth century, was vague about his past. He arrived in Lewiston about 1860, when he was in his early thirties. He built a hotel in the booming town, which at that time was the closest supply center to the gold camps. At first he was considered a fop because of his elegant dress. Even in the mornings he would wear clean, white, starched shirts, and he owned enough suits to wear a different one each day for two months before repeating his attire.

The service in his hotel was superb. Bed linens were changed daily, even for semipermanent guests, and the cuisine

332

in his dining room was the finest to be found between San Francisco and Chicago.

Hill Beachy established himself as a leading citizen in Lewiston when he faced two gunmen in the saloon he owned adjacent to his hotel. No one could recall what started the dispute, but for approximately a quarter of an hour two hoodlums confronted each other at the bar with guns pointed at each other's midriff. The saloon emptied and one of the fleeing patrons ran to Hill Beachy with the news.

The proprietor rose from his desk and strode into the saloon, walking directly over to the two men. "I do not tolerate this kind of behavior in my place of business," he said quietly. "You both shall leave immediately."

"Listen to the dandy," one of the gunman said belligerently.

The bartender said later that Hill Beachy moved so quickly that for a second he was invisible. During that one second, the gunman who had sneered at Hill Beachy landed on the floor of the tavern with a broken arm and the gun he had been holding was in the clenched fist of the hotel proprietor. "Out," Hill Beachy told the other gunman. The man did not move. A split second later his gun went flying from his hand as Hill Beachy put a bullet in his arm. Hill Beachy then suggested for the second time that both men leave, a suggestion they followed with alacrity.

When word of this incident spread around Lewiston, Hill Beachy was shifted to another category. Instead of being thought of as the peculiar dandy who owned the hotel, he now was considered a prominent citizen of the community who certainly was entitled to his few eccentricities. Had he so wanted, he could have been elected mayor, a member of the town council, or sheriff, but Hill Beachy wanted nothing other than to operate his hotel. And this he did unobtrusively until 1863, when he took off on a six-month manhunt that would strain the imagination of even the most inventive Western Americana buff.

Hill Beachy's closest friend in Lewiston was Levi Mac-Gruder, a wealthy young trader who probably collected more gold from the camps in Idaho and Montana than many of the miners who worked them. MacGruder was married, but it is not known whether he had any children. When he was in town, many of his evenings were spent playing chess with Hill Beachy in the lobby of the hotel. The only place Hill Beachy would eat outside of his hotel was in MacGruder's home, and more often than not the finicky Beachy would arrive accompanied by a hotel busboy carrying dinner.

MacGruder's trading trips often involved excursions lasting more than three or four months. Early on the morning of August 3, 1863, MacGruder left Lewiston with a pack train of one hundred mules. His destination was Virginia City, Montana, more than 300 miles away, but his route there was not a direct one. He planned to trace a twisted path, hitting scores of mining camps between the two cities. As usual on these midsummer trips he was shorthanded. Mule skinners were hard to find when the weather was good, and they had been lured away by tales of new strikes in gold and silver.

MacGruder had been gone about two weeks when Hill Beachy received a letter from him, brought back to Lewiston by stagecoach. He wrote that he had been fortunate. On the third day out of Lewiston, his slow-moving train had been overtaken by a group of eight horsemen. One of them was Bill Page, a trapper and a scout known by MacGruder for a long time. He identified three others in the group as Jim Romaine, Dan Lowry, and Dave Howard, all who claimed to be from

334

Lewiston, but who were strangers to MacGruder. The men agreed to sign on the train as mule skinners until they reached Virginia City.

Hill Beachy received another letter from his friend around the first of October. This trip, he said, had been one of the most profitable he had ever undertaken. He had collected more than $30,000 in gold dust and an additional $20,000 in gold coins. Romaine, Lowry, Page, and Howard, along with his regular four mule skinners were returning to Lewiston with the pack train. He anticipated that the journey would be of short duration, providing the snows held off.

October passed the halfway mark and MacGruder had not arrived. There had been a fall blizzard that had delayed the stage for a couple of days, but this would not have delayed MacGruder for much more than the same length of time. Even if he had only averaged thirty miles a day, his arrival was seriously overdue. Hill Beachy saddled up his horse and went looking.

He assumed that MacGruder would follow the stage trail on his return trip, and so Hill Beachy followed this route to Virginia City. At each stage stop he inquired after his friend. Most of the operators at each depot knew Mac-Gruder. Hill Beachy could not find one stage operator in Idaho who had seen the pack train on its return trip until he got high up in the Bitter Root Mountains. Here the proprietor of the stage stop was positive that Levi MacGruder had passed early in October. Hill Beachy narrowed his search between the two stage depots, the one where his friend had been seen and the one he had failed to pass. He found no trace of Mac-Gruder. A lot of snow had fallen in the mountains, covering any clues that might have explained his friend's mysterious disappearance.

Reluctantly Hill Beachy returned to Lewiston. He was puzzled as well as worried. One hundred mules, nine horses, and nine men simply could not vanish without some explanation. If they had been ambushed by Indians, there surely would have been signs of the massacre remaining, which would have been seen by a passing stage. Besides, if the train had been attacked by Indians, MacGruder would have fought, and his men and mules would have scattered. MacGruder was carrying $50,000 in gold. Hill Beachy could not shake this thought.

A break in the mystery came about a week after Hill Beachy's return. A groom who worked in the livery stable that served the hotel guests came to see Hill Beachy in an excited state. "That man who just checked into the hotel is riding Mr. MacGruder's horse," he said.

MacGruder rode a large paint, distinctive because an almost exact copy of the map of Italy was etched in white along one side of the animal. The horse naturally was named Italy and, a short time later when Hill Beachy arrived in the stables, he responded to his name.

The stranger was in the dining room when Hill Beachy returned to the hotel. As the man had just started his dinner, Hill Beachy thought it a good time to search the man's room. He discovered that the man riding MacGruder's horse was a Methodist circuit rider from Boise. Hill Beachy sighed, returned to the dining room, and sat down across from the new arrival.

The traveling minister was nonplused. "I bought that horse from a livery in Walla Walla, Washington, about three weeks ago. I have a bill of sale."

The bill of sale appeared legitimate and Hill Beachy thought it unlikely that a man of the cloth had had anything to do with MacGruder's disappearance. The minister could tell him nothing more than that Italy was one of several horses the livery stable had had up for sale. Before the dinner was finished, the circuit rider no longer owned Italy. He had sold him, at a considerable profit, to Hill Beachy.

The following day Hill Beachy left Lewiston for Walla Walla, riding Italy. The livery-stable operator remembered the paint well. The horse was one of four animals he had purchased from four men early in October. The quartet had said they were miners who had struck it rich and were heading back home. The stable operator had not bothered to inquire where "home" was, but he had insisted upon a bill of sale for the animals. The bills of sale were signed respectively by William Page, D. C. Lowry, David Howard, and James Romaine.

"Did they buy any other horses?" Hill Beachy asked.

"Nope."

"Have you seen them around town?"

"Nope."

Hill Beachy went to the stage company. The four men had departed from Walla Walla by stage for Portland, Oregon, on October 14. He remained overnight in Walla Walla, writing several letters. One went to the sheriff in Lewiston asking that a warrant for the arrest of the four men be sent on to him in Portland. He also wrote to the governors of Washington, Oregon, and California, disingenuously identifying himself as a deputy sheriff and asking that the quartet be "requisitioned" for trial in Lewiston. In none of the letters did he mention a criminal act for which the men reportedly were under suspicion. The next morning, still riding Italy, Hill Beachy set out for Portland.

It was a long and cold journey, but Hill Beachy did not pause to rest once he had arrived in Portland. He picked up the trail immediately. Lowry, Howard, and Romaine had been big spenders while they were in the city. Page had been around, but had spent most of his time in the hotel room. He discovered that all four men had been booked on a coastal steamer for San Francisco, but only Page had shown up. At first Page had boarded the steamer, but then cancelled his passage a few minutes before the vessel sailed. His companions had missed the boat because they were drunk. Ten days before Hill Beachy's arrival in the river-port city, the four men had embarked on another coastal steamer for San Francisco.

Another steamer was not due in Portland for three weeks. Hill Beachy saddled up Italy and took off for San Francisco. The records do not report how long it took him to make the long and arduous trip to the city by the Golden Gate. It is known, however, that when he reached Yreka, not far from the Oregon border in California, he discovered there was a telegraphic link between Yreka and San Francisco. Again, identifying himself as a deputy sheriff, he wired the San Francisco police a description of the four men, which he had picked up in Walla Walla and Portland, along with a request that they be taken into custody. The San Francisco Police Department decided it needed something a little more authentic before launching a search.

When Hill Beachy arrived in San Francisco, the police were still reluctant to cooperate. He was accused of impersonating a peace officer, but no action was taken against him. The San Francisco police agreed to write to the police in Lewiston for confirmation that the four men sought by Hill Beachy were indeed fugitives. Hill Beachy wisely refrained from telling the San Francisco police that all the information the Lewiston sheriff had also came from him.

At this time, San Francisco was already a large city by

338

western standards. There were dozens of hotels and hundreds of boardinghouses in the city, any one of which could house his quarry. The arrival of four more free-spending miners would go unnoticed since the Barbary Coast was full of them.

Hill Beachy, however, was not a man to be easily discouraged. He started with the best hotel, the Palace, and learned that the four men had spent five days there, immediately after their arrival in the city. When they moved on, they had left no forwarding address. He scoured the hotels of the city. Two weeks later, Hill Beachy found William Page. He was living in a small hotel on lower California Street.

The encounter was not a dramatic one. When Hill Beachy asked at the desk for the four men by name, the clerk pointed to a man with an emaciated look sitting in one of the chairs in the lobby. "That's Page," the clerk said. "I don't have the others."

Page seemed relieved when Hill Beachy went over and quietly introduced himself. He told his story to the confidence-inviting hotelier in the lobby of the hotel. He had met his three companions about two weeks before they ran into MacGruder, who had just left Lewiston. All of them were amazed at the hoard of gold MacGruder accumulated as he sold off his wares and supplies. They originally had planned to travel with the mule train only as far as Virginia City. Shortly before they arrived, Page overheard Lowry and Romaine making plans to rob MacGruder. He was caught eavesdropping and was given the choice of participating in the robbery or being killed. Page decided that participation was the lesser of two evils. The four men then volunteered to continue on as mule skinners on the return trip to Lewiston, an offer which MacGruder accepted gratefully.

The night it was Page's turn to stand guard was chosen

as the time for the attack. Lowry killed MacGruder as he slept, striking him on the head with an axe. Romaine and Howard then slaughtered the four regular mule skinners in a similar fashion. One mule was selected to carry provisions and the gold. The other mules and extra horses were then driven over a high cliff into a deep ravine to their death. The bodies of the victims were tossed off the cliff along with the superfluous camping gear.

"How much of the money is left?"

Page shook his head. He had been given only $5,000 as his share. The $20,000 in gold coins was buried at the base of a bluff beside the stagecoach road about a day's ride out of Walla Walla. This had been Lowry's idea. By posing as miners, they could justify the possession of gold dust. But if the bodies were found immediately with the coins still in the bandits' possession, they would be automatically suspect, Lowry suggested, and his two friends agreed. Page added that he believed Lowry planned to return alone and pick up the gold coins.

The former trapper and scout seemed eager to accompany Hill Beachy to police headquarters and tell his story. This time the police listened. Later the same evening the police located Howard, Lowry, and Romaine and arrested them.

It is not known how the four murderers were returned to Lewiston. It is known, however, that they arrived on Christmas Eve, 1863, were tried the following month, and all except Page were hanged on March 4. Page was freed after he testified for the prosecution.

In May, a little more than two months after the triple execution, the snows had melted sufficiently to expose the bodies of the massacre victims and support the story told by

Page. The gold dust that was recovered from the highwaymen was given to MacGruder's widow. In June, Hill Beachy accompanied Page to the area where the $20,000 in gold coins had been buried. It was a futile trip. There were too many bluffs, and Page was confused. The former trapper died in Lewiston the following August.

Hill Beachy's efforts did not go unrewarded. The territorial legislature appropriated $6,244 to be paid to Hill Beachy as reimbursement for expenses incurred during his long pursuit of his friend's murderers.

The $20,000 in gold coins remains secreted at the base of a bluff on the old stage trail between Walla Walla, Washington, and Lewiston, Idaho, about a day's ride by horse outside the old city limits of Walla Walla.

THE LOST CABIN NUGGETS

One of the most spectacular and forbidding strings of mountain peaks in the United States is the Wind River Range in the northwest corner of the thinly populated state of Wyoming. The range of snow-capped peaks continues in a southeasterly direction from Yellowstone National Park and is adjacent to the more publicized Grand Tetons of Jackson Hole. Vast areas of the Wind River Range have never been explored by white men even though gold was discovered in this area more than seven years before the strike at Sutter's Creek triggered the gold rush to California.

Gold was first found in these mountains by a trapper from Georgia. His name has been lost in history, but the story most commonly told about him proves that he was not a greedy man. When he struck gold, he gathered up as many nuggets as he could carry and, with winter approaching, set out for the warmer clime of his native state. As he had no plans of ever returning to Wyoming, he made no secret of where he had found his gold. He was, however, rather vague in his directions, not intentionally, but because he had paid no attention to landmarks on his way out of the mountains.

He cashed in two of his nuggets in Fort Laramie, telling anyone interested where he had found them. By morning of the next day, a party of forty prospectors had been organized and was en route to the area. The following day, the commanding officer of the fort learned of the exodus and, for reasons never made public, sent a detachment of soldiers after the prospectors. The military confiscated all of the miners' equipment and forced them all back to Fort Laramie.

Many years later two of these prospectors who by then were semiretired told a young adventurer named Allan Hurlburt from Walla Walla, Washington, about their experiences. The tale of the homesick Georgian laden with nuggets, and the subsequent confrontation with the military intrigued Hurlburt. He pumped the two oldtimers for all the information they had. He then convinced two friends, Freitag and Smith, to accompany him on a search of the remote Wind River Range for the spot where gold nuggets were strewn around the ground like a sea of pebbles. His friends did not need much to convince them. Tales of fabulous lodes of gold around South Pass City had already reached Walla Walla. South Pass City now had a population of more than four thousand, despite the plethora of hostile Indians in the area. The Wind River Range was just to the west of South Pass City. With no more then these facts to go on, the heavily armed trio set out for what was then Dakota Territory.

The trip to South Pass City was uneventful. When they arrived, with the prospectors' customary reticence they indicated that they planned to look around the Sweetwater Range some miles to the east. They purchased three pack mules and enough supplies to last for several months.

For weeks they traveled up and down the sides of the mountains and through the steep canyons. Game was plentiful and even the sound of rifle shots failed to attract the attention of any hostile Indians. In late August they camped one night beside a small, swift-running stream. As Hurlburt bent over to scoop up some water for coffee, something flashed in the bottom of the stream. A moment later he had recovered a huge nugget of pure gold. The nuggets were not lying around like a sea of pebbles but, within the next hour, the three men found more than a dozen nuggets in the streambed. They obviously had been washed down from an extraordinarily rich vein higher up in the mountains.

For the next several days the men worked the stream on a share-and-share-alike principle, each night dividing the day's take as nearly as possible into three equal parts. After a little more than a week, however, the stream had been cleared of nuggets. Using the camping spot as a base, the three prospectors began working their way farther upstream, searching for the lode.

One night upon their return, they discovered that the gate to the corral was broken, and the mules and horses had disappeared. Hurlburt found bear tracks near the edge of the stream and the three men decided the horses had panicked at the sight of the bear and had crashed open the gate of the flimsy corral. Hurlburt thought it strange, however, that the bear had not gotten into the supplies and that the horses had not returned for feed, since there was little in the way of pasture in the area.

About the middle of September, they found the vein of

gold. It was a streak so pure that it did not need refining. The three men could pack enough out to become multimillionaires. First, however, they had to dig it out, which would take months, and, second, they would need some mules on which they could transport it. A decision was reached. They had plenty of ammunition, game was plentiful, and they were not low on supplies. It would be pointless to leave their discovery and come back to it. They decided to build a cabin in the wide spot by the stream where Hurlburt had found the first nugget. After the cabin was built they would work on the mine until forced to stop by cold or snow. The winter would be spent in the cabin. Come spring, one of the three would go to South Pass City to buy some more mules and horses.

It did not take long to build a log cabin. They even built a fireplace for heat and cooking during the winter. Hurlburt was finishing work on the cabin one chilly day in early October while Freitag and Smith went up to the mine to start work on the excavation. About noon, Hurlburt heard the sound of rifle shots in the distance. They came from the direction of the mine, but Hurlburt was not alarmed. He thought his partners probably were shooting at a wild animal.

He did become alarmed, however, when night fell, and Freitag and Smith failed to return. Leaving the cabin, he climbed up to the mine in the dark. He called out the names of his partners, but there was no answer. There was no possibility of a mine accident, since the shaft had not been excavated to a depth of more than five or six feet. He finally returned to his cabin.

The following morning he again returned to the lode site and in the light of day saw that the ground around the shaft was stained with blood. A short time later he found Smith's body, stripped of its outer clothing and thrown into some brush. As he bent over the body some atavistic sense told him that he was being watched, that he was in danger. He dove over the body of his dead partner and a split second later heard a rifle shot. A bullet ricocheted from a rock in front of him.

Hurlburt rolled down the hill behind Smith's body, narrowly escaping the gunman's bullets. A moment later he reached the sanctuary of a huge boulder. He still held his rifle. After half an hour, he heard footsteps slithering down the shale of the hill. He did not consider himself a heroic man, but he was intelligent enough to know that if he did nothing, he would soon be slaughtered like his partner. He stood up and fired. The force of the bullet threw an Indian flat on his back less than fifty feet away.

The Indian was alone. He wore Smith's pants and carried Smith's rifle. Hurlburt paused only long enough to pick up his partner's rifle, then took a long circuituous route back to the cabin. He planned to stay at the cabin only long enough to pick up as many of the nuggets as he could carry and enough grub to last for the long trek to South Pass City. He knew it was improbable that the dead Indian had traveled alone, but he hoped that the other Indians had not yet discovered the cabin. Hurlburt made a wide circle around the campsite, then approached it stealthily from below.

His hopes were in vain. He heard the Indians before he saw them; a half-dozen were gathered in the clearing. During the time he had made his long circular trip back to the cabin, they had retrieved the body of their companion whom Hurlburt had shot at the mine. They were now wrapping the body in Hurlburt's bedroll, probably preparing to take it back to their village for burial. An unpleasant thought occurred to

346

Hurlburt. Some Indians could well be behind him, having followed his trail from the site of the killing. He thought of the nuggets buried under the dirt floor of the cabin. Before they had buried the nuggets, he and his partners had estimated their worth to be about $30,000 a share. The thought flickered through Hurlburt's mind that with his partners dead, the $90,000 worth of gold was all his. But his life was invaluable. The Indians might watch the cabin for days, expecting him to return. The Indians were not interested in gold, and even if by some slight chance they were, they would know nothing of the nuggets found in the creek bed.

Hurlburt left.

A little more than a month later, a merchant traveling between Miners Delight and Atlantic City, Wyoming, came across a gaunt man staggering along the road. The man could not talk intelligibly, but the merchant took him into Atlantic City where he was treated by a physician for malnutrition and frostbite. The man, of course, was Hurlburt, and by the time he had recovered sufficiently to tell his story, the snows were too deep for him to return to the mountains. Hurlburt had no idea of the route he had taken to get out. Very early in his flight he had discarded Smith's rifle. On the second or third day he had fallen, and his own rifle had slipped from his grasp and disappeared over the side of a steep cliff. He had been caught in two blizzards and chilling cold. He knew that if he stopped moving he would die. He ate snow and bark. Once he killed a porcupine with a rock and carried the carcass with him, eating it slowly for days.

When he had recovered, Hurlburt went home to Walla Walla to spend the winter. The following June he returned to South Pass City. By then the story he had told while delirious in Atlantic City was known in South Pass City, too. Three men followed Hurlburt's trail into the Wind River Range, but Hurlburt was able to shake them.

Early in September Hurlburt once again came out of the mountains. He carried Smith's rusted rifle, which he had found by accident. He had been unable to find the stream or the abandoned log cabin. He tried to enlist some men in South Pass City to go back into the mountains with him, but was unable to organize a group because of the rapidly approaching winter storms.

Hurlburt returned to South Pass City again the following spring. This time he had little difficulty attracting help and, in late April, Hurlburt and four other men once more entered the Wind River Range. During the ensuing months the search party came across several streams, which they followed as closely as possible to their source. None flowed by the former campsite. The cabin, or the ruins of the cabin, could not be found. In August Hurlburt abruptly gave up the search, went back to Walla Walla, and never again returned to Wyoming.

A year later, a prospector named Joe Poole came down from the Wind River Range. He had found the skeleton of a white man who had been shot in the head, he told patrons of a South Pass City tavern.

"How do you know it was a white man?" he was asked.

"Because he had boots on and there was a leather belt around where his belly had been."

It was unlikely that there was anyone in the bar who by then had not heard of Hurlburt's lost nuggets and his experience. The prospector was asked if there was a small stream near the skeleton.

"Yep, there was," Poole replied.

"How about a log cabin. Did you see a log cabin?"

348

Poole had not seen a cabin, but he was confident that he could find the skeleton. It would take about four or five days to reach it. More than a dozen citizens of South Pass City followed Joe Poole into the Wind River Range on the following day. Poole's confidence had been excessive. For more than two weeks he led the group up and down the canyons looking in vain for the skeleton.

The cabin remained lost for about twenty years. Then, shortly after the turn of the nineteenth century, another prospector named J. H. Osborne showed up in South Pass City after the conclusion of a prospecting trip in the Wind River Range. He had in his possession three large gold nuggets. He had found them in a stream, he said, and had spent weeks looking for a lode in the area, but had been unable to find one. If there were any more nuggets in the creek, he had been unable to find them either. Someone else had been there before him because there were the ruins of a log cabin nearby.

Osborne had drifted on before his story reached anyone who recalled Hurlburt.

South Pass City today is almost a ghost town a few miles south of Lander. Some people still live there and many of the buildings still stand. There no longer are hostile Indians in the Wind River Range, but the winters can be severe. It is unlikely that anything remains today of Hurlburt's log cabin other than the stones from a fireplace. But if someone happened across the remnants of a fireplace facing a stream in a cleared area, he could well dig up a fortune in gold nuggets.

TECHATTICUP GOLD

Between Las Vegas and Searchlight in Nevada is the small ghost town of Nelson. It can be reached easily by car. It was a town supported by two mines from which millions of dollars' worth of gold was taken and in which millions more is believed to remain. According to the old-timers still living in the area, the two mines were not shut down because of economic factors, but they were abandoned because they were cursed. There were few mining camps in the West that did not have a high incidence of violent deaths, but few can match Nelson for its record of conspiratorial murder and devious theft.

One of the mines is the Techatticup which, in Paiute Indian dialect, means "plenty for all." The other is referred to by some as the Queen City Mine. Others call it the Savage Mine.

The Techatticup is the older mine, its first shaft dug by Spanish explorers. The ore was nearly pure gold. The first pack train of ore started out for Mexico City in 1703, but before the caravan reached the shores of the Colorado River a few miles away, it was attacked by a horde of Paiutes. Its cargo of nuggets was strewn on the ground. About half of the soldiers escorting the pack train escaped and most of them carried samples of the golden cargo with them. Many also drew maps of the area that were accurate enough to lead a more heavily armed detachment back to the mine the following year.

As soon as the mine was located, soldiers raided several Indian villages for the necessary slave labor to operate it. The Indians retaliated with such ferocity that the Spanish were forced to abandon the venture. Most of the Spaniards were killed but, once again, a few arrived back in Mexico City carrying nuggets, which gave substance to the tales of the fabulous wealth of the Techatticup. With two expeditionary forces to the area virtually wiped out, the Spanish were reluctant to send a third detachment into the hostile area. However, the maps describing the location of the mine were kept in the archives, and, approximately three-quarters of a century later, another group of Spanish soldiers and explorers were sent to the mine.

The Indians had long memories, and they still wanted no part of the white race digging up the land. This massacre was a carbon copy of the first. The Paiutes waited until the first pack train had departed for Mexico, then ambushed it a few miles from the camp. Again the ore and nuggets were scattered on the ground, the members of the caravan slaughtered, and the animals confiscated. The Paiutes then descended upon those who had remained in the camp and killed everyone there.

The Spanish gave up on the project. The maps describing the location remained scattered in profusion around Mexico. Around 1840 a prospector named Jack Nelson acquired one of these maps from a Mexican in El Paso. It was so accurate that it led him directly to the Techatticup, and Nelson was able to load up his pack mule with nuggets and ore and get back to El Paso without attracting the attention of the Paiutes. Legend says that the most surprised person to see Nelson return with the ore was the Mexican who had sold him the map.

Word of Nelson's "strike" spread like fire, and within weeks the hills around the Techatticup were swarming with prospectors. The Paiutes welcomed this invasion with the same enthusiasm they had accorded the Spaniards. One of the first men to fall victim to the Paiutes was Nelson. The fatalities were high on both sides, but there were too many white men this time for the Indians to wipe out. A combine was formed to operate the Techatticup, and the operation was so well guarded that the Indians suffered fearsome losses during the three occasions when they attacked. Soldiers were brought in to protect the property. The gold ore was taken out by steamboats that sailed up the Colorado River to El Dorado Canyon from Yuma, a voyage of more than three hundred and fifty miles. Supplies were brought in the same vessels, successfully blocking the Paiute habit of raiding pack trains.

A quarter of a century after Nelson's discovery, the Techatticup Mine was still living up to its name, "plenty for all." Another mine adjoining it, the Queen City, was equally productive and had been purchased by George Hearst, father of William Randolph Hearst, the newspaper mogul.

Then, around 1865, John Nash arrived in the town of Nelson. Nash came from San Francisco where he had organized the Eldorado Mining Company, which had purchased the Techatticup Mine. Little is known about Nash's background. He was a large man, close-shaven, and usually soft-spoken. He also was dangerous and dishonest.

One day, a few weeks after Nash had taken over operation of the Techatticup, a young man arrived on the river

352

steamer and asked for directions to Nash's house. He was seen going into the house. His body was found a couple of days later on the outskirts of town. Nash blandly denied that he knew the youth and that he ever had seen him, suggesting that the victim was probably a drifter slain by the Indians. Because Nash, through his position as owner of the Techatticup, was above what little law existed in the area, no one seriously questioned his story.

About a year later, another visitor arrived on the steamer and asked for directions to Nash's house. Moments after he entered the dwelling, there was the sound of a gunshot.

"The man is an absolute stranger," Nash said, pointing with his gun toward the body of the stranger lying on the floor. "He started to attack me and I shot him in self-defense."

There were some who said the stranger had been unarmed, and many thought it odd that a man should travel with no identification on his person, but no one bothered Nash.

For reasons probably known only to himself, George Hearst did not operate the Queen City Mine. To protect his claim, Hearst sent in a small crew once a year for development work. Nash coveted the Queen City Mine, and in 1872 an opportunity arose for him to grab it. Only three weeks remained before a full year would have passed since Hearst's agents had appeared for their token development work.

Nash hired three of the toughest thugs he could find to jump the claim, promising to pay each of them $10,000 for holding the property for only three weeks. The leader of this trio was a man named Ray Wareman. The other two were William Pirtle and Jim Jones.

About two weeks after the three had taken possession of the Queen City Mine, Hearst's agents arrived on the river steamer. When they approached their property, bullets whistled over their heads. There were no lawmen to turn to for help, so the agents returned to the steamer and sailed back to Yuma. When word of what happened got back to Hearst, he immediately filed suit in the courts against the "three John Does" who had jumped his Queen City Mine claim. He was much too late. The day after the year ended, the Eldorado Mining Company claimed title to the Queen City Mine, contending that it had been abandoned because no development work had been done on the property during the past year. Nash did not even bother to wait for the issue to be decided by the court. He immediately started working the Queen City.

Wareman, the most dangerous of the three hoods, was paid his $10,000 immediately and left the area. Nash decided on a less costly maneuver to dispose of Pirtle and Jones. He promised to pay Pirtle the entire $20,000 if he would get rid of Jones. Accordingly, Pirtle shot Jones in the back a few mornings later as Jones was bent over a wash basin. The wound was not fatal. Jones grabbed his rifle and killed Pirtle.

Nash expressed shock when he heard about the shooting. "It's time we had some law and order in this community," he said. "Jim Jones should be tried for murder."

One of Nash's men was appointed a town marshal, and he went to Jones's cabin to arrest him. The new town marshal's tenure was extraordinarily short. He was killed when he tried to take Jones from his cabin. Jones apparently decided that his future in the community was bleak, for, despite his wound, he fled. Nash was still not satisfied. "We must have justice," he said. "Cold-blooded murder can no longer be tolerated here."

A posse was formed. By late afternoon, the posse had trapped Jones in a small cave near the bank of the Colorado

River. Before night fell, Jones had killed one member of the posse and wounded another. The group fell back, but kept Jones pinned in the cave during the night. The following morning Nash appeared. "I will talk to him and see if I can get him to surrender," he said. He rode up to the mouth of the cave, calling out his own name as he went. "It's all right, Jim," he was heard to say. "You can come out now."

A moment later Jim Jones lurched out of his sanctuary. He was holding his rifle loosely in one hand, the muzzle pointed toward the ground. Nash waited until Jones was almost abreast of him. Then he whipped out his revolver and shot his former employee twice in the head.

By his action, Nash had successfully eliminated his conspirators in the acquisition of the Queen City Mine, but he probably did not realize that his murder of Jones would alienate him in the community. This town of outlaws and miners had its own peculiar code of ethics. Shooting a man down while he was surrendering was not considered fair play. A day or so later, when Nash was inspecting his newly acquired Queen City Mine, someone shot at him. His horse was killed, but Nash escaped uninjured. A week later someone fired another shot in his direction as he was entering his house.

The second attack apparently frightened Nash more than the first. He left on the next steamer for Yuma, and when he returned he was accompanied by two men. One he introduced as his brother-in-law, Bill Davis, although Nash had never indicated that he was married or that he had any brothers or sisters. The second stranger was William Piette, whose basic function was that of bodyguard. A few weeks later, a third man arrived and moved into the Nash home. His last name was Fuller. His first name has been lost in time.

Both Fuller and Davis were experienced mining men,

and for a while they concentrated their efforts on getting the Queen City Mine into operation. Fuller, however, had an incurable case of prospecting fever. Late in 1873, about a year after his arrival, Fuller found an incredibly rich lode of gold about six miles from the Techatticup Mine. He named his discovery the Bridal Chamber, and not only quit working for Nash, but persuaded Davis to do so and join him as a partner in the Bridal Chamber.

The first shipment of the almost pure ore from the Bridal Chamber shipped by pack mule to the riverfront was hijacked. Davis, accompanying the mules, made no secret of his belief that John Nash was responsible. There are two versions of what happened next. One states that Davis went to see Nash at his home, was welcomed cordially and was invited to have dinner with Piette and Nash. During the dinner, Nash denied any complicity in the hijack, and he offered to buy back the shares that Davis held in the Eldorado Mining Company. Davis agreed to sell his holdings for cash, which Nash gave him.

A few minutes after his departure from Nash's house, Davis fell from his horse, his body twisting convulsively. Piette rushed from the house and carried Davis back inside, then raced into town to summon the town's doctor. Before he arrived, however, Davis was dead. The doctor reported that there were many indications that Davis had been poisoned.

The other version of the story contends that Piette met Davis in a saloon where, acting as Nash's agent, the same deal was agreed upon over the disposition of Davis's stock in the Eldorado Mining Company. This version has Davis collapsing in the saloon a few minutes after the deal was consummated.

Both stories relate that the money Davis was paid disappeared before his body arrived at the town's undertaker and that Piette was the first man at Davis's side when he collapsed.

A few days after Davis was buried, Piette journeyed up into the mountains to see Fuller. It was June, the time of year when the waters of the Colorado were near flood stage, and, when Piette arrived, Fuller was directing a crew of Indians in snagging driftwood to store up for fuel. The wife of one of the crew was in Fuller's cabin when Piette rode up. She ran to fetch Fuller.

The miner angrily ordered Piette from his property, and the bodyguard rode off without a word. That night, while eating his dinner, Fuller was seized by convulsions and died within a quarter-hour. His body was buried near the cabin. A day or so later Nash and Piette arrived and formally claimed possession of the Bridal Chamber.

There was little doubt in the minds of all in the area that Davis and Fuller were poisoned by Piette at Nash's instigation. Several accounts of the apparent double murder even identify the poison as strychnine. Once again, the ethics of the western mining camps were violated. Killing by gunfire was understandable, but poisoning was considered the coward's murder method.

Nash's fate probably will be a mystery forever. He simply disappeared. He did not leave the mining camp. Piette reported that he went to bed leaving Nash sipping a whiskey. When Piette arose in the morning, Nash was gone. There was no steamer at the riverbank. Nash's horses were still in the stable and his personal possessions remained in his home. But there was never again any sign of John Nash himself. Many weeks after he disappeared, a man claiming to represent the Eldorado Mining Company arrived on the supply steamer. He found all three of the mines shut down. The miners would not work without pay and most of them had drifted on. Piette still lived in Nash's house, but did not appear to need funds. The stranger made no attempt to get the mines back in operation. Instead he boarded up the shafts, searched Nash's house thoroughly, and then departed with a suitcase full of papers Nash had left behind.

A few months later, Piette entered into a partnership with two men named Hans Godfritsen and Henry Warner in the operation of a store on the riverfront. It was not a success. With the three large mines shut down, the riverboats appeared only sporadically to ferry out the comparatively meager ore shipments dug out by independent miners. Eventually Warner and Piette quarreled loudly in a tavern. The next day Warner disappeared. A pale and frightened Godfritsen abandoned his interest in the store before nightfall and rode off toward Yuma.

This was too much for the remaining miners in the town to take. Again there are two versions of the tale. The more lurid tells of half a dozen miners surrounding Piette's store and calling for him to come out. When he refused, the attackers emptied their guns into the small frame store, and, when they were sure that Piette was dead, they dragged out his body and threw it into the Colorado River. The other story relates that Piette was visited by a delegation of irate citizens and ordered out of the community. If he returned, they warned, he would be hanged. In either event, Piette disappeared, as had Nash and Warner, and with his disappearance, the murders and mysterious vanishings ended.

None of the three mines ever were reopened. Not long ago, the *Mohave County Miners*, a weekly newspaper, reported "a deep silence lies over all that once was a wild and lawless spot. A curse seems upon the place. Yet these mines contained millions of wealth. Their product is estimated at about $3 million."

The gold is there. So may be the ghost of William Piette.

HONOR AMONG THIEVES

In 1891 a large group of bandits raided the city of Monterrey, Mexico. They held off an army detachment and police in the city, killing a few men while they looted several banks and the cathedral of more treasure than usually was carried in a Spanish galleon. One semiofficial estimate of the loot includes $1 million in diamonds, 39 bars of gold worth $600,000, $90,000 worth of silver coins, plus an undetermined amount of gold statuary, and stacks of gold coins. The value of the booty exceeded by far the wildest estimates of its planners. The raid was a catalyst for a fantastic series of double crosses and counter double crosses and was directly responsible for the naming of Skeleton Canyon in the Peloncillo Mountains on the border of Arizona and New Mexico.

The raid was the idea of Curly Bill Brocius, the leader of a small gang of cutthroats who spent a considerable amount of time in Silver City, New Mexico. For several months they had been preying upon stagecoaches and lone travelers in Arizona, but the rewards had been meager for the risks involved.

Curly Bill called a meeting in his cabin outside Silver City. Those present included Jim Hughes, fluent in Spanish and ranking next to Curly Bill in the gang's hierarchy, Zwing Hunt, Billy Grounds, and Doc Neal. A few years earlier Hughes was identified as the murderer of several people during a stagecoach holdup in Texas and slipped across the Mexican border only a few hoofbeats ahead of a pursuing posse. For a while he lived in Monterrey, where he picked up his proficiency in Spanish and a slowly increasing awareness of the wealth of the city. Hughes later drifted west, but stayed well below the border. In Sonora, he ran across the notorious Mexican bandit José Estrada. Hughes promptly was extended professional courtesy, from one desperado to another, and for several months Hughes roamed the state of Sonora with the Mexican bandit and his gang. One day, the bandits veered to the north to escape a pursuing army patrol, and Hughes slipped across the border back into the United States where, a short time later, he joined up with Curly Bill Brocius.

At the meeting in Silver City, Hughes nostalgically recalled his days in Mexico and, during the course of his conversation, mentioned the richness of Monterrey.

"Why don't we raid it?" Curly Bill suggested.

His suggestion was received enthusiastically. A moment later, the first double cross was conceived by Hughes. If the raid were to be carried out by non-Mexicans, they would easily be recognized as such. Besides the difficulty in getting out of Mexico, the magnitude of the crime might trigger an unfavorable reaction from the United States government. Mexican help was needed, Hughes argued, for the raid must be considered a Mexican operation. Therefore, they would enlist the bandits of José Estrada to conduct the mission.

"Estrada's not going to give us anything just because we gave him an idea," Curly Bill objected.

Hughes had an answer for Brocius. Because of the magnitude of the crime, the Mexican authorities would send an army after the raiders. The only thing that would stop them would be the United States border. In addition, Estrada would have trouble in disposing of his loot in Mexico. Therefore, Hughes would go with Estrada on the raid, travel with the band back to Sonora, then guide them across the border to the sanctuary of the hideout in the Peloncillo Mountains. "By the time we get to the canyon east of Sloan's Ranch, Estrada will be very tired," Hughes pointed out. "I will ride on ahead, and then we will ambush them there," he said.

"And I will remain in Silver City so no one can blame us when they find the Mexicans' bodies," Curly Bill added.

The plan was endorsed unanimously. Time has obscured how long it took to bring the raid to fruition. Hughes went to Sonora and found Estrada to be as enthusiastic about the venture as were his co-conspirators across the border. Although it was many hundred miles from northwestern Sonora to Monterrey, the logistics of the raid were not difficult. The land was sparsely populated and arid for the most part so their trail would be difficult to follow if they had a sufficient head start. Also, it was as customary for Mexicans to flee across the border into the United States to avoid capture by Mexican law enforcement officials as it was for American desperadoes to slip into Mexico when the chase became too close. Thus, Estrada and Hughes reasoned correctly that the pursuit

361

following the raid would be to the nearest point north of the border. It would not occur to anyone that the quarry would be racing west, remaining in Mexico.

The raid was carried out with great success. Estrada, his band, and Hughes pillaged the community for almost three hours. The telegraph wires were cut. Four police officers and an undetermined number of soldiers were slain before the raiders successfully penned them in a barrack. After looting the banks and the cathedral and stealing some pack mules, the raiders vanished.

There is no record of the long overland journey to Sonora. Some reports contend that the Estrada gang buried part of the loot outside of Monterrey and went back for it several months later. Other reports, which are probably more accurate, assert that the bandits fled to the west as planned and were successful in eluding the army patrols sent after them. It is known that several weeks later, the Estrada gang and Hughes, accompanied by a mule train carrying the booty, entered the United States through the Arizona territory along an old smugglers' trail that cut through the Animas Valley.

The gang made camp in an isolated section of the Peloncillo Mountain foothills near the juncture of what is now known as Skeleton Creek and the South Fork Skeleton Creek. Hughes rode on ahead to Silver City where the plans for the double cross were gone over once again. Nothing could go wrong, Hughes promised. Most of the Estrada gang had been paid off in Sonora so, in addition to Estrada, there were only a dozen Mexicans with whom to contend.

Curly Bill remained in Silver City as planned. Neal, Grounds, and Hunt accompanied Hughes to a point a few miles from the Estrada camp. Here they set up their ambush in a canyon so narrow that a pack train would have to pass through it in single file. When the men were positioned, Hughes rode back to his old friend Estrada.

A few hours later the pack mules were loaded, the camp was struck, and the train headed for Silver City with Hughes leading the way. It was late afternoon when the caravan entered the canyon. Hughes started the slaughter when he stopped his horse and fired a bullet into the head of Estrada. A few moments later all of the Mexicans had been killed. The ambush did not go as planned, however. The sound of the gunfire echoed loudly throughout the defile, and the treasure-laden mules panicked at the noise and bolted.

The North American outlaws set off in pursuit. The only way they could stop the fleeing animals was to shoot them. All but two of the animals were killed in the canyon—one was shot about a mile outside the canyon entrance and the other disappeared, last seen heading in the direction of Geronimo's Peak.

The killing of the pack animals posed a problem. There was no way to transport the Monterrey booty to the hideout in the Peloncillo Mountains. Someone had to return to Silver City to get more mules or oxen, and someone had to remain to gather up the treasure, as well as guard it, and bury the dead. While this was being discussed, one of the outlaws questioned the need for Curly Bill's participation in the division of the loot. Although nominally the leader of the gang, he had done nothing to earn a portion of this treasure. It was unanimously decided that Jim Hughes should go back to Silver City and tell Curly Bill that Estrada had escaped. If Curly Bill did not believe him, Hughes would kill him. Hughes then would return with oxen or mules to carry the treasure away. Unfortunately for him, Hughes agreed to this plan.

Hughes was barely out of sight when Neal, Hunt, and

Grounds convened another meeting. It would take a few days for Hughes to make a round trip to Silver City, more if he came back with oxen. There really was no need for him to be cut in on a division of the booty. Doc Neal could buy an ox team from a ranch much closer, and the three of them could load the treasure and be long gone before Hughes returned. The gullible Doc Neal thought this an excellent plan. Taking several gold coins from one of the packs on a dead mule, he cantered off to the west in search of an ox team.

Zwing Hunt and Billy Grounds then proceeded to dig a large hole in a small level spot, about a mile east of the massacre site, in what is now known as Skeleton Canyon. Estimates vary as to how much of the booty they succeeded in burying. The smallest estimate is $80,000. The highest says almost half of the loot wound up buried in Skeleton Canyon.

Doc Neal returned within two days leading a team of oxen. He noticed that many of the treasure pouches had been opened during his absence and that obviously many were missing from the packs of the dead mules. Neal, however, was smart enough to say nothing to his double-crossing companions as they loaded up the ox cart.

For two days, or about fifty miles, the three outlaws drove the oxen east toward New Mexico. Then, near the Arizona-New Mexico border, they veered north into the Peloncillo Mountains. It was then that Doc Neal noticed that Hunt and Grounds often conversed in whispers. Being a practical man, Neal assumed the worst—that his life expectancy would indeed be short if he remained with his companions. Consequently, when an opportunity arose, he galloped back down the mountain. The hail of bullets that accompanied his flight confirmed his suspicions, but he escaped unscathed.

Neal went directly to Silver City, New Mexico, where he found Hughes sleeping in Curly Bill's cabin. Curly Bill was serving a week's sentence in jail for slugging a deputy sheriff in the course of a barroom brawl. Hughes, therefore, had not had an opportunity to tell the gang leader of Estrada's alleged escape. Hughes, understandably, was upset when he learned from Neal of the perfidy of Hunt and Grounds. He and Neal devised a new plan. As soon as Curly Bill was released they would go after Hunt and Grounds. The booty then would be divided in three parts between Curly Bill, Hughes, and Neal.

When Curly Bill was let out of jail he was met by Hughes and Neal. The three men went to a saloon where Hughes told Curly Bill of the double cross pulled by the other two members of the gang. Curly Bill became furious. So great was his anger that he lost control of himself, and when a young barmaid accidently brushed his chair, he whipped out his gun and shot her. Women were scarce in Silver City, and the killing of one was a truly heinous offense.

The three outlaws immediately fled the town, but a posse was after them in less than a half-hour and caught up with them in the New Mexican town of Shakespeare. In the ensuing gunfight, Doc Neal was fatally shot. Curly Bill Brocius and Jim Hughes were captured and immediately hanged from a rafter in the dining room of the Pioneer Hotel in Shakespeare.

Meanwhile, Hunt and Grounds had buried the rest of the Monterrey treasure, except for as many gold coins as they could carry, and had moved on to Tombstone, Arizona. Word of the mysterious massacre had spread throughout the Southwest by this time, but most thought the victims were Mexican smugglers killed by Indians. The two surviving members of Curly Bill's gang spent their money wildly on booze and women.

Grounds had a girl friend in Charleston, a small community a short distance from Tombstone, but he was not the only man in her life. She had a much closer liaison with the town butcher. The butcher, however, did not have as much money as Billy Grounds. This posed a problem for the young woman. If Billy's wealth was temporary, then she would choose the butcher. But if Billy was indeed a man of lasting substance, then she would choose him.

She finally overcame Billy Grounds's reluctance to discuss the source of his riches and his net worth by getting him gloriously drunk. While lying in bed at the side of his beloved, Billy told all. After Billy left for Tombstone on the following day, his girl friend relayed the news to the butcher. When Grounds returned to Charleston that evening, the irate butcher went to Tombstone to tell Sheriff William Breckenridge of the two mass murderers living in his jurisdiction. The woman saw him leave and, in turn, confessed to Grounds what she had done. Grounds immediately raced into Tombstone, found Zwing Hunt and told him the bad news. While Hunt ran to the bank to withdraw the funds he had deposited, Grounds took the time to write a letter to his mother in San Antonio, Texas. He wrote:

> Dear Ma,
>
> I am coming home and will be on my way within the hour. I am tired of this wild life. I wanted to lay my head again in your lap and have you run your fingers through my hair as you did when I was a little tot and came to you with my troubles. I have $80,000 buried which I came by honestly. I will get

this and be home and buy a ranch near Santone and you can live in comfort the rest of your days.

Your loving boy,
Billy

P.S. I am charged with crimes I did not commit and may not get home. So I am enclosing a map showing just where this treasure is buried so you and Sis can get it if I do not get home.

Billy Grounds mailed the letter from Tombstone as he and Zwing Hunt rode out of town. There was no immediate sign of a chase, and, after they covered about ten miles, they thought it safe to spend the night in an empty bunkhouse on a ranch owned by a man named Chandler. It was a mistake. The next morning shortly after dawn they were awakened by a cry from Sheriff Breckenridge to come out with their hands up. Breckenridge was accompanied by two deputies named Gillespie and Young.

Grounds and Hunt charged out of the bunkhouse with guns blazing. Gillespie was shot dead, and Young was felled by a bullet which shattered his leg. The sheriff then shot Grounds in the head with a shotgun and Hunt through the chest with his revolver. Both of the outlaws were carried back to Tombstone in one of the ranch buckboards. Grounds died in the wagon and was buried in the Tombstone Cemetery. Hunt was placed in the local hospital and was expected to die.

Zwing Hunt asked that his brother Hugh be notified of his pending demise, and a short time later Hugh Hunt arrived in Tombstone from Tucson. His stay was brief. Immediately after his arrival he rented a horse and buggy, and after dark, in some unknown manner, smuggled Zwing out of the hospital. The escape was not discovered until the following morning, and the trail was difficult to follow.

Breckenridge, however, was a stubborn man and within a few days deduced from the various reports that came in that the Hunt brothers were heading for the massacre sight in Skeleton Canyon. He resumed the chase. A few miles to the west of where Estrada had been killed, the sheriff and his deputies came across a freshly dug grave at the foot of an oak tree. Carved into the bark of the tree was the name Zwing Hunt. The officers unearthed the grave and found the body of Zwing inside. The men covered up the grave and returned to Tombstone. Hugh Hunt was not worth pursuing.

The map and letter that Bill Grounds sent to his mother on the day before his death are reported still to be in good condition and in the possession of Grounds's sister's son who lives in San Antonio, Texas. No attempt has been made to recover the Monterrey booty by Grounds's descendants.

Many others have searched for it, however, and many have found gold and silver coins, probably scattered by the bolting pack mules, in Skeleton Canyon near the Arizona-New Mexico border. Weldon Heald, writing in *Desert* magazine in 1951, says that Hunt, just before he died, wrote out detailed instructions on how to find the treasure site, which he stated is at the foot of Davis Mountain. Heald repeats the intricate directions, but points out that they are worthless since there is no Davis Mountain in this area of the country.

At this writing the oak tree under which Hunt is buried still stands. A short distance to the east and to the north of Skeleton Creek is the massacre site, and in this area a part of the treasure was buried. The rest of the Monterrey booty is two days' trip by oxen to the east. It should be remembered that everyone who has possessed it since it was looted in Monterrey has died violently.

EPILOGUE

The theme of this volume has concerned treasures of the West that have yet to be found, or, if the location is known, have yet to be recovered. Many skeptics of treasure legends dismiss the existence of these valuable caches on the grounds that if such treasure ever had been buried or lost, they would eventually have been found.

Some treasures may well have been found, and the finder kept the knowledge of his discovery to himself. The location of other treasures has been determined but, for one reason or another, it has been impossible to recover them. The foundered Manila galleon on Nehalem Spit in Oregon is one such case. Some treasure tales are most improbable, particularly those that we mentioned earlier that start out with a deathbed confession.

But before anyone becomes discouraged by these low probabilities, he should consider the case of the late Shorty Wilcox of Colorado. He learned of a treasure from the lips of a dying man, hurried to its location, and found it beyond his physical and financial resources to recover it. Yet, within the passage of a few weeks, he obtained possession of this treasure and spent the remainder of his life playing the stock market and living comfortably in a plush suite in the Brown Palace Hotel in Denver, Colorado.

In the early 1880s, when Shorty Wilcox was in his mid-thirties, Colorado was in the throes of a crime wave. Holdup men swooped down in gangs on banks, saloons, and stores. The state was second only to California in the number of stagecoach robberies tallied. Among those who preyed on stagecoaches was a sadistic trio of young men who killed passengers without reason, and who, for a period of more than four years, left behind no clues as to their identity.

Shortly before this trio began its operations, three young men filed claim upon the Black Prince Mine in Summit County, Colorado. The mine had been abandoned several years earlier after an explosion tapped an underground spring and flooded the main shaft under eighty feet of water. The three new operators were unfriendly. They bought their supplies in nearby Breckenridge and usually stopped in a tavern on their way out of town. Here they spoke only in mono-syllables and only to each other. Their names were known from the claim filing: Alva Davis, Rick Johnson, and Max Smith. They appeared to be making the small mine profitable, for they paid their bills and occasionally brought in ore to be assayed. No one knew how they had drained the water from the main shaft. No questions were answered, and, if a person passed too close to the Black Prince Mine, he was turned away. The merchants and residents of Breckenridge, along with other miners in the area, became used to the taciturn trio and ignored them. More than four years passed before the three became suspects in the wave of stagecoach robberies and killings, and this was not because anyone had become suspicious of their cover.

Another stagecoach robbery had occurred near Alma in

adjacent Park County. One of the gunman emptied his revolver into the coach as he rode away, killing one of the passengers and wounding two others. A posse was quickly formed to give chase; it followed the trail into Summit County. Previously, when outlaws escaped into an adjoining county, a pursuing posse abandoned the chase because the lawmen had passed out of their jurisdiction. In this instance, however, the Park County sheriff continued into Summit County, detaching one member of the posse to ride on to the Summit County sheriff to explain what was going on. The Summit County sheriff responded by forming still another posse and joining the chase.

A short time later, the two posses formed a tight circle around the Black Prince Mine where the trail had ended, and presently discovered that their quarry had fled. Although they searched for more than a day, the men failed to pick up the outlaws' trail again. Their only consolation was that they now had a fairly good idea as to the identity of the killers.

The following day the Park County posse cantered into a small canyon north of Alma and stumbled into the middle of a holdup of a Wells Fargo stagecoach. The gun battle was quick and deadly. When it was over two of the masked outlaws were dead, along with one member of the posse and one stagecoach passenger. The third outlaw escaped. The bodies of the dead outlaws were taken into Alma where they were subsequently identified as those of Alva Davis and Rick Johnson.

Some twenty years later Shorty Wilcox arrived in Breckenridge. For several years he had worked in the large Orizaba gold mine in Cripple Creek until he suffered a permanent injury to his legs when the shoring of a drift tunnel collapsed upon them. He built a cabin on the outskirts of the town and picked up small amounts of money from the women of the

371

community in the role of a handyman. No job was too small or too menial for Shorty Wilcox. He was always polite and cheerful. The wife of the superintendent of the Orizaba Mine described him "as neat and clean as a new needle and with the disposition of a minister."

When Shorty Wilcox became sick, which appeared to happen regularly, the women of the community supplied him with food and took turns nursing him back to health. After these bouts, he would limp around to the homes of his benefactors, personally thanking each one, begging for some small chore to perform as a sign of his appreciation. For almost five years Shorty Wilcox lived this way, until one night a stranger arrived at Shorty's cabin on the outskirts of town.

The stranger arrived on foot, knocked feebly on the door, then collapsed when Shorty opened the door. Shorty dragged him to his bed and made some tea. The beverage restored some color to the stranger's pallid cheeks. "I'm Max Smith," he said presently. "Does my name mean anything to you?"

Shorty shook his head. A quarter-century had passed since the abandoned Black Prince Mine had been used as a bandit hideout.

Max Smith sighed, then clutched his chest. When the pain subsided, his breathing was fast and shallow. He began talking in a rapid monotone, telling Shorty of the robberies and the large sums of money that had been taken. After his partners had been killed, Smith went on, he had fled to Santa Fe in New Mexico territory. Here he had been caught during a burglary and sentenced to twenty-five years in prison. Immediately upon his release, he had headed for the Black Prince Mine.

"I've been up there for the past month trying to figure

372

out how to get it out," he continued. "There's no way it can be done."

Shorty poured his visitor another cup of tea. He waited.

"We put fifty thousand dollars in gold coins, all from the Denver Mint, into a strong box," Smith said after a while. "When the posse started to get close, we tossed it down the main shaft. It was the savings of almost four years."

"Now, why can't you get it out?" Shorty asked curiously.

"Cause the shaft has got more than eighty feet of water in it." Max Smith again clutched his chest and grimaced in pain. "More than four years' savings," he moaned.

All through the night, Shorty remained at the side of Max Smith. Toward dawn, his uninvited guest slipped into a coma, and an hour or so later Shorty limped into Breckinridge to fetch the doctor. When they returned to the cabin, Max Smith was dead.

"Just stumbled against the door last night," Shorty told the doctor. "Said his name was Smith and that he was sick."

The body of the stranger, unrecognized and unclaimed, was buried in an unmarked grave in Breckenridge. A few days later Shorty Wilcox told Mrs. Virginia Petit, wife of the superintendent of the Orizaba Mine, that he was planning to spend more time mining, adding that he thought he would put in a claim for the abandoned Black Prince Mine. When she told her husband he laughed, commenting that Shorty was losing his mind in his old age.

About two weeks later the women of Breckenridge realized that their favorite man-about-town had disappeared. A delegation was dispatched to Shorty's cabin. Shorty was an unusually neat and tidy man, but now there was dust on the table and floor to indicate that its occupant had been gone for a considerable time. Someone recalled Shorty's plan to stake out the old abandoned Black Prince Mine. The next day some of the more energetic women of Breckenridge rode up to the Black Prince. Their fears appeared to be justified. Two planks had been laid across the opening of the main shaft, and on one of these planks was a half-eaten sandwich and half a cup of coffee. Peering over the side of the shaft, the ladies could see the water below. Floating on top of the water was a straw hat that Shorty Wilcox always wore outdoors.

The ladies hurried back to town. Virginia Petit led the group that started the movement to retrieve Shorty's body and return it to Breckenridge where it could be buried with the proper religious rites. The pressure was too great for the practical men of the community to resist, particularly as Mrs. Petit was aware of the existence of a powerful pump kept at the Orizaba Mine.

It took many men several days to haul the heavy pump across the mountains to the Black Prince Mine. There was no power to run the pump and it took a few more days for the men, working in relays, one man on each end of a rocker arm, to pump the water out of the shaft. When the shaft eventually was cleared, however, there was no sign of a body.

While the men and women were mulling over this unexpected development, Shorty Wilcox limped up the trail into the camp. His lined face reflected a combination of anger and surprise. "What are you doing on my property?" he demanded.

If there had not been women present, Shorty Wilcox might have been hanged immediately from a nearby tree by the tired men. There was not a male volunteer present who did not know that he had been tricked into clearing the shaft. The women, however, apparently believed Shorty's story that he had impulsively crossed the mountains to visit a friend at another mine. After Shorty pointed out that he had not requested any help and that everyone present was trespassing, the volunteers packed up and left.

The women did not lose their concern over the well-being of Shorty Wilcox. On the following day, Mrs. Paul Priest and some unidentified friends rode out to the Black Prince Mine to take Shorty a basket of food. An A-frame had been built over the mouth of the shaft and lying on the ground was a block and tackle and a muddy cast-iron hook. But once again, Shorty Wilcox had disappeared. The women returned to Breckenridge. The men of the community were uninterested in his whereabouts. For several weeks the women made periodic visits to Shorty's cabin, but the miner never returned to his small cabin on the outskirts of town.

Several months later Mrs. Priest and her husband checked into the Brown Palace Hotel in Denver. As they turned away from the desk after registering, they saw Shorty Wilcox. He was a picture of sartorial splendor as he limped across the thick-carpeted floor to the open door. An astonished Mr. Priest made some inquiries around the city. The records of banks at the turn of the century were slightly less confidential than they are today, and Priest quickly discovered that Shorty Wilcox had deposited about $50,000 in gold coins in one of the banks a few days after he had last been seen at the Black Prince Mine.

Priest also discovered that Shorty lived in a suite in the Brown Palace. He tried on this and subsequent trips to visit him, but Shorty Wilcox had lost all interest in his former neighbors from Breckenridge. He invested his money wisely and lived luxuriously until his death a few years later.

EPILOGUE

Shorty Wilcox took the words of a dying man seriously, overcame insurmountable odds, and recovered a treasure despite the fact that he was crippled and an old man.

Most legends have some basis in fact. The treasures we have described probably exist, and someone, someday, probably will find them.